Education during the Time of the Revolution in Egypt

COMPARATIVE AND INTERNATIONAL EDUCATION:
A Diversity of Voices

Volume 44

Series Editors

Allan Pitman, *University of Western Ontario, Canada*
Miguel A. Pereyra, *University of Granada, Spain*
Suzanne Majhanovich, *University of Western Ontario, Canada*

Editorial Board

Ali Abdi, *University of Alberta, Canada*
Clementina Acedo, *UNESCO International Bureau of Education*
Mark Bray, *University of Hong Kong, China*
Christina Fox, *University of Wollongong, Australia*
Steven Klees, *University of Maryland, USA*
Nagwa Megahed, *Ain Shams University, Egypt*
Crain Soudien, *University of Cape Town, South Africa*
David Turner, *University of Glamorgan, England*
Medardo Tapia Uribe, *Universidad Nacional Autónoma de Mexico*

Scope

Comparative and International Education: A Diversity of Voices aims to provide a comprehensive range of titles, making available to readers work from across the comparative and international education research community. Authors will represent as broad a range of voices as possible, from geographic, cultural and ideological standpoints. The editors are making a conscious effort to disseminate the work of newer scholars as well as that of well-established writers. The series includes authored books and edited works focusing upon current issues and controversies in a field that is undergoing changes as profound as the geopolitical and economic forces that are reshaping our worlds. The series aims to provide books which present new work, in which the range of methodologies associated with comparative education and international education are both exemplified and opened up for debate. As the series develops, it is intended that new writers from settings and locations not frequently part of the English language discourse will find a place in the list.

Education during the Time of the Revolution in Egypt

Dialectics of Education in Conflict

Edited by

Nagwa Megahed
Ain Shams University, Egypt
The American University in Cairo, Egypt

SENSE PUBLISHERS
ROTTERDAM/BOSTON/TAIPEI

A C.I.P. record for this book is available from the Library of Congress.

ISBN: 978-94-6351-204-6 (paperback)
ISBN: 978-94-6351-205-3 (hardback)
ISBN: 978-94-6351-206-0 (e-book)

Published by: Sense Publishers,
P.O. Box 21858,
3001 AW Rotterdam,
The Netherlands
https://www.sensepublishers.com/

Cover image: A public school in Egypt (photograph by N. Megahed)

All chapters in this book have undergone peer review.

Printed on acid-free paper

All Rights Reserved © 2017 Sense Publishers

No part of this work may be reproduced, stored in a retrieval system, or transmitted in any form or by any means, electronic, mechanical, photocopying, microfilming, recording or otherwise, without written permission from the Publisher, with the exception of any material supplied specifically for the purpose of being entered and executed on a computer system, for exclusive use by the purchaser of the work.

TABLE OF CONTENTS

Acknowledgments   vii

1. Education Amidst Conflict in Egypt: Dialectics of Policy and Practice   1
   Nagwa Megahed

Part I: Dialectics of Citizenship Education and Youth Movement for Peacebuilding

2. The Revolution as a Critical Pedagogical Workshop: Perceptions of University Students Reimagining Participatory Citizenship(s) in Egypt   11
   Jason Nunzio Dorio

3. Egyptian Youth Building a Peaceful Community: The Selmiyah Movement   37
   Shereen Aly

4. Citizenship Education: A Critical Content Analysis of the Egyptian Citizenship Education Textbooks after the Revolution   59
   Soha Aly

Part II: Dialectics of Education for Global Citizenship and Women's Empowerment

5. Global Citizenship Education and Civil Society in Egypt: A Case Study of a Character Education Program   83
   Shaimaa Mostafa Awad

6. Young Rural Women's Perspectives on the Impact of Education Supported Development Projects   109
   Ola Hosny

Part III: Dialectics of Teacher Professional Development and Educational Quality

7. School-Based Teacher Professional Development: Examining Policy and Practice in the Egyptian Context   135
   Amira Abdou

8. Students' Perceptions of the Quality of Higher Education: A Case Study of a Remote Public University in Egypt   155
   Sara Taraman

Author Biographies   171

ACKNOWLEDGMENTS

I would like to express my sincere thanks to Professor Allan Pitman, University of Western Ontario, Canada, who invited me to develop this edited volume; his valuable discussion of my proposal of this book and his support are truly appreciated. My thanks are due to Nazly Abaza for her editorial assistance during the initial stages of developing this volume. My special thanks also go to Michel Lokhorst and to his colleagues at Sense Publishers whose generous time and dedicated efforts made the publication of this volume possible.

NAGWA MEGAHED

1. EDUCATION AMIDST CONFLICT IN EGYPT

Dialectics of Policy and Practice

INTRODUCTION

Understanding the current state of education in a given society requires in-depth analyses of the discourses and actions of different actors at local and global levels. The theme of the 2016 World Congress of Comparative Education Societies (WCCES), "Dialectics of Education: Comparative Perspectives," held from 22nd to 26th August, 2016 in Beijing, China, offered a global platform to present contemporary issues pertaining to educational theories, policies, and practices. The chapters of this book were presented at two panels during the 2016 WCCES, then were further developed, reviewed, and finalized in preparation for publication. The book tackles the roles of different actors, including stakeholders and governmental, non-governmental and intergovernmental organizations, in maintaining or changing the status quo of education and society during the time of conflict, social unrest and political transition in Egypt.

Aligning with the call for ethnographic research and case studies in the field of comparative and international education that examine teaching and learning in local contexts and produces indigenous knowledge that goes beyond the *Eurocentric* analysis and descriptive comparison between nation-states (see Mesemann, 1982; Crossley & Vulliamy, 1984; Phillips & Schweisfurth, 2009; Bray, Adamson, & Mason, 2014; Epstein, 2016), this book focuses on education in Egypt during the time of the revolution as perceived by university students, youth activists, educational professionals, government officials and civil society organizations. Its chapters reveal the tension, contradiction and/or coherence among different players as related to their respective role in education for civic engagement, national identity, global citizenship, peace-building, teacher professional development, and women's and students' empowerment. The book illustrates the dialectics of education in conflict by articulating diverse meanings and perspectives given by Egyptian stakeholders when describing their actions and reality(ies) during the time of the revolution and its aftermath.

Since the January 25th, 2011 revolution, Egyptians experienced and engaged in a daily debate. Controversially, some argued that the conflict and revolts in Egypt, and the Arab region, were neither coincidental, nor the result of a "domino effect" of collective actions by oppressed people against autocratic regimes. Rather, these revolts were the result of mobilization efforts made over decades by several activist groups, as well as national and international non-governmental organizations. Contrary to this view, others claim that despite the rapid economic growth of Egypt in the 2000s, there was a wide gap in the distribution of wealth and economic return, which left the majority of Egyptians suffering from poverty and high rate of unemployment, especially among youth. This, combined with three decades of autocratic governance under Mubarak's regime, provoked the January 25th, 2011 revolution. The latter argument is supported by the chanting of the revolution for "bread, freedom and social justice." Obviously, while national and international economic and political dynamics dominated the daily debate, education remains the forgotten arena amidst conflict. This readdresses Davies' (2009) inquiry concerning the *complexity* of education and conflict and questioning the stand of education in conflict. Davies (2005, 2009) emphasizes the need for further examination of education to be undertaken and contextualized in local communities during the time of turmoil and social chaos. With the exacerbation of conflict between militant extremists and modern states in the region, and most recently in many European countries, it became more important than ever before to understand the dialectics of education in conflict in different local contexts, starting in this book by the Egyptian context.

CONTEXTUALIZATION

Egypt is the largest country in the North Africa and Middle East region in terms of its population. In 2017, the total population reached more than 92 million (92,128,271), with 49 per cent females and 57.2 per cent located in rural areas. Children and youth in the school-age (5–24) represents 39.9 per cent, plus 11.3 per cent aged 0–4. This makes 51.2 per cent of the population in the age of pre-K-12 and higher education (CAPMAS, 2017, pp. 4–6). This marks Egypt as a home to one of the largest populations of school-aged children and youth in the world, with a high annual population growth rate of 2.1 per cent. From a human capital perspective, this constitutes a challenge and opportunity for the nations' development, yet unemployment rate in the first quarter of 2017 was estimated at 12 per cent (CAPMAS, 2017).

Educational services are offered by public and private providers though the public education sector remains the main provider that serves the majority of the population. In the school year 2015–2016, for the pre-K to 12 education, there were a total of 44,787 public schools with a total enrollment of 17,990,836 students versus a total of 7,235 private schools enroll a total of 1,938,751 students. In higher education, there were 24 public universities with 1,835,015 enrolled students comparing to 19 private universities enrolling a total of 111,602, as shown in Table 1 (CAPMAS, 2017, pp. 116–129).

Table 1. Egyptian public and private education, school year 2015–2016

	Sector	No. Institutions	Enrollment
Pre-K-12	Public	44,787	17,990,836
	Private	7,235	1,938,751
Higher Education	Public	24	1,835,015
	Private	19	111,602

Source: CAPMAS (2017, pp. 116–129)

The high demand for educational services in Egypt created a public pressure for improving the quality of learning and teaching and expanding educational opportunities. Thus, since the 1990s till the present, education has been declared as a national priority. During the 1990s, several educational reform projects and initiatives were undertaken and partially or fully funded by international bilateral and multilateral organizations (i.e., the World Bank, the European Union, and the United States Agency for International Development). Examples of these reforms included Basic Education Improvement Project, Secondary Education Enhancement Project and Education Reform Program. These state-led reforms aimed at improving opportunities and access to basic education, enhancing the quality of education (focusing on teacher professional development, use of technology, and school quality assurance and accreditation), and establishing a supportive, decentralized system for continuous quality improvement. In addition, attention were given to community education including, community schools, supported by UNICEF since 1992, and girls' friendly schools (Ministry of Education, 2014). Similarly, in higher education, attention was given to enhancing its quality and relevance to the labor market. In the 2000s, the Ministry of Higher Education with support from the World Bank embarked on a major Higher Education Enhancement Project that tackles different areas such as quality assurance, faculty and leadership development, and information and communication technology (Ministry of Higher Education, 2010).

In 2003, the document of national education standards was released, followed by the establishment of the National Authority for Quality Assurance and Accreditation in Education and the founding of the Professional Academy for Teachers. All these national bodies have functioned in parallel to the Ministry of Education and its equivalent entities for quality assurance and in-service training, already existed at different levels of the system (the state, province, district, and school levels). The situation in higher education was not much different. Although public universities maintain a level of autonomy, they were all obliged to establish units and centers for quality assurance and accreditation as well as for faculty and leadership development. On the one hand, these reform initiatives have duplicated the arms of the state and strengthened its control over professionals. On the other hand, they resulted in the intensification of duties of teachers and other educators who felt burdened by many additional administrative tasks and requirements. In the meantime, the persistence of problems such as a high-stake exam system, widely spread practice of private tutoring, low educational quality, and high unemployment rate among youth – reached 30 per cent in 2008 (Megahed & Lack, 2011, p. 414) – increased the level of dissatisfaction among educators, parents, students and other stakeholders.

A brief portray of educational and socioeconomic statistics reveals the continuation of serious problems, such as school drop-out, illiteracy, inequality and poverty in Egypt in 2011. According to the Ministry of Education (2014), "the state has been able to absorb more than 90 per cent of the population at the age of basic education [grades 1 – 9]" (p. 7). Yet, in 2011, the drop-out rate estimated an average of 6 per cent, with higher rate than average in 14 out of Egypt's 27 governorates (provinces). The illiteracy rate reached 28 per cent in the age group 15–35, totaling 17 million people, and 40 per cent in the age group of 15+ (34 million people). It is worth noting that two-thirds of the latter group were female illiterates and about 64 per cent of all illiterate people were in rural areas (Ministry of Education, 2014, p. 9). In addition, a high level of poverty (equivalent to two dollars a day), especially in rural areas continues to be a major challenge. The rate of poverty among children under the age 15 is reported to be 23 per cent and among youth-aged 15–19 is 28 per cent. Poverty is concentrated in rural than urban areas with 30 per cent versus 12.16 per cent, respectively (Ministry of Education, 2014, p. 10).

By filling the gap of the state's social and educational services, Islamist groups, mainly the Muslim Brotherhood, gained popularity in local communities, especially in rural and remote areas. It is well known that the conflict between the Muslim Brotherhood and the Egyptian state is dated back to the time of 1952 revolution, when the Brotherhood opposed Nasser's (the president of Egypt, 1952–1970) socialist approach of nation-state building. This longstanding conflict included phases of conciliation and confrontation during the presidency of Sadat (1970–1981) and Mubarak (1981–2011) (see Ginsburg & Megahed, 2002; Megahed, 2015). Thus expectedly, following the January 25th, 2011 revolution, the two main political forces prevailed were the Egyptian Armed Forces, representing the Egyptian state, and the Muslim Brotherhood. During the Brotherhood's one-year rule in Egypt in 2012, several confrontations took place between the Islamist government and political activists who called for liberal democracy and social justice. Several protests broke out and a movement, known as *"Tamarud"* (the Rebel Movement), against the Brotherhood's rule was initiated by young Egyptian men and women. The *Tamarud* movement quickly gained popularity and led to the uprising of June 30th, 2013 which ended the Brotherhood's rule. The support of this uprising by the Egyptian Armed Forces caused global controversy, yet it was celebrated nationally. Clashes, confrontations and violent actions took place in Egypt during the aftermath of June 30th, 2013 (Megahed, 2015). Nonetheless, in 2014 the Egyptian constitution was amended and two elections for the people assembly (parliament) and for the state presidency took place. Nowadays, Egyptians are heading toward a new presidency election to take place in 2018 while gaining the support of regional and global communities in "eliminating terrorism" and countering extremism.

In this national context, all chapters of this book were developed. The chapters are based on original research and fieldwork conducted in Egypt from 2012 to 2015. During these years and in anticipation of this book, I supervised and supported the work of many dedicated graduate students, research fellows, and visiting scholars at the American University in Cairo, some of whom I worked closely with throughout the development of their research and the refinement of their work, to the finalization of their included chapters. The authors of the book chapters investigate the discourses and actions of diverse groups during the time of revolts and uprisings, illustrating the dialectics of citizenship education, peace-building, global citizenship, women's empowerment, teacher professional development, and educational quality.

DIALECTICS OF CITIZENSHIP EDUCATION AND YOUTH MOVEMENT FOR PEACE-BUILDING

The dialectics and policy discourses of citizenship education, youth movement and peacebuilding are examined in three chapters. In Chapter 2, Jason Dorio employs critical pedagogy to connect participatory citizenship and citizenship education in the context of the Egyptian revolution. Illustrating this "historical moment in Egypt," Dorio presents an overview of the revolutionary Egypt, starting from January 25, 2011, through the 18th days of demonstrations and uprisings, to the aftermath of political change and unrest during the past five years (2011–2016). Dorio claims that "revolutionary transitions, such as the January 25th Egyptian Revolution, can be a critical pedagogical workshop where citizens engage with new forms of political intervention and resistance, critically reflecting upon consciousness-raising events, and experimenting with relationships between agency and power." In support of his claim, Dorio discusses participatory citizenship and citizenship education in Egypt and relays on qualitative data with in-depth interviews conducted with Egyptian university students during the 2014–2015 academic year. Dorio focuses on the narratives and perceptions of two university graduate student-instructors that reveal their perceived realities prior to, during, and post the revolution. His chapter demonstrates the characteristics of critical pedagogical workshops in the time and space of the January 25th Egyptian Revolution and subsequent events and concludes by implications of participatory citizenship(s) for universities in Egypt.

In Chapter 3, Shereen Aly focuses on a youth movement, known as "Selmiyah" (peaceful or in-peace) to articulate the actions and perspectives of Egyptian youth in promoting peace in local communities. Aly argues that throughout the period of conflict in Egypt since 2011, "it became clear that the Egyptian society is not as tolerant as it would like to be, there is still discrimination against religion, ethnicities, social classes, and political ideologies, etc. There has been a dire need to create a culture of tolerance, acceptance and co-existence that emerged and become obvious in the Egyptian scene." Aly questions the role of education in the Egyptian community;

"what are Egyptians educating for and can peace education be a viable solution?" She focuses her analysis on peace education, with attention given to a group of youth-led initiatives and organizations who in 2012 created a movement called "Selmiyah." She employs a qualitative approach where in-depth interviews and participant-observation were conducted with this group of youth activists. Her chapter clarifies the motivation and drives for this group of Egyptian youth to focus on peace education. Moreover, she explains the structure of their initiatives and whether they fit within Ian Harris (2007) categorization and model of peace education. Aly's chapter discusses the dynamic of creating a collective movement, and how this has affected the initiatives of peace education during the period of transition in Egypt.

While Jason Dorio and Shereen Aly focus on the dialectics and discourses of university students and youth activists, Soha Aly analyzes the state discourse as presented in the national textbooks of citizenship education. In Chapter 4, she presents a critical content analysis of six textbooks issued by the Ministry of Education and taught in public secondary schools during the school-years 2011–2012 through 2014–2015. Her content analysis tracks the extent to which the concepts and principles of citizenship education influenced by political unrest and conflict during the examined period. In other words, she explores to what extent have the curricula of citizenship education changed in terms of the type of citizen to be constructed among Egyptian youth. Soha Aly's chapter reveals how far did the political regime, after the January 25th revolution, influence the content of citizenship education in national curriculum in order to accommodate the revolutionary status among Egyptian youth who seek change for better political, social, and economic conditions.

DIALECTICS OF EDUCATION FOR GLOBAL CITIZENSHIP AND WOMEN'S EMPOWERMENT

The dialectics of education for global citizenship and women's empowerment in the Egyptian context are presented in Chapters 5 and 6. Shaimaa Awad conducts a case study that focuses on the experience of a civil society organization in implementing a character building program for Egyptian children during the time of uprising and conflict. The program intends to contribute to the state's efforts for restoring social cohesion and promoting global values of citizenship. Awad employs a qualitative approach, using a survey with open-ended questions and semi-structured interviews, along with observation of the program implementation. Awad's chapter reveals the extent to which the civil society organization examined in this case study and its education program supports school and community in building well-rounded Egyptian characters who possess moral values and manifest those values in their relationships with others during a challenging time of conflict and unrest.

In Chapter 6, Ola Hosny gives attention to young women in rural, poor areas in Egypt. She examines some education development projects undertaken in the post-2011 revolution, and explores the perceived impact of these projects on young rural women. She focuses on three developmental projects implemented in the south of

Egypt (known as Upper Egypt governorates). Qualitative and quantitative data were collected from a group of young women who participated in these projects. Hosny's fieldwork also included interviews with project staff, parents, and community leaders to better understand the local community and the impact of its culture on women. Hosny's chapter identifies socio-cultural factors that enabled or hindered the potential impact of developmental projects on young rural women, the most deprived segment of the population in Egypt.

DIALECTICS OF TEACHER PROFESSIONAL DEVELOPMENT AND EDUCATIONAL QUALITY

Focusing on school teachers, Amira Abdou examines school-based teacher professional development, which has been promoted as part of the state's reform initiative prior to and post- the 2011 revolution. In Chapter 7, Abdou analyzes the Egyptian policy discourse for school-based teacher professional development, then explores the extent to which this approach has been implemented in Egyptian public schools and how it has been perceived by teachers. Conducting fieldwork in an urban public school that includes primary and secondary education levels, Abdou's chapter identifies the gap between educational policy discourse and practice, highlighting problems and challenges confronting teachers and affecting educational quality at school level.

At the level of higher education, Sara Taraman explores university students' perceptions of the quality of education and whether there was any major improvement or change occurred after the January 25th revolution. Conducted her fieldwork in one of the public universities located in a remote area in Egypt, Taraman presents the university students' perspectives on educational quality, in terms of institutional facilities/infrastructure; organizational culture, especially in relation to students' freedom of speech; teaching and learning experience; and education for career pursuit and community service. Her research has been conducted in four university colleges, representing students in sciences and humanities majors. Taraman's chapter demonstrates the continuation of students' dissatisfaction in the post-revolution Egypt and clarifies the urgent need for genuine reform that would improve the quality of higher education for students in remote areas.

REFERENCES

Bray, M., Adamson, B., & Mason, M. (2007). *Comparative education research: Approaches and methods*. Hong Kong: Comparative Education Research Centre, University of Hong Kong.

CAPMAS. (2017). *Egypt in figures*. Cairo: CAPMAS.

Crossley, M., & Vulliamy, G. (1984). Case-study research methods and comparative education. *Comparative Education, 20*(2), 193–207.

Davies, L. (2005). Evaluating the link between conflict and education. *Journal of Peacebuilding and Development, 2*(2), 42–58.

Davies, L. (2009). Comparative education in an increasingly globalised world. In J. Zajda & V. Rust (Eds.), *Globalization, policy, and comparative research* (pp. 13–34). Berlin: Springer Science + Business Media.

Epstein, E. (Ed.). (2016). *Crafting a global field: Six decades of the Comparative and International Education Society*. Hong Kong: Springer/Comparative Education Research Centre.

Ginsburg, M., & Megahed, N. (2002). What should we tell educators about terrorism and islam? Some considerations in the global context after September 11, 2011. *Educational Studies, 33*(3), 288–310.

Masemann, V. (1982). Critical ethnography in the study of comparative education. *Comparative Education Review, 26*(1), 1–15.

Megahed, N. (2015). The pursuit of democracy: Women's activism, education and gender equity in Egypt and Tunisia. In S. Majhanovich & R. Malet (Eds.), *Building democracy in education on diversity. Comparative and international education: A diversity of voices*. Rotterdam, The Netherlands: Sense Publishers.

Megahed, N., & Lack, S. (2013). Women's rights and gender-educational inequality in Egypt and Tunisia: From colonialism to contemporary revolution. In D. Napier & S. Majhanovich (Eds.), *Education, dominance and identity. Comparative and international education: A diversity of voices* (pp. 201–222). Rotterdam, The Netherlands: Sense Publishers.

Ministry of Education. (2014). *Strategic plan for pre-university education 2014–2030*. Cairo: Ministry of Education.

Ministry of Higher Education. (2010). *Higher education in Egypt: Country review report*. Cairo: Strategic Planning Unit, Ministry of Higher Education.

Phillips, D., & Schweisfurth, M. (2009). *Comparative and international education: An introduction to theory, method and practice*. London & New York, NY: Continuum International Publishing Group.

Nagwa Megahed
Ain Shams University
and
Graduate School of Education
The American University in Cairo (AUC)

PART I

DIALECTICS OF CITIZENSHIP EDUCATION AND YOUTH MOVEMENT FOR PEACEBUILDING

JASON NUNZIO DORIO

2. THE REVOLUTION AS A CRITICAL PEDAGOGICAL WORKSHOP

Perceptions of University Students Reimagining Participatory Citizenship(s) in Egypt

INTRODUCTION

The January 25, 2011 Egyptian Revolution was driven, to a large extent, by the indignation and democratic aspirations of a broad-based coalition of Egyptian people. The chants of "*Aish, Horreya, Adala Egtema'eya*" (Bread, Freedom, and Social Justice) embodied the pursuit for an Egypt that is governed in a more equitable manner, demanding greater dignity and opportunities for Egyptian citizens to civically, politically, and economically participate in the future development of their country. However, subsequent instability and a second Revolution on Jun 30th, 2013 (some refer to it as a popular coup) have revealed contention surrounding emerging models, concepts, and policies of citizenship and the future role of the Egyptian state. Yet, the current turmoil does not reflect a cultural inaptitude towards democracy, but rather a long and complex road toward reimagining Egyptian models of participatory citizenship.

With over one-third of the Egyptian population under the age of 30 (UNHDR, 2010), Egyptian youth are playing a significant role in forging new definitions of Egyptian citizenship through alternative civic and political engagement and social spaces (British Council, 2013; Herrera, 2014; Laiq, 2013). As the precarious and dynamic political transition in Egypt materializes and Egyptian youth seriously consider the kind of state they want and their relationships to said state as well as to their fellow citizens, a spill over into the fundamental institutions of the Egyptian state, most notably Egyptian universities, has resulted from this debate.

Intertwined within the unsettled role of the Egyptian state, Egyptian universities provide a vital site for qualitatively exploring experiences of university students and educators as they navigate the hopefulness as well as challenges of participatory citizenship during the current historical moment in Egypt. Through the lens of participatory citizenship and citizenship education, my research is situated within the contentious struggle to redefine citizenship during the current revolutionary era in Egypt. The broad focus of this research is concerned with the experiences of university students, particularly emphasizing meanings of participatory citizenship and citizenship education, situated within the context of the January 25th Egyptian

Revolution and the subsequent socio-political transitions. Moreover, this chapter is grounded in the notion that revolutionary change can provide a process of learning. Paulo Freire (1996) argues, "Citizenship is a social invention that demands a certain political knowledge, a knowledge born of the struggle for and reflection on citizenship. The struggle for citizenship generates a knowledge indispensable for its invention" (p. 113). When learning is considered outside of the classroom and into everyday life, it provides the basis for understanding how revolutionary processes, and social and political movements can be a moral and political education that teaches and shapes (as well as being shaped by) the way people think and act as citizens and strive for active citizenship. I maintain that revolutionary transitions, such as the January 25th Egyptian Revolution, can be a critical pedagogical workshop where citizens engage with new forms of political intervention and resistance, critically reflecting upon consciousness-raising events, and experimenting with relationships between agency and power. In the context of revolutionary processes, "critical pedagogy would take on the task of regenerating both sense of social and political agency and a critical subversion of dominant power itself" (Giroux, 2004, p. 33).

It is from the premise of the January 25 Revolution as a critical pedagogical workshop that I ask the question, to what extent has the experiences of the January 25th Egyptian Revolution and subsequent socio-political events impacted the perceptions and actions of participatory citizenship for university students and educators in Egypt? To address this question, I focus on the experiential perceptions and narratives of two university graduate student-instructors struggling to engage their reimagined visions of citizenship as they navigate spaces of teaching and learning within the university as well as within the broader Egyptian society. Participants learn what it means to be a citizen from various sources and how to practice those ideas in multiple spaces. Moreover, the Revolution and subsequent socio-political events, in combination with other influences, have significantly impacted the perceptions of participatory citizenship for participants. Although, participants currently face a number of challenges to participatory citizenship in Egypt, I conclude that the Revolution and subsequent socio-political developments are critical pedagogical workshops for participatory citizenship, fostering, and reinforcing senses of belonging, awareness, and duties of participation in various forms as an Egyptian citizen.

BRIEF BACKGROUND: THE HISTORICAL MOMENT IN EGYPT

In January 25, 2011 it took only 18 days, for a broad-based coalition of pro-democracy demonstrations and strikes to significantly challenge the authoritarian regime; ousting the long-term President Hosni Mubarak on February 11, 2011. The political system under Mubarak was dominated by the military, maintained an extensive security service, and established a one-party rule, based upon an economy driven by crony capitalism (Mitchell, 1999). The national unity and optimism towards social justice and democracy that generally characterized the Egyptian

THE REVOLUTION AS A CRITICAL PEDAGOGICAL WORKSHOP

Revolution and was epitomized by mass demonstrations in the streets and squares such as *Midan al-Tahrir* (Tahrir Square) has now been replaced with a great social rift torn by political and ideological divisiveness, social breakdown, and bouts of violence over the emerging models and concepts of Egyptian citizenship and the future identity of the Egyptian state.

Over the past five years (2011–2016), Egypt has been governed by four different political leaders, two of whom have been democratically elected, and witnessed a second mass uprising in June 2013 that led to the ousting of Egypt's first democratically elected President, Mohamed Morsi. Additionally, Egyptians are suffering from voter fatigue having been called to polls to vote for three constitutional referendums (The ratification of two new constitutions occurred in 2012 and again in 2014), for three houses of parliament and for two presidents. Thus, Egyptians have had a total of eight elections, with multiple phases and runoffs.[1] There have also been a number of deadly clashes between police and protesters, state repression against freedoms of assembly and speech for secular, Islamist, and youth activists alike, which has been met with occasional tactics of bombings, kidnappings, and assassinations by some violent oppositional groups. Additionally, in Northern Sinai and on the border with Libya, the Egyptian military has led campaigns against militants as well as strikes against *Daesh* (the Islamic State) and other terrorist organizations in Syria, Iraq, and Yemen. Moreover, the social and political instability has also drastically contributed to a flailing economy and significantly impacted the vital tourist industry.

Even though the recently ratified 2014 constitution mandates the new Egyptian state to be formed as a "democratic republic based on citizenship and the rule of law," the extent, practices, and implementation of citizenship is yet to be determined.[2] Brown et al. (2013) argue, the Egyptian state is currently in a "process of redefining itself," as the competition for the authority of state between the economically powerful military, Islamist groups, bureaucracy, an entrenched set of patronage networks established by the National Democratic Party, and the protesters is still unresolved (p. 224). As a result, the current political transition in Egypt provides a unique historical opportunity for analyzing how Egypt's political and civic participation will transform under a new state.

WHY CITIZENSHIP?

The euphoria mixed with instability and uncertainty that characterizes the so-called Arab Spring began in Tunisia in December 2010 and was soon followed by a wave of popular protests and revolts in the majority of Arab League states.[3] Consequently, against this seeming rise in political and civic participation in the Arab world, a renewed interest into questions of what does it mean to be a citizen, and how can— and how do—people exercise their rights as citizens are defining political, social, and intellectual discourse within the current era of the Arab uprisings. For instance, a recent quantitative study focusing on political participation in Egypt concluded, "The revolution of January, 2011 has changed the concept of political participation in Egypt and encouraged people to take part at both formal and informal levels. Whilst the former still enjoys greater levels of support than the latter, it is important to note that just as concepts and means of political participation evolve over time so can citizens' perceptions of them" (Refaei, 2015, p. 21). Furthermore, there have been many recent conferences dedicated to the topic of citizenship held throughout the Arab world. Additionally, citizenship pertaining to various areas such as the nature of the Egyptian state, youth participation and education is mandated within 2014 Egyptian Constitution. Furthermore, the Egyptian government has featured the rather ambiguous term of "citizens happiness" as one of four main goals within its 2030 development agenda entitled *Sustainable Development Strategy: Egypt's Vision 2030* launched in March 2015 during the Egypt Economic Development Conference in Sharm al-Sheikh.[4] Thus, these examples are but few illustrations of the growing demand to develop deeper insight into the theories, realities, and struggles of citizenship within Arab states in general, and within Egypt specifically. But, what is citizenship?

An insightful analogy provided by Parolin (2009) describes citizenship "as an ellipsoid, its main intersection points can be expressed in terms of membership, rights, participation or status, variously considered from the legal, philosophical, political or sociological planes. When the models of each focus change, the entire figure reshapes" (p. 19). This quote underscores the complexities of analyzing citizenship, and highlights the fact that from Ancient Greek philosophers to present day scholars, politicians, and ordinary citizens, many have debated, negotiated, and fought over the multifaceted and contested terrain of citizenship.

Citizenship generally contains the three elements comprised of membership, rights, and participation within the nation-state (Bellamy, 2008). Simply stated, "citizenship, at least theoretically, confers membership, identity, values, and rights of participation and assumes a body of common political knowledge" (Knight Abowitz & Harnish, 2006, p. 653). *Membership* in a political community is concerned with identity and who is a citizen, conferring membership in a polity, while excluding those who are not members (various means of exclusions of citizenship have been based upon ethnicity, gender, levels of property ownership, and education, etc.). Associated with membership in the polity are those who receive collective benefits and *rights*. These rights are based upon negotiated standards of decency and civic virtues that regulate social relations, and provide the ability for individuals to make claims against others, including governments, when rights are abused. The duty to uphold as well as expand citizenship rights is related to *participation* in a community's political, economic, and social processes. Participation is connected with multiple forms of social and political agency. In addition to these three elements, citizenship can also be distinguished as a form of *knowledge*. From this perspective, citizenship education, as a form of citizenship knowledge and development, can pertain to a formal as well as informal educational endeavors intended to bestow civic and political knowledge, skills, and virtues necessary to transform youth into informed, responsible, and participatory citizens (Torres, 1998). Therefore, the four elements of citizenship above are connected to the range of problems linked to the relationships between citizens and the state (the social contract), and among citizens themselves. I argue that citizenship should be understood as a social practice and knowledge that extends beyond legal and social norms. Citizenship therefore arises out of social struggle (Turner, 1990). Moreover, citizenship should be viewed as an unfinished project; a continual struggle that people strive for and that every generation must renegotiate and reimage its meanings. This study will focus specifically on two elements of citizenship: participatory citizenship and citizenship education in Egypt. Thus, during times of tremendous political and social transition, such as that occurring in Egypt, participatory citizenship and citizenship education, to a varying extent, get redefined and renegotiated to either accommodate or suppress emerging actors within a renewed political system.

Participatory Citizenship in Egypt

Participatory citizenship is based upon the theory that in democratic societies political and civic participation is a duty and responsibility needed to foster the preservation of membership and rights of citizens. Participation is a citizen's involvement in civic and political life, ranging form formal and informal forms and spaces, including voting, standing for office, volunteering, and public discussions. Participatory citizenship can also be the basis for agency on which people build their rights to seek justice and to demand active participation within their societies, assuming greater civic and political participation and increased awareness of the social, political, and economic issues facing local and national communities. Turner (1990) describes the notion of 'active and passive citizenry' and the importance of 'struggle', arguing particular social struggles are a driver of citizenship, naming this 'citizenship from below.' In this way, social movement theory and citizenship rights and participation are linked, and the oscillations between 'passive' and 'active', 'demobilization' and 'mobilization,' and 'depoliticization' and 'politicization' make for dynamic models of participation (Meijer, 2014).

The right to participate, in all of its various forms, has been increasingly endorsed and promoted through global and regional institutions and has—at least theoretically—became a global norm.[5] However, as Parolin (2009) reminds us, "exploring citizenship in the Arab world requires first a disentanglement from all those ideas, images and suggestions that have settled into the concept in the course of European political thought" (p. 25). The extent, processes, and stakeholders of participatory citizenship are relative to particular individuals and structural challenges. Resources, the nature of the political system, and citizenship education, and skills can all influence the form and intensity of civic engagement and political participation.

In Egypt, prior to the Revolution, political rights and civil liberties[6] have been deeply defined and controlled by the state apparatus, limiting the extent of participation of its citizens. Within the Egyptian context, Refaei (2015) states, "one must bear in mind the overall low levels of political awareness and participation and limited means available for citizens to engage informally in the political process or influence government decision-making. In a society where voices of dissent have rarely been tolerated, it is interesting to note that dissenting views are often only associated with informal means of political engagement, whereas in some other countries formal channels serve the same purpose" (pp. 5–6).

Yet, from another perspective, the civic and political participation that occur outside the formal channels sanctioned by the Egyptian state is of considerable importance. For example, Alhamad (2008) argues that in Egypt, "political participation goes beyond the formal realm and that the subtle, seemingly non-political actions by citizens carry considerable political meaning. Such participation often takes place through loosely based, informal vehicles, many of which serve multiple purposes—social, political, occupational—and are often indigenous to the region" (p. 36). Bayat (2010), for instance, examines agency and participation of the subaltern[7] in Egypt, and how through everyday acts of defiance and the "art of presence," citizens are redefining participation. In addition, conducting research on youth participation and civic engagement in North Africa, researchers from UNICEF (2011) identify youth participation ranging from participating in family and school, to participation within the public arena (community, national, and emergencies). Therefore, since the type of state cannot guarantee or predict all the particular forms and spaces of participatory citizenship, this research is guided by a more nuanced understanding of participation in Egypt.

Consequently, within the realities of the changing Egyptian state, participation in Egypt can include, but is not limited to, voting, community service and participation in civil society groups, actively participating in the wellbeing of family members, individual activism, and participation in social movements. A broad-view of participatory citizenship in Egypt is needed in order to reveal the potential range of local interpretations of participation. Therefore, participatory citizenship exists on a continuum of participation, from those formal participation policies authorized and taught by the Egyptian state, to more alternative modes of participation that seek to challenge participation norms and carve out spaces of expanding civic and political participation.

CITIZENSHIP EDUCATION

It is well recognized that various forms of schooling and education have been given the duty and promise by national governments to foster the knowledge, skills and virtues necessary for youth to become valuable citizens that participate in the construction of the 'good society' (Hillygus, 2005; Torney-Purta, 2002). However, critics have argued that historically the instrumental rationality of citizenship education (CE), with few exceptions, has been to develop a submissive citizenry in order to maintain and reproduce particular economic, social, and political structures of society (Giroux, 1980). Therefore, a considerable tension exists between education that "can be used as a tool for maintaining the status quo," and education towards "empowering individuals and groups to struggle for emancipatory change" (Schugurensky & Myers, 2003, p. 1).

Citizenship education can be criticized for contributing to producing, on the one hand, passive, apathetic, consumer-driven, and/or possessive individualistic citizens. On the other, CE can produce overly patriotic and narrowly nationalistic citizens leading to citizens who favor exclusionary, ethno-nationalistic, and xenophobic visions for society. Furthermore, since schools are fundamentally undemocratic institutions, unless schools provide students with opportunities to have a voice in the decision making process, it is difficult for such environments to instill in students the virtues, commitment, and skills necessary for CE to have a proper impact. However, it is too simplistic to suggest that X school produces X citizen; a more complex and multifaceted approach to the pedagogical subject and reproduction should be taken (Morrow & Torres, 1995).

Formal institutions of education within the nation state are not the sole place where youth can acquire citizenship knowledge and skills. There are many agents of political socialization, and therefore CE can occur in formal (school), non-formal (community-based), and informal (family, media) spaces of learning and education. Political socialization, as an important element of CE, can be explained as the means and processes connected to the acquisition of political knowledge, perceptions, and behaviors greatly shaping citizenship. Political socialization can be the ways political and social systems are legitimized, reproduced, as well as challenged. The agents of political socialization commonly include: family, teachers and schools, peers, mass media, political leaders, state institutions, institutions of religion, and social movements to name a few. However, a main premise of this chapter is that major political and social events such as revolutions should also be acknowledged as formative agents of political socialization and CE.

By problematizing CE and agents of political socialization away from functionalist perspectives, researchers can at least theoretically carve out spaces where momentous political and social events, such as the January 25 Egyptian Revolution, can become a significant pedagogical catalysis for raising the consciousness and participation of citizens in Egypt. First, youth as a pedagogical subject are not merely objects waiting to be filled with political knowledge, but co-construct their political knowledge, perceptions, and behaviors *with* agents of political socialization (Freire, 2007). Second, citizenship is not merely a package of rights that may or may not be exercised at the prudence of the citizen (such as the right to vote). It is a kind of freedom, a capacity that involves a particular set of knowledge, skills, virtues, networks, and resources. Citizenship is not a material item to be bought or sold that one chooses to own and use; it is a process towards a better and good society. It is a kind of social being that through struggle one can cultivate and pursue. Third, political socialization is strongly dominated by the state through formal institutions. Thus, there are often tensions between the values and identities students possess and those pedagogies and values promulgated through CE that is fostered by the state. That is not to say that political socialization, which promotes oppositional ideas and practices, does not occur within formal institutions such as public schools and universities. The important point is that the monopoly of CE controlled by the state often creates struggles and contentious citizenship between the "official knowledge" of CE (Apple, 1993) projected by the state and citizenship knowledge and actions supported by dissenting and oppositional groups. Therefore, there is a constant struggle over the various models of citizenship between the various agents and among pedagogical subjects themselves. Finally, in the current era of globalization, agents of political socialization are not restricted to the borders of the nation-state. Accordingly, knowledge, skills, and virtues—more so than ever before—can be readily exchanged through the transnational mobility and migration of people, the Internet, social media networks, and global cable news channels, which may challenge, uphold, or compliment CE within the nation-state.

Citizenship Education in Egypt

Within the context of the reverberations of the Arab uprisings, CE takes on a particular importance that has led various authors to encourage the growth of social and cultural responsibilities necessary to support democratic changes in the Arab world (Hibbard & Layton, 2010). For example, Faour and Muasher (2011) argue that in light of the Arab uprisings students need to learn "what it means to be citizens who learn how to think, seek and produce knowledge, question, and innovated rather than be subjects of the state who are taught what to think and how to behave" (p. 1).

In Egypt specifically, scholars have called on implementing critical visions of citizenship at all levels of education (Bali, 2013; El-Mikawy, 2012). Muhammad Faour highlights three rationales for CE.[8] First, CE attempts to consolidate democracy, which thrives only in cultures that accept diversity, different view points, tolerates dissent, and regards truths as relative. Second, CE generally includes values central to human development (freedom, women's rights, and democratic governance). Last, CE promotes 21st century skills, such as problem solving, critical thinking, consensus building, collaboration, creativity, and communication. However, even though historical research has demonstrated that Egyptian universities have long been central to the project of nation building and citizenship development (Makdisi, 1981; Reid, 1990), the overwhelming majority of empirical research on citizenship education in Egypt focuses exclusively on primary and secondary education (Baraka, 2008; El-Nagar & Krugly-Smolska, 2009; Faour, 2013; Faour & Muasher, 2011; Zaalouk, 2006).

The perspective that universities have an important role as well as responsibility to foster the skills and values necessary for a new era of Egyptian citizenship guides the present study. First, universities have traditionally produced Egyptian leaders that have been instrumental in influencing citizenship discourse and policies. Second, universities in Egypt have not only been important sites for developing multiple forms of citizenship, but have also been battlegrounds of the contention that arises out of divergent ideologies which greatly shape the understanding and practice of citizenship (Abdalla, 1985; Herrera, 2006; Mazawi, 2005; Megahed & Lack, 2011). Finally, when factoring in the significant youth bulge (Chaaban, 2009) in Egypt, universities and other institutions of higher education have an extraordinary role in harnessing the talent, creativity, and productivity of Egyptian youth. Therefore, not only are Egyptian universities vital locations for analyzing university students' perceptions of participatory citizenship, but can also provide researchers with microcosms for observing the turbulent moment occurring throughout the larger Egyptian society.

However, there has been a significant amount of research that calls into question the recent role of Egyptian universities cultivating citizenship participation. For instance, as a result of the centralized control over campus-life during the period prior to the January 25 Revolution, universities played a rather diminished role as sites that foster the skills and knowledge necessary for the construction of democratic citizenship (Herrera, 2010, 2012; Shehata, 2008; Sika, 2012). To a large extent, formal political and educational institutions were replaced by non-formal organizations such as NGOs and civil society groups (Gerhart Center, 2011), virtual social networks (Herrera, 2012), and social movements (Beinin & Vairel, 2011) where Egyptian youth gained civic and political engagement skills, experience, and citizenship education.

Currently, in the aftermath of the ousting of Mubarak, reports have indicated that universities have increasingly become reinvigorated sites where young people discuss, mobilize, and even clash about grievances related to their universities as well as issues faced by the broader Egyptian society (Levy, 2011; Lindsey, 2012; Lynch & Mahmoud, 2013). For example, a recent report by *The Economist Intelligence Unit* found that during the 2013 fall semester alone there were 1,122 student protests carried out at universities and schools in Egypt.[9] It appears that Egyptian students are testing the boundaries of participatory citizenship and are attempting to carve out spaces of agency where their grievances about political, social, and educational issues are brought to the forefront. Consequently, empirical research is also needed to analyze the extent of universities as revived spaces that foster participatory citizenship in Egypt. Since humans are complex pedagogical citizens, who learn through various processes and participate in various spaces, it must be acknowledged that universities—although a revived space for CE—are but one important institution and agent of political socialization that can foster CE in Egypt.

METHODOLOGY AND METHODS

Hermeneutic Phenomenology

To explore the perceptions and practices of citizenship, I employed the qualitative research methodology known as Hermeneutic Phenomenology (HP). Phenomenology as a research methodology is often described as studying the meanings of lived experience, and hermeneutics as studying the processes of interpretation and meaning. Therefore, a HP approach is both descriptive and interpretive. As Van Manen (1990) explains, HP "is a descriptive (phenomenological) methodology because it wants to be attentive to how things appear, it wants to let things speak for themselves; it is an interpretive (hermeneutic) methodology because it claims that there are no such things as uninterpreted phenomena" (p. 180). Consequently, HP "aims at gaining a deeper understanding of the nature or meaning of our everyday experiences" (Van Manen, 1990, p. 9).

As a qualitative research method well received and validated within the field of education (Henriksson & Friesen, 2012), HP diverges from other qualitative research methods, and also from traditional phenomenological approaches. In addition to providing depth and richness of meanings of lived experience, "it rejects the claim of some phenomenological methods that ideal "essences" of experience or consciousness can be isolated outside of the researcher's cultural and historical location" (Henriksson & Friesen, 2012, p. 1). Contemporary phenomenologists are then concerned with understanding social phenomena and the range of experiencing a phenomenon from the perspectives of people involved. Van der Mescht (2004) explains that phenomenologists "'language' participants' physical, emotional and intellectual *being-in-the-world*" (p. 3). Therefore, rather than subscribing to a positivist understanding of reality being stable, measurable, and existing "out there", phenomenologists understand that reality is socially constructed and interpretive, and often co-construct knowledge with their participants, having the prospect for more critical and empowering research (Merriam, 2009, pp. 8–9).

Hermeneutic phenomenology is therefore a valuable methodology for unearthing the rather complex and highly contextualized nature of participants' perceptions and practices of participatory citizenship and its relationship to the university. The purpose of using a HP approach for the present study is to provide specific and deep understandings of participatory citizenship in Egypt and how citizenship may be related to experiences and meaning-making within the university as well as throughout the broader Egyptian society.

An important method of data collection in a hermeneutic phenomenological study is the semi-structured phenomenological interview (Van Manen, 2014). The phenomenological interview "serves the very specific purpose of exploring and gathering experiential narrative material, stories, or anecdotes that may serve as a resource for phenomenological reflection and thus develop a richer and deeper understanding of a human phenomenon" (Van Manen, 2014, p. 314). Therefore, the flexibility of semi-structured questions was designed to elicit experiential accounts that are rich and detailed, focusing on participant's experiences and interpretation about participatory citizenship and citizenship education.

Participants

As a "Scholar without Stipend" affiliated with the Graduate School of Education (GSE) at the American University in Cairo (AUC), I spent 8 months (August, 2014 to March, 2015) in Cairo, Egypt conducting interviews on the campus of AUC as part of my dissertation fieldwork. Although the current chapter focuses on the interviews of two participants, it is part of a larger dissertation research projected that included interviews with 24 university students and educators (educators refer to professors, instructors, and/or researchers in a university or educational institutions). Interviews were conducted in English within quiet spaces on the campus of AUC, and ranged from 20 to 60 minutes each. Participants were selected by maximal variation and information-rich sampling (Patton, 2002) as well as snowball sampling techniques (Creswell, 2008). Although the main criterion was that all participants had to be Egyptian citizens, ranges of identities were represented including various genders, ages, socio-economic statuses, governorates, religious affiliations, educational levels, faculties, and type of institutions (public and private). For the present chapter, the two participants, Ahmed and Nadia (pseudonyms) represent most of these identities (see a more detailed explanation under the section of the findings). It should be noted that regardless of the range of identities of participants, a qualitative study by nature is not designed to assemble statistically large sample sizes. Although the study is relevant, the findings cannot be extrapolated to a larger set of the population and does not represent the multifaceted and complicated experiences of all Egyptians. For many Egyptians, daily survival takes precedence over focusing on forms of participatory citizenship.

Thematic Analysis

The analysis of the interview data was guided by Max Van Manen's approaches to theme analysis for HP research. Van Manen (2014) refers to thematic analysis as "the process of recovering structures of meanings that are embodied and dramatized in human experience represented in a text" (p. 319). Van Manen (2014) describes the process of thematic analysis for HP research, including the different ways of extrapolating various levels of meaning from the text. First, the researcher conducts a thematic reading of the transcript or edits the transcript into a shorter anecdote by deleting excess material. Next, a "themaitzation" of the anecdote occurs. As a way to identify thematic expressions, phrases, and/or narratives, the anecdote is submitted into one or all of levels of various thematizations. Last, the themes are used for exemplary HP reflective writing—"where themes can further be extrapolated by the using side headings for more explicit organization of the themes and added material that would supplement the text" (p. 322).

For the purposes of this study, I started with the selective reading approach.[10] I highlighted phrases and statements that at first glance appeared to be relevant to my research question, by using In Vivocoding (Saldana, 2013) or my own interpretive phrases as labels. Then after a second reading, I took chunks of combined selective reading excerpts and formulated them into a larger anecdote that could be expressed by a single *wholistic phrase*[11] for a particular participant. Shown in the next section, the wholistic phrases for this paper were: "the Revolution, when it happened, it got me angry" and "the beauty of the Revolution." The anecdotes of these two phrases address the research question: how have the experiences of the January 25 Egyptian Revolution and subsequent events impacted the perceptions and actions of participatory citizenship for university students and academics in Egypt? Last, the anecdotes were broken into sub-anecdotes and then excerpts from the selective reading approach were used set up each anecdote, discuss themes, and conclude each anecdote. I felt that it was easier for readers to follow if the phenomenological reflective writings were included before and after the sub-anecdotes rather than following strictly to the Van Manenian process of page-long sections of anecdotes followed by large sections of phenomenological writings. Additionally, for the purpose of this chapter, I did not include a detailed reading approach due to space restraints.

FINDINGS

During times of social and political conflict, ideas about citizenship and the role of the state becomes greatly contested, which can significantly impact people's perceptions of citizenship. Turner (1990) argues "it is important to put a particular emphasis on the notion of social struggles as the central motor of the drive of citizenship" (p. 193). As a recent social struggle, the January 25, 2011 Egyptian Revolution and subsequent social and political turmoil has left a deep impression on how Egyptians view themselves as citizens and their relationship to society and to the state. The section provides evidence to support the assertion that for the participants interviewed, the January 25 Revolution and the subsequent turbulent era are transformative critical pedagogical events for developing perceptions and practices of participatory citizenship. Using In Vivo (Saldana, 2013) excerpts from the thematic phenomenological analysis, in this section I present some of the relevant perceptions of two participants during their complex trajectories of their citizenship development. Their perceptions are organized in thematic sections including before the Revolution, during the Revolution, influences of citizenship, after the Revolution, teaching as an political act of citizenship, and current challenges.

The Revolution fostered self and experiential learning about meanings and practices of citizenship, and created awareness about politics and being political. For participants, the Revolution forced them to confront their various forms of identities and membership as an Egyptian, struggling with new senses of belonging and duties, and in turn participants transformed learning and experiences into new and renewed forms of participatory citizenship. These participants demonstrate a significant shift from an inability to connect with Egypt as a citizen before the Revolution, to a deeper connection and an overwhelming duty to participate as a citizen after the Revolution. Consequently, teaching becomes a manifestation of the Revolution as a critical pedagogical event for participatory citizenship, as participants perceive teaching as an action of citizenship and in turn foster participatory ideas and skills of citizenship for their students.

'The Beauty of the Revolution:' Ahmed

Ahmed is from Cairo, in his mid-30 s. He has a bachelor's degree in Language Arts from a public university and is currently a graduate student enrolled in a masters of education program at a private foreign university. Ahmed is an English language instructor at the same private foreign university and also manages teachers at a community center that teaches English, citizenship education, and technology to underserved teenagers. Ahmed is also a practicing Muslim. The experiences of Revolution gradually helped Ahmed to not only connect with being an Egyptian citizen and made him feel pride in his country, it helped to instill duties trying to make a better Egypt through his various forms of participatory citizenship and his teaching.

Before the Revolution

Prior to the January 25th Egyptian Revolution, Ahmed did not feel connected to Egypt as a citizen. Although Ahmed always viewed his teaching as a service "helping the community," that service was driven by the need to help students have better job opportunities, rather than teaching them to be active citizenship. Ahmed explains:

> Before the Revolution I can't say that I was even aware [what it means to be a citizen]. Before the January 25 Revolution…I didn't feel that I was a citizen and I couldn't frame it in this way. I just felt that I'm in a place. Going to work, earning my living and that's it. Working as a teacher…I felt that that I was helping the community, because I was teaching English. It would help my students have jobs and have a good future. Maybe that would help the progress of the whole country…but still the idea that I am a citizen or I can call myself a citizen I never felt. I could not say I am an Egyptian citizen. I never felt like that.

For Ahmed, there was a lack of knowledge about being a citizen and ways of participate. Egypt was just a "place" where he goes to work and earns a living and "that's it." The sense of belonging, the sense of community or of duties and having rights generally characterizing citizenship were "never felt" by Ahmed before the Revolution. However, as Ahmed states in another excerpt, "When the 25th [Referring to the January 25, 2011 Egyptian Revolution] came, that was an eye-opener!" The following sub-anecdote showcases his transition from not feeling that he was a citizen to a sense of confusion about the dynamic developments of the Revolution.

Confusion during the Revolution

This sub-anecdote describes the often-confusing trajectory of Ahmed's experiences during the Revolution ending with the awakening Ahmed had during his first day that he visited Tahrir Square after Mubarak was ousted.

> On the 25th people were calling for protests. And I wanted to go, but then I had people telling me "why are you going, this doesn't make sense; they are just a bunch of kids. You don't need to go." So I listened to all of the people around me telling me this bullshit and then I stayed at home. I was the only one within

my circle who wanted to really go and join. This showed that I had the passion to be a part of it. The last years before the Revolution, things go so worst that people were dying at bread queues. There were also other incidents of deaths by police. It was so bad and the corruption became so noticeable.

For Ahmed, the Revolution was a confusing time. Initially he recognized the corruption, deaths, and lack of economic opportunities that plagued Egypt before the Revolution and was sympathetic to the protesters in Tahrir. However, his circle of friends persuaded him not to take part in the protest. As events unfolded Ahmed become more confused about joining the protests:

Then the Friday, Day of Wrath [January 28, 2011], I saw on TV…it was a strange moment. Then the media started the war. They said prisoners were set free. And then you got so worried about your neighborhood and thinking of the thousands of prisoners that were on your street. So we had to have committees that would protect the streets. But I remember seeing on TV people saying, "still if prisoners were on the street we are not leaving Tahrir. Some of us will stay to protect the neighborhoods and some of us will stay in Tahrir." The persistence that they had was strange for me. I got so confused. I was in a state of confusion.

Then I heard rumors that people in Tahrir were taking money [to protest]. And I found even my neighbors repeating the same thing saying, "my friend is in Tahrir and he is taking 100 pounds for the day." When you hear it not only from media, but also from people that was also confusing.

On the one hand you have people saying these people are traitors and they are taking money, and the country is falling. And you have the other camp saying, no this regime should be toppled; it should be ousted right away. So I was in such a state of confusion to the extent that I sympathized with Mubarak when he gave his famous speech.

Subsequently, the fear of prisoners in the streets and the alleged bribes paid to protestors, promulgated by the media, and the violence and destruction made him "sympathize with Mubarak" and dissuaded Ahmed for participating in any demonstrations.

Then the Battle of the Camel [February 2, 2011] happened. I didn't know what was going on. When you see Egyptians killing each other, in a strange scene where you have horses and camels running over people in Tahrir. After the Battle of the Camel, Cairo was on fire, and this [media] guy said, "This is not the Cairo that I love." When he said that and I saw Cairo on fire, I got emotional and I hated everything that was happening. I felt that my city and my country were on fire. Like it's going to hell.

Even my mom was so worried about us… she refused that we would be part of anything. She felt that she was going to die or have heart attack if we just started to discuss anything or started to talk about things. She got in such a medical condition, that she had to take medication because she was so afraid of what she saw on TV.

With the city that he loves on fire and unrecognizable, he felt like the city was "going to hell" and he wanted stability. The confusion and disappointment of the developments that Ahmed felt was exacerbated by medical issues experienced by his mother, ultimately deterred him from joining the protests as well as prevented him from discussing current events at home. However, the overall confusion and obstacles that Ahmed initially faced was soon eclipsed by a newly found appreciation of the Revolution and greater connection to Egypt.

Influences

The following excerpts shows how although initially his peers and the illness of his mother greatly dissuaded Ahmed from joining the protests before the ousting of Mubarak, his mother was actually excited about Mubarak's departure and persuaded him to go the demonstrations. In addition, actually witnessing and participating on the streets of Tahrir, not relying on the opinions of his friends, the media, or his neighbors, transformed his opinion about the Revolution and eventually (in the following excerpts) transformed his sense of membership, agency and community as an Egyptian citizen.

> On the day when Mubarak was ousted [February 11, 2011], I found my mother crying happily. She was jumping and she said Mubarak left, Mubarak's ousted. Let's go to the street! I was surprised. She kept all of this inside her all of these days, because she was afraid for us to be a part of it…but when it happened, she couldn't believe it. So we went right away to the streets joining and you'll find all the streets full of people around Tahrir and all the people were very happy and they were celebrating. Different people, different groups, different beliefs. Rich and poor, Christians and Muslims, those with beards, like Islamists maybe, and without, veiled and unveiled, everybody together. Those with special needs and those without all together in Tahrir. And that moment was amazing.

> Then I saw with my eyes the field hospitals, and I saw the people who slept the nights in the streets. That was the happiest moment in my life. That was what I need help seeing. The beauty of the Revolution and all of that. It's amazing. The happiest day was when Mubarak was ousted, that day was amazing.

With his mom's surprising support of the Revolution and her persuasiveness to go out into the streets after the ousting of Mubarak, Ahmed got to finally experience the "beauty of the Revolution" firsthand, which he needed "help seeing." He witnessed the unity of the Egyptian people, the sacrifices people had made through the endless protests sleeping on the streets during the winter as well as the makeshift "field hospitals" that took care of the injured and killed revolutionaries. It was "the happiest moment" in Ahmed's life. However, "the beauty of the revolution" soon took an ironic twist.

After the Revolution

After the Revolution, when SCAF[12] took control of Egypt's government, Ahmed was willing to give the leadership a chance to change the situation in Egypt.

> Then I waited because I believed that now the Supreme Council would take over and things will change. So I was that person that thought okay the Supreme Council took over and we don't need to be in the streets…But then I found that I was fooled again. Because nothing happened, and all that I heard was just talk. So I started going to the streets from then on. Because now the picture's clear. I don't have any more confusion. Since then I was on the streets.

Although Ahmed was willing to support SCAF, the social, political, and economic changes that they were promised by SCAF failed to materialize quick enough for Ahmed. The lack of change in Egypt promised by SCAF appeared to bring some clarity to Ahmed's position. He felt that he was fooled by SCAF and decided to once again join the protests and be "on the streets," participating in various demonstrations and movements. Additionally, actively being involved in protests, which not only ultimately gave him a newfound connection to Egypt, but also help him to recognize his work for social change in Egypt through education. Currently, amidst the restrictions placed on various forms of social and political participation (e.g., The Protest Law, governmental controls on civil society, and etc.), Ahmed views education—over participating in formal politics—a more viable path for social change.

Growth as a Citizen: Teaching as a Political Act of Citizenship

The following excerpt specifically states that the Revolution and education was important to the development of Ahmed definition of citizenship.

> Actually when I think of myself before the Revolution and also before doing the masters, I would say that education and the Revolution they helped me to have a more comprehensive and developed definition of citizenship. I have duties and rights towards my community and the whole world.

Overall the revolution helped Ahmed to grow as a citizen. Similar with other participants, Ahmed participated in various avenues and had a greater sense of belonging, of social and political awareness, of hope and of community. The following sub-anecdote encapsulates Ahmed's experiences during the revolution and highlights the impacts of the revolution on his understanding and actions of citizenship:

> The revolution gave me the chance to unite with other Egyptians, to make change happen, to see the intensity of our social problems, to evaluate my perception

for the whole surrounding that I did not think of before the revolution. Yeah, being part of the marches, protests, watching political problems extensively, talking to other people and trying to understand their viewpoints. I think it was a journey of self-learning; I was deprived of politics throughout my whole life and I decided to take an intensive course [metaphorically]. I guess that was the case with many.

And even being part of politics that was also totally new. And having the power to change that was also new. Because I never felt it, and I never even thought about it [before]. It wasn't something to think about it before... I started to feel that I'm a citizen after The Revolution. I started to feel I'm citizen when I heard people say, "raise your head up, you are Egyptian." And then I started thinking and started to even feel proud that I am Egyptian. I am proud because people are changing things and they have the power to change, and they own the country, it's theirs and they have rights, and they have duties, and all of that. So that all happened after The Revolution...

Now, I practice citizenship by educating myself more and more. I watch political or serious programs whenever I get a chance. I broaden my academic knowledge by reading a lot in the field of education and see how I can come up with practical solutions to some of our problems. The social can make a change in the country, but it will take like more time to reach the political change I am aiming at, but it is possible.

The "beauty of the Revolution" for Ahmed was unity he felt with other Egyptians and being part of the political scene, understanding others view points and going through "a journey of self-learning," all things he was deprived of before the Revolution. Chants such as "Raise your head your Egyptian," helped him to unite with his country and made him feel proud his was an Egyptian citizen. He has recognized the power that people have to make changes in their country, and as citizens they have rights and duties. Now he has made efforts to educate himself on various social and political issues. Additionally, he sees himself and his students as agents of change, and his role as a teacher as not only a duty to his country but also a space where he practices citizenship. Ahmed states:

> So I am going for the possible. I believe that helping my students become critical thinkers, active citizens, confident, courageous, knowledgeable will lead to a great change in society. I hope I can do this with the marginalized and underprivileged since they are not given the chance to get real education and they form the majority of the population.

Ahmed is helping his students to become "critical thinkers, active citizens, confident, courageous, [and] knowledgeable," which he believes "will lead to a great change in society."

'The Revolution, When It Happened, It Got Me Angry:' Nadia

Nadia is in her late-20s and currently a graduate student in an education program at a foreign private university. After receiving a bachelor degree in computer science from another foreign private university, she was convinced by a professor to become an instructor for undergraduate students at the same university when she is pursuing her master's degree. Although she was born in Cairo and therefore retains the rights of an Egyptian citizen, her family migrated from a neighboring Arab country, which creates an interesting tension for her during the Revolution. Nadia is also a practicing Christian.

Before the Revolution

Growing up, Nadia and her family maintained their cultural and ethnic heritage by speaking English, French, and their Arab dialect and surrounding themselves within a community of family and friends from their country of origin. Attending international primary and secondary schools, she never thought of herself as an Egyptian, she identified more to her home community. But, it was never really an issue until she started her university career. During her time at a private university, Nadia was exposed to and forced to socialize in Egyptian Arabic, very distinctive from her home dialect of Arabic. Nadia shared:

> People there [the university] didn't speak English all the time, so I had to speak in Arabic. Then I realized my Arabic is different. Even in my community, the church, the club, or wherever we go, it is always, almost the same. It is a very closed community, which I never liked, and my parents never forced it on me, so when I decided never to go back again they were okay with that. That is why it was contradicting, because I was never raised…I could never say Egypt belonged to me, and I never said I belong to Egypt.

Before the Revolution Nadia felt that she was an outsider. She spent very little time on campus, refused to make friends or attend social events, and never participated in community service or civic engagement activities outside her cultural and ethnic community. She never felt that she was an Egyptian citizen, "I could never say Egypt belonged to me, and I never said I belong to Egypt."

During the Revolution and Influences

The Revolution has drastically challenged not only her sense of belonging but also her commitment to Egypt. She explains:

> I didn't even know the Revolution happened, until 24 hours after it happened. When the Revolution happened in Egypt…I was like its just fine let it happen, but then when it affected me personally, it affected people that I loved, and

people pasted-away. Literally, I had no idea, and I was like oh wow. It [The Revolution] was a slap in my face. I was like, I belong here, why didn't I think of it. It really made me to rethink everything, rethink my ideology, rethink my perception of myself in this place [Egypt].

Because I started to understand the system better; The Revolution when it happened it got me angry. It got me very angry at myself, because I didn't know about it. And then at the people that were opposing what was happening, because I felt that it was their right. But again it was their right; I never said it was my right until later on, when I felt that if my brother was getting into the Army then I am a part of this.

For Nadia, the Revolution was an unexpected and abrupt event, as she described a "slap in my face." She now feels a sense of belonging; "I belong here." This new sense of belonging sparked by the Revolution forced her to rethink her ideologies and perceptions as an Egyptian, especially now that her brother got conscripted into the Army. She further shared that the Revolution has forced her to learn about and follow Egyptian politics and current events: "to understand the system better."

Admittedly, the Revolution was not the sole event that led to her re-evaluating pervious understandings of what it means to be an Egyptian citizen. The conscription of her brother and people she loved died from police violence while protesting, also reinforced her newfound identity as an Egyptian citizenship. Consequently, Nadia felt she now had a role to play in Egyptian society and shared many personal stories and people who had helped her to realize her present relationship to Egypt.

Growth as a Citizen: Teaching as a Political Act of Citizenship

Currently, while working on her master's degree, she is a university instructor teaching critical thinking and writing classes to undergraduate students at a private university. She especially pointed to her role as a teacher as important part of her newfound sense of belonging and duty to Egypt. Discussing her recent experiences as an instructor, Nadia discusses the need for her students to be connected to Egypt:

So, I cannot change the world, but at least I can change the life of my students. At least when I am in class we do talk about rights, we do talk about freedom. I always make it a point to talk about these things. To open up their perspectives and their perceptions of certain things. And to listen to what they have to say.

So a lot of them [her undergraduate students] are not connected to their country. A lot of them do not know their rights. A lot of them are just focused on how to get out of here [Egypt] and with this always-negative feeling and thought that they have that this [Egypt] is the worst place to be. Yes, this may the worst place to be, but you have a role to do here. They don't understand that they have a role to do.

Nadia comments on Egypt being "the worst place to be," which may be a sentiment of her students, but it also shows her own frustrations with the multifaceted issues facing Egyptian society. While many students at the university are focusing on emigrating out of Egypt, Nadia attempts to foster within them a sense of belonging, an awareness of their rights, and helping them to understand they have a role to play in the future of Egypt. Regardless of the current turmoil, Nadia still believes that her and her students have "a role" in Egyptian society. For example, in addition to being an instructor at the university she is committed to volunteering with groups working to empower girls and women in underprivileged areas in Cairo. Nadia explains:

> I help out in the slums to teach children. And even just to talk about hygiene, or have an activity to do in the summer. Or whenever they would say we are going to collect money for this cause, I would help people collect. Or I held cloth drives, especially in the winter. We used to work a lot with kids in the recycling area, in the *Zabbaleen* [garbage collectors] area. Working with orphans and girls, I go a lot to visit them and see what they need. We would have women's group were we would talk about experiences and just to be able to share.

Comparing these sub-anecdotes to the one explaining her perceptions before the Revolution, Nadia has grown a deeper connected to Egypt and, through her growth, she is committed to changing the life of her students as well as marginalized communities. The overall anecdote provides evidence to the argument that the Revolution was a pivotal event for Nadia in the process of a deeper relationship with her Egyptian identity and a greater commitment to an active Egyptian citizenship. Similar to Ahmed, the Revolution, in combination with other influences such as experiences with family, friends, and education, was not the sole event that fostered a re-imagination of citizenship for Nadia. However, many participants interviewed shared similar stories of how the political and social struggles of the Revolution have greatly shaped their convictions of what it means to be an Egyptian citizen and how to actively practice those convictions for the social, political, and educational betterment of Egypt. Therefore, the Revolution appears to be an important catalysis for participants identifying as an Egyptian citizen and promoting a sense of duty to actively participate as a citizen in various spaces, thus participatory citizenship. However, participates also shared some of the current challenges they face.

Perceptions of Current Challenges to Participatory Citizenship

In the face of raising state repressions of freedoms of speech and assembly, on and off university campuses, as well as the postponement of parliamentary elections, the dynamic socio-political situation in Egypt has the potential to degenerate into restrictive and apathetic environments similar to the era preceding the Revolution. Five years after the Revolution, both Ahmed and Nadia shared their frustrations to current challenges to participatory citizenship.

Ahmed feels that he does not have anybody to represent him politically and "it is very difficult to voice concerns or to be part of any political entity." Furthermore, he commented "the political status is very disappointing and made me feel very disappointed and upset that I wanted to leave the country." The frustrations felt towards developments within the formal political arena in Egypt was common among participants as was the desire to leave the country. Ahmed's initial euphoria and hopefulness of the Revolution now has turned to cautious opportunism, and has forced Ahmed to focus more on "trying to make a change in some social aspects" such as in his classrooms and with community organizations, away from more formal political participation, hoping in "the long run" it will led to political changes.

The challenges shared by Nadia highlights gender issues and the struggle for the rights of women in the Egyptian society. Nadia feels that even though she believes she is equal to men, she states in society, "I am not really equal." One of her hopes is that "as a female that I am free. I am free to express myself, to do what I want." She shared that she wants to be free to dress how she wants, and to be able to walk in public without the fear of being harassed. Nadia attempts to create awareness about gender issues through discussions and various assignments with her students.

CHARACTERISTICS OF CRITICAL PEDAGOGICAL WORKSHOPS FOR CITIZENSHIP IN EGYPT

So, how have the experiences of the January 25th Egyptian Revolution and subsequent events impacted the perceptions and actions of participatory citizenship for university students and academics in Egypt? For the participants, the Revolution and subsequent events have been transformative critical pedagogical workshops where people have gained knowledge and agency towards participatory citizenship in Egypt. The well-know Egyptian novelists and political commenter, Alaa Al Aswany proposes, "A revolution is not just a political act, it is a major humanitarian evolution. People are one thing before a revolution and another after they take to the streets and protest; it is always this way."[13] Al Aswany points to the transformations that occur to citizens during the revolution. The current socio-political era in Egypt appears to be raising the consciousness of citizens in Egypt. The experiences of the participants demonstrate a form Freirean praxis of citizenship in Egypt. Paulo Freire explains that in order to transform oppressive realities, humans must confront reality critically, by simultaneously reflecting and acting upon their world (Freire, 2007). For Freire, critical pedagogy is deeply intertwined with praxis, a reflection and action upon the world to transform it. As Freire states, "discovery cannot be purely intellectual but must involve action; nor can it be limited to mere activism, but must include serious reflection: only then will it be a praxis" (Freire, 2007, p. 65). Participants are reflecting about the situation around them and taking action by attempting transform the world around them. In a complex combination with other influencers such as family, friends, education, and the media, the Revolution and subsequent events are critical pedagogical workshops for participatory citizenship.

The generous narratives shared by the participants can provide an outline for some characteristics of the Revolution and subsequent socio-political as critical pedagogical workshops for participatory citizenship.

First, for both Ahmed and Nadia, the Revolution helped to foster a *deeper identity, connection,* and *sense of belonging* as an Egyptian citizen. Along with the Revolution, both Ahmed and Nadia were influenced by other experiences with family, friends, the media, and education, a complexity that goes beyond what Parolin (2009) narrowly focuses on kin, religion, and the state. Second, as the sense of belonging increased, the need to *learn more about politics and issues of Egyptian society* were shared by both participants. Third, this new or renewed identity as an Egyptian and knowledge about politics and issues encouraged both Ahmed and Nadia to *participate in various forms as an Egyptian citizen.* However, their forms of participatory citizenship differed slightly. While Ahmed participate in protests, social movements, formal politics, as well as in community programs, Nadia tends to participate more in community groups. Where they aligned was in their commitment to teaching as form of participatory citizenship. Forth, they both view their *role as a teacher* both in the formal university setting as well as within the marginalized communities as an important part and action of their reimagined citizenship. They see their role as a teacher as means to transform society, where they intend to foster in their students an active citizenship that includes critical thinking, an awareness of issues, and a commitment to better their society. Last, they both identified struggles that they are addressing and creating awareness as part of their commitment to being a teacher.

RECOMMENDATIONS FOR DEVELOPING UNIVERSITIES FOR 'BREAD, FREEDOM, AND SOCIAL JUSTICE'

The recently ratified 2014 Egyptian Constitution can provide an important legal guide for working towards university reforms. The 2014 Constitution mandates that the new Egyptian state be formed as a "democratic republic based on citizenship and the rule of law" (Article 1), explicitly stating that participation of citizens in public life is a national duty (Article 87), guaranteeing youth engagement to participate in public life (Article 82), based upon the goals of education "to build the Egyptian character, preserve the national identity, rooted in the scientific method of thinking, develop talents and promote innovation, establish cultural and spiritual values, and founded on the concepts of citizenship, tolerance and non-discrimination" (Article 19), and for universities, specifically, the state shall "guarantee its independence of universities and scientific and linguistic academics in accordance with international quality standards" (Article 21) and shall "teach human rights and professional values and ethics of the various academic disciplines" (Article 24).

Universities have an obligation to capitalize on this unique period of raised consciousness and willingness on behalf of young people to participate in the betterment of Egyptian society. Participants conveyed a need for both public and private universities to become more active with student and community engagement. There is a long list of recommendations towards active-universities by those interviewed. Notable recommendations embraced calls for incorporating citizenship-based knowledge and skills throughout the curricula in all faculties; fostering meaningful and equal student-professor and student-counselor relationships; upgrade the quality of teaching, labs, and libraries; enhance inclusive and safe spaces for student dialogue of critical issues (inside and outside the classroom); increase the number and accessibility of inclusive clubs/programs that focus on civic and political empowerment and social entrepreneurship; increase social and academic partnerships with surrounding communities, especially the underprivileged; fostering social and academic partnerships across universities and other educational institutions; provide travel opportunities (nationally and internationally) for study, internships, and conferences; and promoting social justice orientated research that address social, political, and economic issues in Egypt and beyond. Failure of universities to encourage and foster spaces and resources necessary to empower active citizens run the risk of creating apathetic, passive, and uncritical student-citizenry plagued with ambitions of leaving Egypt and apprehensive about bettering Egyptian society.

NOTES

[1] *Mada Masr*, October 31, 2015, Elections commission: There have been lower turnouts, http://www.madamasr.com/sections/politics/elections-commission-there-have-been-lower-turnouts

[2] The quote was from Article 1 of the 2014 Arab Republic of Egypt Constitution. English translation retrieved from http://www.sis.gov.eg/Newvr/Dustor-en001.pdf

[3] The Arab League is an assembly of states generally unified by the predominant language of Arabic. These states include: Algeria, Bahrain, Comoros, Djibouti, Egypt, Iraq, Jordan, Kuwait, Lebanon, Libya, Mauritania, Morocco, Oman, Qatar, Saudi Arabia, Somalia, Sudan, Syria (recently suspended), Tunisia, the United Arab Emirates, Yemen, and Palestinian.

[4] Government of Egypt (2015). *Sustainable Development Strategy: Egypt's Vision 2030*. The Government of Egypt. http://www.mop.gov.eg/Vision1.pdf

[5] See the UN Universal Declaration of Human Rights at http://www.un.org/en/documents/udhr/index.shtml.; See the UN Millennium Declaration at http://www.un.org/millennium/declaration/ares552e.htm.; See the African Union Youth Charter at http://www.au.int/en/sites/default/files/AFRICAN_YOUTH_CHARTER.pdf

[6] *Political rights* generally refer to norms such as free and fair elections for the chief executive and the legislature; the ability of citizens to organize in multiple political parties and compete in elections free from interference by the military, religious, or other powerful groups; the absence of discrimination against cultural, ethnic, religious, or other minority groups; and transparent, accountable, non-corrupt government. *Civil liberties:* freedom of expression and belief, freedom of association and organization, the rule of law, and individual rights (Angrist, 2013, p. 6).

[7] Bayat (2010) defines the subaltern in Egypt as "the urban dispossessed, Muslim women, the globalizing youth, and other urban grass roots" groups who strive to affect change in Egypt "by refusing to exit from the social and political stage controlled by the authoritarian state, moral authority, and neoliberal economy, discovering and generating new space within which they can voice their dissent and assert their presence in pursuit of bettering their lives" (p. ix).

[8] Faour, M. (2013). Education for citizenship in the Arab World: Key to social transformation. Keynote, *Education for Citizenship in the Arab World*, The AUC Graduate School of Education, Cairo, Egypt, December 3, 2013, http://www.aucegypt.edu/GSE/Documents/EdforCitizenshipDec2013(1).pdf

J. N. DORIO

[9] The findings of The Economist Intelligence Unit report were posted in the *Middles East Monitor*, December 15, 2013, https://www.middleeastmonitor.com/news/africa/8824
[10] Selective Reading Approach: after reading the text several times, particularly revealing or essential statements and phrases of the phenomenon are highlighted (Van Manen, 2014, p. 320).
[11] Wholistic Reading Approach: the anecdote is taken as a whole, and the main significance emerges. The meaning of the whole anecdote is express in a phrase (Van Manen, 2014, p. 321).
[12] The Supreme Council of the Armed Forces (SCAF), headed by Field Marshal Tantawi, ruled Egypt from the ousting of Mubarak on February 11, 2011 to June 30, 2012 when Mohamed Morsi was elected President.
[13] *Al Ahram*, October 22, 2013, Al-Aswany weaves threads through Egypt's Revolutions, http://english.ahram.org.eg/News/84488.aspx

REFERENCES

Abdalla, A. (1985). *The student movement and national politics in Egypt, 1923–1973*. Cairo: The American University in Cairo Press.

Alhamad, L. (2008). Formal and informal venues of engagement. In E. Lust-Okat & S. Zerhouni (Eds.), *Political participation in the Middle East* (pp. 33–47). Boulder, CO: Lynne Rienner Publishers.

Angrist, A. P. (2013). The making of middle east politics. In M. P. Angrist (Ed.), *Politics and society in the contemporary Middle East* (2nd ed., pp. 1–29). Boulder, CO: Lynne Rienner Publishers.

Apple, M. W. (1993). The politics of official knowledge: Does a national curriculum make sense? *Teachers College Record, 95*(2), 222–239.

Bali, M. (2013, August 19). Critical citizenship for critical times. *Al Fanar: News and Opinion about Higher Education*. Retrieved August 20, 2013, from http://www.al-fanar.org/2013/08/critical-citizenship-for-critical-times

Baraka, P. E. (2008). Citizenship education in Egyptian public schools: What values to teach and in which administrative and political contexts? *Journal of Education for International development, 3*(3), 1–18.

Bayat, A. (2010). *Life as politics: How ordinary people change the Middle East*. Stanford, CA: Stanford University Press.

Beinin, J., & Vairel, F. (2011). Introduction: The Middle East and North Africa beyond classical social movement theory. In J. Beinin & F. Vairal (Eds.), *Social movements, mobilization, and contestation in the Middle East and North Africa* (pp. 1–23). Stanford, CA: Stanford University Press.

Bellamy, R. (2008). *Citizenship: A very short introduction*. New York, NY: Oxford University Press.

British Council. (2013). *The revolutionary promise: Youth perceptions in Egypt, Libya, and Tunisia* (Summary). Cairo: British Council. Retrieved June 14, 2013, from www.britsihcouncil.org/sites/default/files/documents/revolutionary- promise-summary.pdf

Brown, N. J., Shahin, E. E., & Stacher, J. (2013). Egypt. In M. P. Angrist (Ed.), *Politics and society in the contemporary Middle East* (2nd ed., pp. 217–249). Boulder, CO: Lynne Rienner Publishers.

Chaaban, J. (2009). Youth and development in the Arab countries: The need for a different approach. *Middle Eastern Studies, 45*(1), 33–55.

Creswell, J. W. (2008, November 21–24). *Educational research: Planning, conducting, and evaluating quantitative and qualitative research* (3rd ed.). Upper Saddle River, NJ: Pearson Education, Inc.

El-Mikawy, N. (2012, Noevmber 21–24). *Civic education and the Arab spring: A historic opportunity. Keynote*. Participation now! citizenship education and democracy in times of change, Cordoba. Retrieved July 19, 2013, from http://www.bpb.de/veranstaltungen/netzwerke/nece/137606/ programme

El-Nagar, A. M., & Krugly-Smolska, E. (2009). Citizenship education and liberal democratic change: The Egyptian case. *Canadian and International Education, 38*(2), 36–54.

Faour, M. (2013). *A review of citizenship education in Arab nations*. Washington, DC: Carnegie Endowment for International Peace.

Faour, M., & Muasher, M. (2011). *Education for citizenship in the Arab world: Key to the future*. Washington, DC: Carnegie Endowment for International Peace.

Freire, P. (1996). *Letters to Cristina: Reflections on my life and work* (D. Macedo, Trans.). New York, NY & London: Routledge.

Freire, P. (2007). *Pedagogy of the oppressed* (30th Anniversary ed.). New York, NY: Continuum.
Gerhart Center. (2011). *Youth activism and public space in Egypt*. Cairo: American University in Cairo. Retrieved June 14, 2013, from http://www.aucegypt.edu/research/gerhart/Documents/YouthActivismandPublicSpaceinEgypt.pdf
Giroux, H. A. (1980). Critical theory and rationality in citizenship education. *Curriculum Inquiry, 10*(4), 329–366.
Giroux, H. A. (2004, Winter). Critical pedagogy and the postmodern/modern divide: Towards a pedagogy of democratization. *Teacher Education Quarterly, 31*(1), 31–47.
Henriksson, C., & Friesen, N. (2012). Introduction. In N. Friesen, C. Henriksson, & T. Saevi (Eds.), *Hermeneutic phenomenology: Method and practice* (pp. 1–16). Rotterdam, The Netherlands: Sense Publishers.
Herrera, L. (2006). Higher education in the Arab world. In J. F. Forest & P. G. Altbach (Eds.), *International handbook of higher education* (pp. 409–415). Dordrecht: Springer.
Herrera, L. (2010). Egyptian youth's quest for jobs and justice. In L. Herrera & A. Bayat (Eds.), *Being young and muslim: New cultural politics in the global south and north* (pp. 127–143). New York, NY: Oxford University Press.
Herrera, L. (2012). Youth and citizenship in the digital age: A view from Egypt. *Harvard Educational Review, 82*(3), 333–352.
Herrera, L. (Ed.). (2014). *Wired citizenship: Youth learning and activism in the Middle East*. New York, NY: Routledge.
Hibbard, S., & Layton, A. S. (2010). The origins and future of Egypt's revolt. *Journal of Islamic Law and Culture, 12*(3), 197–214.
Hillygus, D. S. (2005). The missing link: Exploring the relationship between higher education and political engagement. *Political Behavior, 27*(1), 25–47.
Knight, A. K., & Harnish, J. (2006). Contemporary discourses of citizenship. *Review of Educational Research, 76*(4), 653–690.
Laiq, N. (2013). *Talking to Arab youth: Revolution and counterrevolution in Egypt and Tunisia*. New York, NY: International Peace Institute.
Levy, D. (2011, May 22). Egypt: The Tahrir Square spirit lingers on campus. *University World News*, p. 78. Retrieved November 28, 2011, from http://www.universityworldnews.com/article.phpstory=2011052018333727
Lindsey, U. (2012, September 4). *Freedom and reform at Egypt's universities*. Washington, DC: Carnegie Endowment for International Peace. Retrieved April 10, 2013, from https://www.carnegieendowment.org/2012/09/04/freedom-and-reform-at-egypt-s-universities/drak#
Lynch, S., & Mahmoud, M. (2013, October 30). Looking behind the Egyptian student protest. *Al Fanar Media*. Retrieved November 1, 2013, from http://www.al-fanarmedia.org/2013/10/looking-behind-the-egyptian-student-protests/
Makdisi, G. (1981). *Therise of colleges: Institutions of learning in islam and the west*. Edinburgh: Edinburgh University Press.
Mazawi, A. (2005). Contrasting perspectives on higher education governance in the Arab states. In J. C. Smart (Ed.), *Higher education: Handbook of theory and research* (pp. 133–189). Dordrecht: Springer.
Megahed, N., & Lack, S. (2011). Colonial legacy, women's rights and gender-educational inequality in the Arab world with particular reference to Egypt and Tunisia. *International Review of Education, 57*, 397–418.
Meijer, R. (2014). Political citizenship and social movements in the Arab world. In Hein-Anton van der Heijden (Ed.), *Handbook of political citizenship and social movements* (pp. 628–660). Northampton, MA: Edward Elgar Publishing.
Merriam, S. B. (2009). *Qualitative research: A guide to design and implementation*. San Francisco, CA: Jossey-Bass.
Mitchell, T. (1999). Dreamland: The neoliberalism of your desires. *Middle East Report, 29*(210), 28–33.
Morrow, R. A., & Torres, C. A. (1995). *Social theory and education: A critique of theories of social and cultural reproduction*. New York, NY: State University of New York Press.

Parolin, G. P. (2009). *Citizenship in the Arab world: Kin, religion and nation-state*. Amsterdam: Amsterdam University Press.
Patton, M. Q. (2002). *Qualitative research and evaluation methods* (3rd ed.). Thousand Oaks, CA: Sage Publications.
Refaei, M. M. (2015). *Political participation in Egypt: Perceptions and practice*. Cairo: Baseera.
Reid, D. M. (2002). *Cairo university and the making of modern Egypt* (Vol. 23). Cambridge: Cambridge University Press.
Saldana, J. (2013). *The coding manual for qualitative researchers* (2nd ed.). Thousand Oaks, CA: Sage Publications.
Schugurensky, D., & Myers, J. P. (2003). Citizenship education: Theory, research and practice. *Encounters on Education, 4*, 1–10.
Shehata, D. (2008, October 23). Youth activism in Egypt. *Arab reform initiative brief*. Retrieved June 15, 2013, from http://www.arab-reform.net/en/node/377
Sika, N. (2012). Youth political engagement in Egypt: From abstention to uprisings. *British Journal of Middle Eastern Studies, 39*(2), 181–199.
Torney-Purta, J. (2002). The school's role in developing civic engagement: A study of adolescents in twenty-eight countries. *Applied Developmental Science, 6*(4), 203–212.
Torres, C. A. (1998). *Democracy, education, and multiculturalism: Dilemmas of citizenship in a global world*. Lanham, MD: Rowman & Littlefield Publishers.
Turner, B. S. (1990). Outline of a theory of citizenship. *Sociology, 24*(2), 189–217.
UNHDR. (2010). *Egypt human development report 2010*. New York, NY: United Nations Development Program.
UNICEF. (2011, December 8–11). Youth, actors of development. *North Africa Development Forum*. Retrieved from http://www.uneca.org/sites/default/files/uploads/overview.pdf
Van der Mescht, H. (2004). Phenomenology in education: A case study in educational leadership. *Indo-Pacific Journal of Phenomenology, 4*(1), 1–16.
Van Manen, M. (1990). *Researching lived experience: Human science for an action sensitive pedagogy*. Ontario: University of Western Ontario.
Van Manen, M. (2014). *Phenomenology of practice: Meaning-giving methods in phenomenological research and writing*. Walnut Creek, CA: Left Cost Press.
Zaalouk, M. (2006). *The pedagogy of empowerment: Community schools as a social movement in Egypt*. Cairo: American University in Cairo Press.

Jason Nunzio Dorio
Graduate School of Education and Information Studies
University of California, Los Angeles (UCLA)

SHEREEN ALY

3. EGYPTIAN YOUTH BUILDING A PEACEFUL COMMUNITY

The Selmiyah Movement

INTRODUCTION

Focusing on youth movement in Egypt during the time of unrest and revolts, this chapter is based on my research that explores the potential insights and lessons that can be deduced from the case of *Selmiyah* (peaceful), a grass-roots movement that is aiming to spread the culture of peace through different dimensions and channels. This movement includes over 40 initiatives, whose founders and participants are primarily youth, illustrating collaborative efforts across various civil society organizations (CSOs) in Egypt, where there are a few movements working together on the ground (CIVICUS, 2005). Most of the initiatives within Selmiyah are undertaken within the non-formal sector, while some of them are working in collaboration with educational institutions such as schools or universities. This research offers a description of 15 initiatives within the Selmiyah movement that were selected to demonstrate a comprehensive example of youth contribution to development in Egypt during the period of transition and unrest. Of particular interest is understanding the motives for creating these initiatives, their structure, the framework and methodology they follow, and the organizational and financial sustainability. The research questions the dynamics of creating this movement; why the different civil societies' initiatives chose to join the Selmiyah movement and what are the benefits of being part of its network? I use a peace education model developed by Ian Harris to analyse the comprehensive nature of the initiatives within Selmiyah; the Harris model will be explained later in this chapter. This research offers insights to all CSOs who are interested in the field of peace education, to educators who would like to reflect on how to integrate such concepts within educational institutions, and policy makers who can think of ways to integrate this work into school reforms.

This research adopts a qualitative approach, where 23 in-depth interviews were conducted with founders of initiatives and coordinators of the Selmiyah network. The purpose of using qualitative methods is to understand in depth youth-led initiatives and to gain insight on their motives and target goals. It is of essential importance to this research to document and present the views of the youth, who are involved in these initiatives, about the community, their role and the targets they hope to achieve, i.e., hearing their voice. In the field of youth research, there is availability of quantitative research in the form of reports (see Abdelhay, 2005; El-Rouby, 2007; Handoussa, 2010; Population Council, 2011), and while these reports provide valuable data, they lack the quality of in-depth analysis that is needed to complete the picture. This research is an attempt to fill in the missing gaps within the total picture of how youth can contribute to the development of Egyptian society. This research is an attempt to fill the gap within the existing literature, by showing a clear example and successful model of youth contribution to the development of Egyptian society, at a time where many reports view that youth do not participate in civil society and are not heard from policy and decision makers (see Abdelhay, 2005; El-Rouby, 2007; Handoussa, 2010; Population Council, 2011; Mahgoub & Morsi, 2013).

What Is Peace Education?

Peace education is a notion that began in the Western hemisphere and is slowly finding its way towards the Arab region. Peace Education is defined differently in the reviewed literature, yet there are common dimensions or levels mentioned. Peace education has to do with changing the mindset or perception, with gaining the skills needed for peace building, and with the ability to practice these skills through providing channels and alternatives (Danesh, 2006, p. 56). Another important dimension is to provide successful models, as this is a new culture that is being promoted. Peace education is seen by researchers as essential to build a new holistic non-discriminating worldview that can contribute into bettering humanity's approach to life, "peace education is the only route to true civilization and true civilization is both peaceful and peace creating" (Danesh, 2006, p. 57). Based on this vision, the UNICEF considers peace education as an essential component of basic education, and thus is not only necessary in countries where there is conflict but everywhere (Fountain, 1999).

"Youth" a Transition Phase

What is "Youth" Phase? Youth by definition is an intermediate or transition phase between childhood and adulthood, from dependence to independence (UNESCO, n.d.). UNSECO identifies the age group of "youth" to be from 15 to 24, for statistics and research purposes. The African Youth Charter (UNDESA) identifies the youth age group to be from 15 to 35 years (UNDESA, n.d.).

In the 1980s, there was a shift in the "youth" narrative in the US influenced by the new youth development movement. One of the key concepts that contributed to a more positive image of youth by viewing them as an asset is the concept of human capital, a neoliberal approach that dominated literature for some time, producing several policies aiming at maximizing the utilization of youth as a resource in the global economy (Sukarieh & Tannock, 2011). This approach translated into focusing on education, health, and employment as the key issues related to youth so that they become productive members of the society.

Overview of Egyptian Youth Status

Egyptian youth are facing several challenges on several levels. On the social level, youth suffer from poverty, unemployment, access to education and high dropout rate, and differentiation in the quality of services based on location, where around 60% of young people live in rural areas and the rest in urban or informal urban areas (Population Council, 2011). When it comes to basic education, it is reported that "27% of young people aged 18–29 have not completed basic education" (Handoussa, 2010, p. 4), and access to education does not necessarily mean access to equal quality of education. It is also worth noting that 90% of the unemployed in Egypt are aged less than 30 years (Handoussa, 2010).

On the institution level, there hasn't been consistency in terms of the governing body that addresses youth issues; responsibilities have alternated between a national council and the Ministry of Youth for almost two decades now (Abdelhay, 2005), and currently there is a Ministry of Youth and Sports (MoYS). In addition, there is not currently a declared national policy for youth and development; the current MoYS website does not state a common vision that would provide a framework for the legislations and policies related to youth.

On the legislative level, there has been contradicting legislations that confuse the definition of youth (in terms of their age group) in Egypt and confuse it partly with children (Abdelhay, 2005). A publicly issued plan of how youth are expected to contribute to societal development remains missing. Abdelhay (2005) concludes that there is a dire need to issue a "youth law" similar to the "child law", which defines clearly the jurisdiction of all governing bodies and the overlapping of all ministries involved, and facilitates addressing all youth issues from a comprehensive perspective (p. 7). On a participatory level, some reports show that youth in Egypt did not fully participate in public life, and did not actively engage in volunteer activities or other form of civic engagement activities (Handoussa, 2010; Population Council, 2011). This narrative changed slightly after the January 25th revolution, recording a spike in the engagement of youth in all forms of public life (UNV, 2013; British Council & Gerhart Center, 2013).

However, there is a lack of representation of youth in the management of NGOs and especially in decision making positions, which contributes to the small participation levels that are reported (El-Rouby, 2007). According to El-Rouby (2007), the World Bank 2007 report, "Mapping Organizations Working with and for Youth in Egypt", defines what is considered a youth organization or initiative; this definition is adopted in this research. Youth organization or initiative is described as matching the following four criteria:

(1) Number of youth in the board exceeds 60%; (2) The programs/services of the organization are directed mainly to youth and children; (3) Number of employees under 35 exceeds 70%; and (4) The organization depends on youth volunteers in planning and implementing its activities. (El-Rouby, 2007, pp. 8–9)

It is important at this stage to further understand the notion of civil society and CSOs and the role they play in youth related issues, especially that civil society organizations are the main vehicle for social and political participation for youth.

ROLE OF CIVIL SOCIETY IN PEACEBUILDING

Definition of Civil Society and It's Role in Peacebuilding

Civil society is a complex term that has several definitions that try to define its form, whether it is a subsystem in society or a crosscutting system (Barnes, 2005; Rucht, 2014), its role in society, and the values that govern it. Definitions explore as well which organizations are within civil society framework; some say that civil society includes all the entities and organizations and communities that are not state governed, that civil society comprises of all the non-governmental and not-for profit organizations (Rucht, 2014). Other scholars see that it is difficult to set the boundaries between civil society and the state due to the complex relations and dynamics of today's world (Kopecký & Mudde, 2010).

Another way to define civil society is through its function within society, some see that its function is "cultivating civic values and practices" (Barnes, 2005, p. 8), others see that it has a political role in providing the space for citizens to engage in public life and voice their interests through certain channels of communication with the state. Another perspective is based on the wider view of society and the sub-systems that operate within it, where civil society with the social dimension it represents can balance the power of the capitalist market-based economies and the authoritarian sates (Rucht, 2014). Within this framework, the idea of "civil" raises questions, where scholars have debated the part that civility plays in this scope, and what to do with uncivil societies or groups (Rucht, 2014). Here Rucht invites scholars to adopt a paradigm shift, "a shift from the concept of civil society (defined as a distinct space or sub-system) to practices of civility in society as a whole" (Rucht, 2014, p. 18).

With the notion of "practices of civility", civil society organizations (CSOs) can play a role during conflict times and can contribute to the peacebuilding process. Choosing to handle any conflict, whether internal or external, in a peaceful or violent way is partially the responsibility of civil society, and sometimes is led by civil society groups. Its role is essentially related to structural prevention, which is working within the community to eradicate all the causes of structural violence, such as unequal distribution of resources, human rights issues, discrimination, and prejudice. The remaining stages of peace building include escalation of violence where the CSOs' role is to highlight this (early warning) and lobby for support to prevent it. During the conflict where the role is related to negotiations and providing safe spaces for conflicting parties; and towards the end of conflict, the role becomes more about consolidating peace efforts and putting measures to prevent reoccurrence of war or violence.

While CSOs have a viable role in peacebuilding, it is important to remember that they cannot achieve peace on their own since there are other players, like governments, politicians, and military leaders, who need to be on board for the process to reach positive outcomes. CSOs need to be able to persuade these parties to come to the table and negotiate, and need to ensure people support all the time to maintain power balance. From here comes the importance of forming partnerships and networks on a local, regional, and global level (Serbin, 2005, p. 52). Serbin (2005) is inviting structured partnerships that are planned and done strategically rather than ad-hoc partnerships or collaborations that might not be as effective.

Overview of Civil Society in Egypt

In 2011, it was indicated in the CSO sustainability index that there are over 45,000 CSOs registered with the Ministry of Social Solidarity (MoSS) (USAID, 2011), a Ministry that is in charge of managing non-governmental organizations (NGOs) in Egypt and ensuring that they abide by the governing law number 84 of 2002 (Khallaf, 2010). Some research shows that the organizational capacity of NGOs in Egypt is not high. There are variations between the urban and rural capacities, and between NGOs in Cairo and Upper Egypt with regards to the caliber of who can handle operations and management capacities. Most of the time, NGOs cannot maintain full-time employees due to irregularity and fluctuation in funds.

Regarding financial capabilities, most CSOs receive funding from International non-governmental organizations (INGOs), international agencies, local and international corporations and community members. The funds are inconsistent and short-term which leads to many challenges and obstacles. Overall, the Law 84 of 2002 prohibits any organization from receiving any money from foreign organizations without prior approval from the MoSS (USAID, 2011), however the process of approval is a very long and can take years, which poses a threat on the financial resources of some CSOs.

With regards to creating relations and bonds among CSOs, there were several federations, councils, and unions formed, although their effectiveness is under question, and cross-sectorial cooperation is not high. Moreover, the cooperation between CSOs and the business sector is increasing due to the rise of the concept of corporate social responsibility (CSR) in Egypt (CIVICUS, 2005).

When it comes to public image, many small and medium size CSOs do not have the capability or resources to manage media campaigns or any other marketing campaigns, while the big local CSOs have been able to sustain a rather good image in Egypt (USAID, 2011). Towards the end of 2011, the government launched an aggressive campaign against NGOs in general with accusations of foreign agendas and treason, an act that confused the Egyptian community about the whole sector and raised many questions on the corruption level within civil society (USAID, 2011).

OVERVIEW OF PEACE EDUCATION

Definition of Peace Education

Peace education has several definitions. One category of definitions stipulates that there are different layers or levels within peace education. These include understanding the roots of the conflict, understanding the alternatives to conflict and learning new skills of conflict resolution and dialogue, and learning more about human rights, international, and local laws and environment friendly approaches to promote a more peaceful approach to life in general (Danesh, 2006; Fountain, 1999). Another categorization of peace education is related to how peace is perceived whether it is inner peace, which is mainly individual and is more of a state of mind, or outer peace, which is more of practices and attitudes that affect the society, culture, and the larger community (Harris, 2007).

Peace education mainly combines knowledge that is constructed with the participation of the students, skills that are needed to progress through life without violence, and attitudes that are a natural product of the interactive and contextualized process that students undergo. This requires a pedagogical shift from teacher-centered approaches to student-centered approaches, which would have great impact on how curricula are developed and practices within the classroom (Ashton, 2007; Fountain, 1999).

UNICEF considers peace education as an essential component of basic education, and thus is not only necessary in countries undergoing armed conflicts or social emergencies but is needed everywhere. It also recommends that peace education is integrated within the education system rather than becoming a separate subject. The main reason is the belief that instilling peace values within a given society is a long-term process, and it requires the whole community to be involved (Fountain, 1999). To explore this idea further, some scholars and international agencies created models of peace education introducing the framework that could be the foundation of a curriculum. Among these models is Ian Harris Model which is used to form the theoretical framework employed in the analysis of this case study of *Selmiyah movement*.

Ian Harris Model of Peace Education

Several scholars and international agencies created models of peace education based on the ideas mentioned above. Ian Harris (2007) developed a model that includes five key components or pillars within peace education: international education, human rights education, development education, environmental education, and conflict resolution education (Harris, 2007). More details about each component will be demonstrated in the below table. The reason behind choosing this model is the level of detail Harris reached in clarifying the components and creating links between them. The main components of peace education in the Harris model are further explained in Table 1.

Table 1. Ian Harris' peace education model

Pillar	Core concepts/skills	Why is it important?
International Education	1. Understanding international and state laws. 2. Understanding the positive and negative dimensions of globalization and how it impacts nation states.	• Understand how wars start over territory divisions and imaginary man-made borders. • Construct a new narrative of the "other". • Realizing that globalization is a key factor of the spread of Peace education; however it is also playing a major role in increasing religious extremism, violence and discrimination.
Human Rights Education	Understanding commonalities and differences among people, engaging in dialogue, sharing human experiences and creating new solutions for co-existence.	Reduce all ethnic, religious, political, ideological and gender-based forms of discrimination.
Development Education	1. Understanding the components of social injustice and creating new development strategies to eliminate these components. 2. Focusing mainly on positive peace,[1] the root causes of its absence and how it can be achieved.	• To eliminate all forms of social injustice, through active citizenry and participation within the community. • To include the people suffering from social injustice in the planning and implementation process, to avoid issues of social marginalization and monopoly of resources by the "elites".
Environmental Education	1. Understanding the issues facing the environment. 2. Developing personal conviction towards saving the environment.	To create a culture of environmental and ecological awareness.
Conflict Resolution Education	1. Building needed skills to promote peaceful resolutions to conflict.	To provide peaceful effective alternatives for students, teachers and the community in general to the normal violent techniques used to resolve conflicts.

From the above table, it is clear that Harris model includes several aspects, some that might not even be categorized within peace education, such as environmental education. However, this model offers a comprehensive approach towards all issues related to countering structural and cultural violence, thus helps educators plan for peace education from an integrated and multi-disciplinary perspective. It is also important to note that this model integrates several levels of education (awareness, attitude, skills and actions), which makes it more of a holistic approach in the teaching and learning of peace for diverse students.

RESEARCH DESIGN AND METHODOLOGY

This research is exploring the potential benefits and challenges to developing a peace education model that is suitable to Egyptian context in an informal set-up. It uses the case study design, to examine a specific movement in Egypt called "Selmiyah" that is working towards spreading the culture of peace. Case studies have several definitions; for the sake of this research the definition proposed by John Gerring (2004) is used where a case study is defined as,

> An intensive study of a single unit for the purpose of understanding a larger class of (similar) units. A unit connotes a spatially bounded phenomenon—e.g., a nation-state, revolution, political party, election, or person observed at a single point in time or over some delimited period of time (Although the temporal boundaries of a unit are not always explicit, they are at least implicit). (Gerring, 2004, p. 342)

In its essence, this case study is a critical-constructivist piece, where I designed the research tools and constantly modified and revisited throughout the research, while maintaining focus on social change and the impact of the work being done on society. This approach is, thus appropriate to the topic and nature of the research, having done the field work with people who are categorized as social activists and who are striving towards social transformation (Carspecken, 1996).

Case Selection

This research focuses on a network and movement in Egypt called "Selmiyah" as a case or single unit as per above definition. "Selmiyah" as a movement includes over 40 initiatives, a network of partner civil society organizations, and more than one-thousand individuals. To achieve a deep understanding of the initiatives undertaken by this movement, 15 initiatives were selected for examination in this study, as further explained below. Participants included the co-founders of the Selmiyah movement and active members who were/are involved in the coordination of the movement since its launch, but also who are engaged in undertaking the selected initiatives. The sample included 23 participants, 43% of whom were women and the average age was 32, ranging between 21 to 50 years of age.[2]

Selmiyah was officially launched in June 2012; many of the initiatives that joined had started long before the movement launch. Furthermore, the initiatives involved in the network are diverse in terms of scope, structure, age groups, etc. Therefore, the selection criteria of the initiatives were designed to maintain a balance between: (a) old and new initiatives in terms of the time of launching their activities and when they joined the movement; (b) different structures that exist within the movement's initiatives; (c) different age group included in these initiatives; and (d) the fields of work or focus areas of the initiatives and projects.

The last criterion was added during the course of the research, as I tried to categorize initiatives similar to the components of the Harris model to make the process of the analysis easier. The final sample of peace education initiatives is shown in Table 2.

Table 2. Summary of peace education initiatives included in the study

Name of group/initiative	Type	Year of establishment	Registration date in selmiyah	Categorization according to Ian Harris model
Initiative A	Informal Group	2002	Sep-13	Art for Social change
Initiative B	Company	2004	Sep-13	Conflict Resolution Education/Human Rights Education
Initiative C	NGO	2007	Sep-13	Development Education
Initiative D	NGO	2008	Sep-13	Conflict Resolution Education
Initiative E	Company	2009	Sep-13	IT integration
Initiative F	NGO	2011	Dec-13	Cultural Exchange
Initiative G	Company	2012	Sep-13	Development Education/ Human Rights Education
Initiative H	Informal Group	2012	Sep-13	Development Education/ Human Rights Education
Initiative I	NGO	2005	May-14	Art for Social change
Initiative J	Informal Group	2011	NA	Environmental Education
Initiative K	Company	2009	Sep-13	Development Education/ Art for Social Change
Initiative L	NGO	2007	Sep-13	Development Education
Initiative M	Company	2007	Sep-13	Art for Social change
Initiative N	NGO	2005	Sep-13	Development Education
Initiative O	Informal Group	2011	Sep-13	Development Education/ Human Rights Education

45

Data Collection

For this study, data was collected in the forms of semi-structured interviews, non-participant observation and documents' review. Interviews were carried out with one founding member of each selected initiative, co-founders of "Selmiyah" movement, and the coordinators of the movement. Two interview protocols were developed for this study. The first is the version for the initiative founders, and the second for the founders and coordinators of the movement. The interview with the initiative members asked about the experience of the initiative in developing their idea and structuring their interventions. The interview protocol for the movement co-founders and coordination team asked about the experience of creating the movement, sustaining it, and developing it further.

In addition, *Participant Observation* was conducted to gain additional insight into the implementation process in the organization and to see some workshops or trainings implemented by the selected initiatives. Main points of focus were the relationship between team members as facilitators during preparation and facilitation, their relationship with the participants throughout the workshops and camps, and the methods of delivering the content. Moreover, available documents that describe the activities, purposes, targets, and/or curriculum of the selected initiatives were gathered and reviewed. It is important to note that I am a part of the Selmiyah network, and have volunteered to assist in coordination and maintaining coherence within the network. This made accessibility to many of the participants easier, even though I personally did not know almost 35% of the sample involved in the study. However, I was able to access them through contacts within the network. Being in the same network had an impact on the trust factor, and thus participants may have been willing to share more insights and reflections during interviews. Some of ideas that were suggested by participants in the interviews were used to enhance the coordination of the network, and some processes are being developed currently based on the feedback the participants shared.

Data Analysis and Validation

The typological technique for analysis and coding was used, which means that the researcher was "dividing everything observed into groups or categories on the basis of some canon for disaggregating the whole phenomenon under study" (Hatch, 2002, p. 152). Credibility for this study was achieved using the validation strategies of triangulation. The data was triangulated with the various forms of data that were collected in this study; i.e., interviews, observations, documents, and field notes.

FINDINGS

The richness of data collected and the sample chosen to include different and common characteristics (age group, interests, etc.) reveal different aspects of the

Selmiyah movement (and its network of initiatives). Focusing on the purpose stated earlier for this case study, I focus my discussion of the research findings on the following themes:

- Motivation of youth in developing initiatives within the field of Peace Education and its context.
- Structure of initiatives and projects.
- Methodology of Developing Frameworks.
- Harris Model vs. Selmiyah Model.
- The Movement Dynamics.

MOTIVATION AND CONTEXT

The trigger to start the examined initiatives differed. For some the trigger was a phenomenon in society that indicated intolerance and prejudice. Incidents were related to religious discrimination and led to physical and verbal violence within the community. Founders of these initiatives were able to identify that these were indicators of societal issues that needed to be addressed. Some initiatives were part of an already existing network or project, so the teams did not develop the idea but they made it more relevant to the emerging needs, changing context or developed their own approach. For instance, a participant states, "when there are events, when there is a project that we can offer, for example during the constitution voting period, we did a seminar about the constitution, without any political orientation towards a certain party" Many initiatives share the feature of developing their ideas across time, based on the experiences they gain from working on the ground, and on their constant readings and observations.

The January 25th revolution had impact on the founders and their initiatives. For some participants, it was an eye-opener on the reactions of people towards the old regime; for others it was more eye-opening on the youth movement. Some initiatives had to slow down their activities because they could not cope with the fast changes and the dynamics that were occurring during the first period of the revolution. For some, these same dynamics were the force that gave birth to the idea and pushed the people to work, such as initiative H. The participants also shared some core differences between the times before and after the revolution related to freedoms, mobility, awareness of society, and position towards civil society. Below is a summary of the points they raised.

Before the Revolution

> People did not want to talk or to discover their differences, so it was very hard getting people to engage in dialogue or finding people who request that.
>
> People did not see the need to work on coexistence and conflict resolution.

"Peace" had a political connotation and it meant normalization with Israel, now people understand that it can be societal peace.

Terms like non-violence and alternatives to violence did not have any meaning or relevance to reality.

The access to public spaces and government-owned spaces was limited. People were not used to seeing street performances and public spaces weren't open for use, either by artists or anyone else.

After the Revolution

People saw the need for dialogue in the community and the awareness was much higher, so requests increased for dialogue, consensus building, dealing with difference, and conflict resolution. After the 30th of June events in 2013, people don't want to engage in dialogue again especially after the political polarization that occurred.

As people experienced both violence and non-violence, the terms became familiar.

The revolution deepened the idea of public ownership, so people started using the public spaces, especially activists and artists.

The revolution events brought together groups who were working on the ground, which led to the growth of networks and connections among them. This had huge impact on the collaboration and outreach levels among initiatives. Right after the revolution, the Egyptian society was supportive of civil society and there were a lot of donations and volunteers.

After the 30th of June events in 2013, there was a lot of attack on NGOs, accusations of foreign funding and treason, and this impacted the way the community looks at civil society in general and youth groups specifically.

STRUCTURE OF INITIATIVES

Goals and Framework

During the interviews, each participant shared the goals of their initiative; these goals were grouped and categorized to include: (a) goals related to achieving peace on an individual level, (b) goals related to achieving peace on a community level, and (c) goals related to achieving peace on a societal level. On an individual level, some initiatives aimed at creating spaces for communication and deep understanding of oneself and the others. They wanted people who engaged in their activities to know what peaceful coexistence is, that there is this option, and to have the skills and tools to practice it.

On a community level, there were goals related to spreading the culture of dialogue within youth groups and among them. Some projects strived to create enabling spaces for people to discover themselves and meet one another, through that they achieve forgiveness, creativity, and peace. Within that goal, providing models of non-violent conflict resolution, such as mediation is important. Some aimed at enabling the marginalized communities in solving their own problems, helping them to build upon the human resources who exist in the area to make their lives better, and thus increasing their participation in decision-making. One initiative saw that the main goal was to have real coordination and collaboration among people who are working on the ground, to build on what has been done already, and benefit from other people's experience in this field or in this location.

On a societal level, part of the goals of some projects was focused on creating an alternative community for people who want to live according to peaceful values, through building partnerships between different communities and creating spaces for working together towards a common goal. And through raising awareness, for example on the importance of art for social change, and how arts can contribute to the community's prospering; and providing art services that speak to the people which help in bringing art to the street.

For some initiatives, they developed these goals after a few years of working on the ground; assessing actual needs based on first-hand experience in the field, and choosing which area they will focus on. Others knew their area of focus from the beginning and they worked on refining their articulation of it throughout the years.

Legal and Organizational Structure

Regarding the legal status, the Selmiyah initiatives choose different levels of legalization, depending on their conditions and scope of their work (see Table 3). Some choose to be Limited Liability Companies, others choose to register as NGOs, and others choose to be unregistered. This choice has an impact on the financial and organizational sustainability. Some initiatives depend on team contributions whether monetary or voluntary, while others depend on funds, services, income generating activities, and strategic partnerships with donors or INGOs. In the meantime, for activities and services targeted students, these specific initiatives depend on membership fees. On the other hand, some initiatives rely on donations from the local community and connections. These initiatives needed to build trust with their donors through their work. A participant explains, "we were able to build trust and good reputation …our reputation is good, people know we do real work on the ground, even if it is on small scale, and this is what I tried to really focus on."

The initiatives also varied in their organizational structures. Unregistered initiatives depend mainly on volunteers while companies have part-time staff, a few full-time staff, and consultants who are hired for certain tasks along with volunteers and interns. Some NGOs have trainers and animators who only conduct workshops and are not considered staff. One NGO has a flat management system with no hierarchy where decision-making process is done collectively, and another includes their young volunteers in all phases of planning and execution. A summary of the legal and financial resources for all initiatives within this case study is shown in Table 3.

Table 3. Summary of legal status and financial model of initiatives within study

Name of group	Year of establishing	Legal status	Financial model
Initiative A	2002	Initiative	Minimum Costs
Initiative H	2012	Initiative	No need for money, self-funded
Initiative J	2011	Initiative	No need for money, self-funded
Initiative O	2011	Initiative	No need for money, self-funded
Initiative C	2007	NGO	Donations from community members
Initiative D	2008	NGO	Providing Services and local Partnerships – Facing difficulty in receiving any foreign funds
Initiative F	2011	NGO	Fund by local NGO for part of the project
Initiative I	2005	NGO	Funds, donations and provide paid services
Initiative L	2007	NGO	Member fees
Initiative N	2005	NGO	Donations from community members
Initiative B	2004	Company	Service-based model, no funds accepted
Initiative E	2009	Company	Based on human capital: mostly all work is done by volunteers
Initiative G	2012	Company	Key partners with some international NGOs that have offices in Egypt
Initiative K	2009	Company	Service-based model
Initiative M	2007	Company	Mostly self-funded – Received one grant through a local NGO

METHODOLOGY OF DEVELOPING FRAMEWORKS

Many of the initiatives have developed documents that explain the principles, vision and mission that guides their work and the different activities or steps they follow. Most of them have developed these documents across time based on research, experiences on the ground, and readings. Some initiatives focused on producing materials (i.e., handbooks, books, documentaries, and videos) for a wider dissemination of their work and for their interest in encouraging people to reapply their model.

Values and principles are key terms that are used in the documents of all the initiatives. Based on these values and principles the framework is built and this forms the foundation for the activities and practices within the workshops. It also defines how the team members themselves would interact with one another. For example, one of the initiatives, which focused on dialogue, published a handbook for anyone who is interested to learn more about the topic or to organize dialogue workshops. As stated in its introduction: "In this book, you can read about the principles for dialogue and get ideas for planning. You can also get inspiration for exercises that create dialogue. And you gain understanding of the role of the workshop leader and facilitator." The handbook addresses in the beginning the values or principles of dialogue (trust, openness, honesty, and equality) and defines them. A participant during the interview explained the process of creating this handbook:

> The process by which this handbook was written is completely dialogical. We could have done it in three months … it took above a year because we had to make sure that it was a dialogical process that integrates everyone and that we all kind of reach some level of consensus on everything that was written … I am super proud of how this handbook was written, because it was more about the process rather than the content.

The activities included in the handbook are interactive; they are inviting participants to think critically, to revisit their ideals and habits, and to reflect on their experiences.

Experience through Practice

It was a common feedback among the interviewed participants that many of their work and their concepts developed over time and with practice, whether working in training and workshops, community organizing and participation, arts for social change, activities with children, environmental mobilization, and remote or marginalized areas. This experiential approach to developing the curricula promotes further flexibility and ability to adapt to the context and the audience, and this addresses a core concept in curricula development, that Dewey talks about when he says, "the essence of education is the continual reforming and reshaping of activities, and this requires plasticity – the ability to reach new and more complex adjustments" (Dewey, 1899, pp. 32–33).

For one initiative that works mainly on many aspects of peace education, there was a document that explains the theoretical framework and methodology that their curriculum is based upon, which are mainly:

- The relevance of the content to the lives of the participants and their experiences;
- Activities are diverse, interactive and strongly based on participants' experience, whether simulated on site or borrowed from real life events;
- The knowledge is built–rather than transmitted—through the awareness, sharing, and evaluation of the participants' experiences and their exposure to new or different ones;
- Emphasis is put on the process of learning together and through each other in a climate of openness and respect;
- Individual differences in learning, experiences, opinions and values are acknowledged and respected.

Research-Based Approach

Another common feedback among groups was the factor of research, readings, and trainings that had an impact on developing their framework and curricula. For some initiatives, members joined graduate studies related to the field, for others they were looking for available training related to their field. One initiative had several university professors involved in their work and mentoring the team on different aspects. This passion for learning and developing ideas shows a commitment to the value of openness, which is one of the underlying values of peace. Another dimension that was mentioned by some participants was reflections, that there were organized and periodic sessions for reflection. This develops the cognitive skills of the members and also helps them articulate the experiences and lessons learnt. The combination between research and experiences on the ground and reflections is powerful, and this is why the documents that have been developed so far are very rich and comprehensive.

HARRIS MODEL VS SELMIYAH MODEL

When it comes to compatibility between the Ian Harris model and the initiatives within Selmiyah, some interesting points arise. First, regarding International Education and Human Rights Education, there are not any initiatives within Selmiyah working mainly on these components. However, several initiatives do address these topics within their work. One participant saw that diversity as a concept is missing from Harris' model and she saw it as a core concept with regards to viewing the "other". She explains: "I feel what is really missing is diversity which is not just international education so I know who is outside, I need to first understand who is inside... we [the group who works on this initiative] have a concept called social dynamics which most probably we invented, inside the community how the different groups deal with each other and why ... dealing with diversity within society and the dynamics of diversity within society."

There are many initiatives within Selmiyah that are operating within the pillar of Development Education; in fact, they are the majority of the initiatives. The scope of these initiatives varies, as shown before, from raising awareness to actual interventions. Initiatives combine addressing structural violence and encouraging people to participate in resolving their own problems. Most of the initiatives within Selmiyah did not have an environmental approach to their work, except for one initiative (initiative J). Even for this initiative, their work was more related to campaigning and mobilizing people to support environmental issues. It included a dimension of raising the awareness of people about the importance of the environmental issues and their direct impact on their daily lives.

Many of the initiatives within Selmiyah are working within conflict resolution pillar. Many participants shared that they saw this as a crucial area to work in, because Egyptian society needs to see alternatives to violent resolution of issues, as one of the participants explains, it is important for citizens "to see how to resolve conflicts through mediation instead of resolving it through fighting or vengeance or through courts that decide that you are right and you are wrong, [and] how mediation will help us reconcile instead of the courts that will make us fight." Here the idea is not just finding a solution, it is in reaching a state of satisfaction from both sides, otherwise the conflict will continually resurface, and one day it might explode into extreme violent acts.

WHY DID INITATIVES CHOOSE TO BELONG TO SELMIYA MOVEMENT?

What are the reasons behind joining the Selmiyah network and what are the added and contributing values by joining this movement? The answers of these questions are discussed in this section based on the interviewees' perspectives, supplemented by the perception of the co-founders and coordinators of the movement.

When asked why they decided to join the Selmiyah network, participants who lead the examined initiatives expressed the following reasons:

- Finding common values between Selmiyah and the initiative, such as promoting culture of peace, coexistence and accepting diversity;
- Supporting the idea of collaboration and believing in it strongly;
- Being trustful of the community due to the group of people within Selmiyah community;
- Sharing the goal of creating a network but didn't know how to do it;
- Working with some partners within Selmiyah was comfortable, thus decided to join;
- Seeing the added-value that the initiative can bring to Selmiyah and that Selmiyah can bring to the initiative;
- Wanting to be part of this network because it includes many initiatives and projects that are rich in terms of experience and content.

Mutual Added Value

All interviewed participants were asked to identify the added value that they think they bring to the network and that they gain from Selmiyah. In response, the interviewees perceived their contribution in relation to the goals and activities of their respective initiative, such as dialogue, creating a values-oriented culture, creating opportunities for practicing on the ground with different communities, etc.

On the other hand, the added value of Selmiyah to the joined initiatives was highly recognized, as it created a channel through which people can collaborate to overcome some of the challenges they face during implementation of activities, it also created a support system, especially to the new initiatives who might get frustrated at the beginning of their road and might give up. Another key added value is that each of these initiatives on its own doesn't have enough resources to work on some of the key challenges, like raising awareness of the idea of conflict management and coexistence, or changing the image of the development field to attract new talents or donors, or even challenging the current perceptions of the term "peace education" in the Middle East and North Africa region. Therefore, being together with a readiness to collaborate and partner, and a commitment to support each other is a substantial asset that might help each initiative maintaining its sustainability and further develop and expand their scope.

CONCLUSION

Selmiyah network offers a unique model of association between CSOs in Egypt, this collaboration and partnership model has generated common goals for peace education on the ground, which would motivate other CSOs to develop a similar joint structure. Such bonds within civil society are highly needed to improve (a) coordination among different initiatives, (b) minimize redundancy, (c) maximize the benefit of resources, and (d) undertake activities and produce materials that would have a better impact and sustainability. The findings of this study revealed that the Selmiyah movement with its joint network of different initiatives for peace building is a needed bottom-up movement of collaborative efforts towards promoting a culture of peace among Egyptians. Despite challenges confronted, Selmiyah has a pool of resources and the potential for expanding its partnerships and cooperation between Selmiyah and other similar local and global movements.

The initiatives within Selmiyah offer several lessons from the structure of their framework to the methodology of practice. All the examined initiatives adopt a participatory experiential approach, whether working with children, youth, adults, and communities or working within a learning framework, community organizing framework, or arts for social change framework. Developing these frameworks and their related curricula depends on well-thought and clearly articulated values, practice and experience as well as on extensive research. The idea of involving the target groups in the initiatives of peace building in order to engage them in the learning process from its planning to implementation is particularly in line with Freire's ideology of education for liberation. In his words,

> education as the practice of freedom–as opposed to education as the practice of domination–denies that man is abstract, isolated, independent, and unattached to the world. Authentic reflection considers neither abstract man nor the world without people, but people in their relations with the world. In these relations consciousness and world are simultaneous: consciousness neither precedes the world nor follows it. (Freire, 1921, p. 81)

An interesting finding of this study is the unintentional organic way in which Selmiyah movement was created and the fact that all the initiatives within the movement address different aspects of peace education in society, these aspects integrate and form a comprehensive model comparable with the model designed by Ian Harris.[3] The added value of Selmiyah network was found to be offering the needed collaboration and supportive system that would contribute to the dissemination and sustainability of the initiatives and projects within the network.

In the post-revolution Egypt, it became obvious that there is a need within Egyptian society for the frameworks, values, and materials that are being introduced and produced by the Selmiyah initiatives for promoting peace education. On the same note, even though there is exclusion and marginalization of certain sects of Egyptian society such as youth (Population Council, 2011), this did not stop these young people from engaging actively in their community, and developing ideas that are desperately needed within the society. The Selmiyah movement offers demonstrated examples of initiatives for peace education that encourage marginalized groups to engage back in society and to adopt a constructive approach, through a mindset shift of how they are perceived and what they can contribute to the development of their society.

ACKNOWLEDGEMENT

I would like to thank Dr. Jennifer Skaggs, Assistant Professor at The American University in Cairo for her supervision of my MA thesis where the initial research of this chapter was conducted.

NOTES

[1] Johan Galtung, a Norwegian peace researcher who started the intellectual work done in this field in the 1960s, defines positive peace as: "a condition where non-violence, ecological sustainability and social justice remove the causes of violence. Positive peace requires both the adoption of a set of beliefs by individuals and the presence of social institutions that provide for an equitable distribution of resources and peaceful resolution of conflicts" (Harris, 2007, p. 12).

[2] The database of the Selmiyah network was used as reference and the official registrations were shared with the researcher by the coordinator, along with the database updates until end of November 2014.

[3] Ian Harris explains the key components that should be included in a peace education model while Selmiyah Model offers a demonstrated example of a youth-led movement to form a network of CSOs' initiatives for peace education.

REFERENCES

Abdelhay, A. T. (2005). *Studies on youth policies in the Mediterranean partner countries.* MarlyleRoi: EUROMED.

Ashton, C. V. (2007). Using theory of change to enhance peace education evaluation. *Conflict Resolution Quarterly, 25*(1), 39–53.

Bacani, B. R. (2004). Bridging theory and practice in peace education: The Notre Dame University peace education experience. *Conflict Resolution Quarterly, 21*(1), 503–511.

Barnes, C. (2005). Weaving the web: Civil-society roles in working with conflict and building peace. In P. Van Tongeren, M. Brenk, M. Hellema, & J. Verhoeven (Eds.), *People building peace II.* Boulder, CO: Lynne Rienner Publishers.

British Council & Gerhart Center. (2013). *The revolutionary promise: Youth perceptions in Egypt, Libya and Tunisia.* Cairo: British Council.

Brown, B. B., & Larson, R. W. (2002). The kaleidescope of adolescence. In B. B. Brown, R. W. Larson, & T. S. Saraswathi (Eds.), *The world's youth: Adolescence in eight regions of the globe* (pp. 1–16). New York, NY: Cambridge University Press.
Carspecken, P. F. (1996). *Critical ethnography in educational research.* New York, NY: Routledge.
CIVICUS. (2005). *Civil society index report for the Arab Republic of Egypt: Executive summary.* Cairo: CIVICUS.
Creswell, J., & Miller, D. (2000). Determining validity in qualitative inquiry. *Theory into Practice, 39*(3), 124–130.
Danesh, H. B. (2006). Towards an integrative theory of peace education. *Journal of Peace Education, 3*(1), 55–78.
Dewey, J. (1897). My pedagogic creed. *The School Journal, 54*(3), 77–80.
Dewey, J. (1899). *Lectures in the philosophy of education.* New York, NY: Random House, Inc.
El-Rouby, H. (2007). *Mapping organizations working with and for youth in Egypt.* Cairo: World Bank.
Fountain, S. (1999). *Peace education in UNICEF.* New York, NY: United Nations Children's Fund.
Freire, P. (1921). *Pedagogy of the opressed.* New York, NY: Continuum International Publishing Group.
Gerring, J. (2004). What is a case study and what is it good for? *American Political Science Review, 98*(2), 341–354.
Guido, F. M., Chavez, A. F., & Lincoln, Y. S. (2010). Underlying paradigms in student affairs research and practice. *Student Affairs Research and Practice, 47*, 1–22.
Handoussa, H. (2010). *Egypt human development report.* Cairo: UNDP.
Harris, I. M. (2007). Peace education theory. *Journal of Peace Education, 1*(1), 5–20.
Hatch, A. J. (2002). Analyzing qualitative data. In A. J. Hatch (Ed.), *Doing qualitative research in education settings* (pp. 147–211). Albany, NY: State University of New York Press.
Helde, M. L. (2013). *The dialogue handbook: The art of conducting a dialogue and facilitating dialogue workshops.* Copenhagen: Danish Youth Council.
ICNL. (2014, November 25). *NGO law monitor: Egypt.* Retrieved December 5, 2014, from http://www.icnl.org/research/monitor/egypt.html
ILO, CAPMAS, & IPEC. (2012). *Working children in Egypt: Results of the 2010 national child labour survey.* Cairo: ILO.
Jones, T. S. (2005). Education that makes a difference. In P. Van Tongeren, M. Brenk, M. Hellema, & J. Verhoeven (Eds.), *People building peace II* (pp. 245–254). Boulder, CO: Lynne Riennen Publishers.
Kamara, E., & Neal, K. (2005). Food, education, and peacebuilding: Children's learning services in Sierra Leone. In P. Van Tongeren, M. Brenk, M. Hellema, & J. Verhoeven (Eds.), *People building peace II* (pp. 257–263). Boulder, CO: Lynne Rienner Publishers.
Kendall, N. (2009). International development education. In R. Cowen & A. Kazamias (Eds.), *International handbook of comparative education* (pp. 417–435). Berlin: Springer Science + Business Media.
Khallaf, M. (2010, January 28). *Civil society in Egypt.* Retrieved December 5, 2014, from http://foundationforfuture.org/en/Portals/0/Conferences/Research/Research%20papers/Civil_Society_in_Egypt_Mahi%20Khallaf_English.pdf
Kopecký, P., & Mudde, C. (2010). Rethinking civil society. *Democratization, 10*(3), 1–14.
Kurhasani, V. (2005). Young Kosovars help themselves: The Kosovar youth council. In P. Van Tongeren, M. Brenk, M. Hellema, & J. Verhoeven (Eds.), *People building peace II* (pp. 167–173). Boulder, CO: Lynne Rienner Publishers.
Lekaa, L. A. (2013). *Yearly report 2013.* Cairo: Lekaa.
Mahgoub, N., & Morsi, R. (2013). *EURECA documents.* Boulder, CO: Lynne Rienner Publishers. Retrieved April 15, 2014, from http://www.aucegypt.edu/research/conf/eureca/Documents/URJ%20V3/Nahla%20Mahgoub%20Reham%20Morsi.pdf
Ministry of Youth and Sports. (n.d.). *Goals.* Retrieved May 26, 2014, from http://www.youth.gov.eg/pages/goals
Naguib, K. (2006). The production and reproduction of culture in Egyptian schools. In L. Herrara & C. A. Torres (Eds.), *Cultures of Arab schooling: Critical ethnographies from Egypt* (p. 77). New York, NY: State University of New York Press.
Population Council. (2011). *Survey of young people in Egypt.* Cairo: Population Council.

Roushdy, R., Rashed, A., & Salemi, C. (2015). *2014 panel survey of young people in Egypt: Preliminary findings*. Cairo: Population Council.

Rucht, D. (2014). Civil society, civility, and democracy. *Civic education conference documentation* (pp. 16–21). Cairo: Goethe-Institut.

Serbin, A. (2005). Effective regional networks and partnerships. In P. Van Tongerern, M. Brenk, M. Hellema, & J. Verhoeven (Eds.), *People building peace II* (pp. 45–58). Boulder, CO: Lynne Rienner Publishers.

Sukarieh, M., & Tannock, S. (2011, May 16). The positivity imperative: A critical look at the 'new' youth development movement. *Journal of Youth Studies, 14*(6), 675–691.

UNDESA. (n.d.). *Youth definition*. Retrieved May 26, 2014, from http://www.un.org/esa/socdev/documents/youth/fact-sheets/youth-definition.pdf

UNESCO. (n.d.). *Definition of youth*. Retrieved May 26, 2014, from http://www.unesco.org/new/en/social-and-human-sciences/themes/youth/youth-definition/

UNV. (2013). *Arab youth volunteering for a better future*. Cairo: UNV.

USAID. (2011). *The 2011 civil society organization sustainability report for the Middle East and North Africa*. Cairo: USAID.

Zahidi, S. (2013, October 24). *Top 10 most gender equal countries in the world*. Retrieved May 12, 2014, from https://www.weforum.org/agenda/2013/10/top-10-most-gender-equal-countries-in-the-world/

Shereen Aly
Graduate School of Education
The American University in Cairo (AUC)

SOHA ALY

4. CITIZENSHIP EDUCATION

A Critical Content Analysis of the Egyptian Citizenship Education Textbooks after the Revolution

INTRODUCTION

Citizenship education is the means to develop individuals, who can act as effective citizens in their societies. Many scholars and politicians have written about the importance of viewing citizenship as a priority for achieving social/national cohesion. Dewey (1915), an educational reformer, stated that the school should reflect what is happening in society in order to achieve its educational purpose towards the community. It is the school's role since it is the only formal learning institution that gathers young citizens of all categories and segments of a democratic society, for extended periods of time. The school is an entity that comprises school culture, curricula, teachers, pedagogy and other activities.

With the unrest that Egypt has been experiencing since the January 25th, 2011 revolution, concerns have been raised by youth about the meanings of citizenship promoted through and by the Egyptian educational system. This research examines how the Egyptian authorities through the Ministry of Education (MOE) have approached these concerns through curricula development, in order to raise generations who would hold and understand the meaning of being a 'good Egyptian citizen.' Special attention is given to Citizenship Education textbooks for secondary stage students, particularly those textbooks that have been produced during the aftermath of the revolution, since 2011 to 2014. This research analyzes the content of these textbooks and intends to propose recommendations to enhance citizenship education curricula in Egypt, questioning; to what extent have the curricula of citizenship education (as presented in the MOE textbooks) changed in terms of the meaning of citizenship to be constructed among Egyptian youth? And, how far did the political regime, after the January 25th revolution, influence the content of citizenship education to accommodate the national revolutionary status of being optimistic and enthusiastic for change and better general conditions?

This research intends to clarify how far the information given in the Egyptian citizenship education textbooks is relevant to the common goals and principles of education for citizenship as identified in scholarly publications. Through literature review focusing on the purposes and goals of citizenship education, indicators are then developed for analyzing the content of citizenship education textbooks.

Therefore, the research and its findings could help educational policy makers and curricula developers in improving citizenship education offered to secondary stage students in Egypt. In addition, it would promote a better understanding of how the national discourse of citizenship, constructed through schooling, could be preserved or changed during the time of political transition and social unrest.

CONCEPT AND CONTEXT OF CITIZENSHIP EDUCATION

With its long history prior to and post colonialism, Egypt presents a case where the meaning and characteristics of citizenship are worth examining. After being part of the Ottoman Empire, Egypt was colonized by the British for several decades (1882–1952). Since gaining its full independence by the 1952 revolution, the country has been trying to define its own identity and restore its sovereignty. With the building of nation-state in Egypt, similar to other countries, the concept of citizenship constitutes a basic foundation to attain and maintain a democratic society. One may argue that Egypt has hybrid social and political perceptions of citizenship, which was developed and accumulated throughout its history. Egypt has been subjected to Western citizenship perceptions and influences under Roman, French, and British colonialism and has also been influenced by Islamic citizenship perceptions under the Islamic caliphate.

Although understanding the construction and meaning of citizenship in Egypt may appear contested, as it has been influenced by various and diverse constituents, the January 25th, 2011 revolution and its aftermath magnified the importance of respecting civic rights and duties in nation-building. Lee and Fouts (2005) in agreement with Ian Lister, who noted that politics and education are intimately and profoundly connected. Both aim to influence how the society is structured. They pointed out that oftentimes writers on politics are also great writers on education. Hence, schools are usually made responsible for producing *good* citizens, which is quite difficult when there isn't a clear definition of the term (Lee & Fouts, 2005).

Before examining citizenship education in Egypt, it is important to address the purpose and goals of citizenship education in general to establish the conceptual basis needed to critically analyze the content of citizenship education textbooks in the Egyptian context.

Citizenship Education Purpose and Goals

Asserting that becoming a citizen is a process, Gonçalves e Silva specified that it is imperative that education plays a role in developing "civic consciousness and agency" within students. Hence, education has specific goals towards citizenship, the most important is to help students acquire knowledge, attitude, and skills needed to create a democratic multicultural active citizen. In addition, citizenship education should help students understand their global citizenship, acquire and develop attitudes and commitments towards global justice and equality (Banks, 2004). Researchers and activists assert that citizenship education plays an important role in shaping students' characters and perceptions, as it is inspiring and motivational for young people due to its relevancy to the concerns of their everyday lives (Faour & Muasher, 2011).

However, some educators express their concern about the discrepancy of citizenship education in theory versus practice. They argue that there is a lack of connection between what is being offered in textbooks and what students experience in reality. From this perspective, effective citizenship education should be attained through experience and interactions in real life and during the daily ritual in schools. This would enable students to understand and practice the concepts of democracy and citizenship where they engage in observation and analysis of the context in which they live, then identify what is lacking and actively seek justice and equality (Banks, 2004). Yet, Banks (2004) explains that among the challenges for citizenship education is embedded in its definition and goal, as being the process of constructing an "inclusive pluralistic nation-state" (p. 12) that respects common values as well as diverse cultures, and perceives them as legitimate to all.

From an Egyptian perspective, many scholars have tackled the definition of citizenship and the history of the concept. Focusing on the role of education and how it could add to the concept of citizenship. In their analysis of the definition of citizenship education by Egyptian scholars, Rifai and Abuzayd (2005) and Qasim (2006) explain that several Egyptian scholars agree with El-Bielawy (2005) that citizenship education is a back-and-forth, give-and-take relationship between school and society. They argued that citizenship is a sense of identity, which incorporates citizens' rights and duties. It is a process where students are prepared to becoming actively involved in the development of society through economic, political, and democratic participation. Moreover, El-Bielawy (2005) adds that citizenship is a set of core values that create a community; through these common values individuals feel belonging to the wider community, rather than only to their families and friends.

The purpose and goals of citizenship education are further defined in relation to lifelong learning and the knowledge and skills of the 21st century. According to Faour and Muasher (2011), education for citizenship plays a key role in promoting most of the 21st century skills and lifelong learning, by which students can acquire opportunities to practice civic skills such as problem solving, persuasive writing, collaboration, and consensus building, as well as developing dialogues with public officials about issues of concern. To achieve these learning outcomes, a teaching and learning approach that emphasizes open discussions and active learning is proven to be far more effective than the didactic lecture-based approach. From their perspective, Faour and Muasher (2011) explain what they term 'education for citizenship' to incorporate two notions; 'education about citizenship' and 'education through citizenship.' The former provides knowledge and understanding of history and politics. The latter enhances students' learning through involvement in civic activities inside the school, such as voting for the school council, and outside the school, such as joining an environmental group in the community.

The above two notions associated with 'education for citizenship' are further clarified by Qasim (2006) in his explanation of six dimensions of citizenship education, which include the following: (1) Active Citizenship, defined as a sense of belonging to a state and performing the rights and duties identified by the state law and its constitution; (2) Public Interest, focuses on developing citizens' perceptions and knowledge about public matter and political issues to be able to observe and demand rights for the common good; (3) Community Service, aims at not only engaging citizens in collaborative activities and services to enhance their societal interaction skills, but also raising their awareness of the needs and rights of their local communities to prevent abuse of power by government officials; (4) Pluralism and Diversity, seek the development of citizens who accept and respect multiculturalism and support pluralism to achieve coexistence, through discussions and evaluation of common values and ethics as well as through pedagogies for diverse learners; (5) Cultural Identity, identifies the common heritage and characteristics of citizens in a given society based on shared customs, traditions, beliefs and history, as all these elements together constitute the nation's s distinguished identity that presents and integrates its diverse citizens in the global society; and (6) Political Literacy, entails the required theoretical knowledge and interactional social capital that citizens should acquire to be able to engage in and pursue political participation.

Citizenship Education and Curriculum

Educators discuss different approaches for the inclusion of citizenship education in the school curriculum. Some approaches tend to favor the integration of citizenship education in traditional courses that are regularly taught at schools while others prefer to introduce it as a separate course or activity. Kjellin, Stier, Einarson, Davies, and Asunta (2010) introduce three approaches for teaching citizenship. Firstly, the content-focused approach, which focuses on the content being taught to students. This approach uses typical, traditional teaching method that relies on the knowledge-content of different subjects and assesses student learning outcomes based on quantitative measures through test scores. Secondly the result-focused approach, which focuses on the intended learning outcomes and uses the knowledge-content to achieve these outcomes. Hence, students' achievements are evaluated by using different assessment techniques during the learning experience and not only test scores. And thirdly, the process and development-focused approach that focuses on the learning experience of students and engage them in activities and hands-on experience to develop citizenship values and skills, such as using problem solving and project-based strategy to enable student acquiring critical thinking skills. Hence, choosing which pedagogical approach would depend on the expected political consciousness that the government wants for its citizens. In other words, whether the government wants to develop passive citizens who are disengaged in public interests or active citizens who are aware of their rights and duties, thus able to address and serve public interests and issues.

In his analysis of Richard Pring's work, Crick (2001) argued that citizenship education in formal schooling is influenced or shaped by the government's political agenda and interests in a given society. Thus, the discussion about 'Citizenship and Schools' solidifies the argument about how important 'political literacy' is in building and enhancing students' civic skills, understanding and knowledge, which in turn enable them to participate in fostering democracy in their society. However, he posed some questions in order to critically think about how to construct the curricula of citizenship education and how to assess its learning outcomes. He questioned if moral or social qualities could be objectively measured, and assessed according to what?

In addition, Crick (2001) considered citizenship education as a humanities discipline, accordingly, he argued that the structure of its subject content should be a mixture of history, philosophy, anthropology, and other humanities subjects. With this interdisciplinary nature of citizenship education, it cannot really achieve its objectives and learning outcomes unless it is enriched with discussions and dialogues about life experiences, incidents and situations. This leads to another point, which is the attitude to deliberation. The Crick (2001) discussion questions the challenge that might face an open democratic society when dealing with consensus and disagreements among diverse groups, in which both are built on rationales and evidences. He raised this query to point out the manner by which students need to learn how to use logic to acquire, understand, and deal with reliable and factual information but also to have the tendency to respect differences and value diversity. In that, the reliability of assessing Citizenship Education is also questionable, as it is a subject that aims to develop students' characters for a lifetime, not only for school.

Parallel to the previous point and in relation to the development-focused approach in teaching citizenship, service learning is examined as a teaching strategy that would foster citizenship values. In his case study, Rhoads (1998) found that service learning enabled students to: (1) develop a better understanding of the theoretical knowledge covered in classrooms, (2) connect theoretical knowledge to actual experience, (3) interact with diverse groups in local communities, and (4) provide an opportunity for real experience of tackling certain social problems and find solutions for these problems. Soutphommasane (2011) added another teaching strategy following the developmental approach to develop 'Patriotic Thinking.' This strategy focuses on engaging diverse groups of students in discussions and debates about national problems.

Education for Citizenship in Egypt

In focus of the Egyptian case, Baraka (2008) discussed the gap existing within students' social and political awareness in Egypt, and how schooling could narrow this gap if policy makers could appreciate the significance of curricula reform; asserting the interrelation of education and politics. This can be illustrated by examining how the purpose of citizenship education differed during different political administrations in recent Egyptian history. A historical overview of education for citizenship in Egypt offered by El-Naggar and Krugly-Smolska (2009) explains this difference and variation.

According to El-Naggar and Krugly-Smolska (2009), in the beginning of Egypt's modern history, some educational developments were made by the rulers like Mohamed Ali and Khedive Ismail to initiate a national sense of belonging. Afterwards under the British colonial rule, the curriculum and textbooks in general expressed the superiority of the imperial British culture. In 1919, the Egyptians united for the first nationalist revolution against the British occupation. Four years later the first Egyptian constitution was written. During this period, the educational syllabi for Citizenship Education was drafted to promote an Egyptian-centered national identity countering the previous curriculum developed by the occupiers. Decades later and after the 1952 revolution and under Nasser's administration, curricula were modified to include social justice, equity, and socialist democratic values (El-Naggar & Krugly-Smolska, 2009). Nonetheless, this major change is described to be a doctrinaire fashion. It intentionally neglected different viewpoints that oppose socialism, and even falsified them to establish a socialist democratic ideology (Baraka, 2008). In addition, Arab nationalism was developed during Nasser's period, yet it was more of a sentiment than an achieved citizenship. In this regard, the Egyptian curricula focused on promoting Egyptian ties with the Arab world (El-Naggar & Krugly-Smolska, 2009).

Later on, Sadat succeeded Nasser but with a different perspective. Sadat's regime was working towards political, economic, and social liberalism. He aimed to achieve democracy through political plurality and freedom of speech. During Sadat, curricula were more open asserting the values of unity and the role of Egypt in the Middle East. Values of patriotism, pride, and identity were stressed with the focus on the 6th of October 1973 victory and Camp David Peace Accords. Also under Sadat, the Islamic discourse was pretty much developed in textbooks and formal education (Baraka, 2008; El-Naggar & Krugly-Smolska, 2009).

Finally, under the regime of Mubarak and during the 1980s, education reform prioritized quantitative expansion by building more schools over funding quality education; consequently, less attention was given to curricula development, including citizenship education (Baraka, 2008). While attention was given to improving educational quality during the 1990s and the 2000s, national efforts supported by international organizations focused on teacher professional development and standardization rather than curricular reform and development (Megahed, 2008; Megahed et al., 2012). Thus, despite educational reform efforts, public criticism of the poor quality of education prevailed in Egypt and marked the era of Mubarak's regime (Faour & Muasher, 2011).

Explaining how education for citizenship is shaped by and contributes to shape political, economic and social dynamics, El-Naggar and Krugly-Smolska (2009) touched on the influences that negatively affect citizenship and accordingly citizenship education in Egypt. They described Mubarak's rule coming after Nasser and Sadat as a combination of nationalism and liberalism that was neither clearly perceived by the public nor correctly implemented by the government. This along with poor institutional structures and poor performance in many public sectors led Egyptian citizens to lose trust in public institutions and officials, and in turn felt discouraged. For example, although citizenship principles and values are identified in the Ministry of Education publications, teachers were left under-informed about, lack understanding of, and do not grasp the meaning of these principles in practice. Therefore, they lacked the competency needed for teaching citizenship education offered in schools at all grades (Baraka, 2008).

During the 1980s, the purpose of education focused on developing knowledgeable, skilled and productive citizens who are capable to serve their local communities. As El-Naggar and Krugly-Smolska (2009) mentioned, the Egyptian state law no. 139 issued in 1981, article 16 states that:

> The purpose of basic education is developing the students' abilities and readiness, and providing them with the necessary and sufficient values, knowledge, and scientific, vocational skills that are suitable for different local environments. Furthermore, enabling the pupils who complete basic education to pursue education in a higher stage, or after intensive vocational training. This is required in order to prepare the individual to become a productive citizen within their environment and community. (cited in El-Naggar & Krugly-Smolska, 2009, p. 46)

In the 2000s, emphasis on the Egyptian identity, values and heritage was reinforced. Baraka (2008) explains that a policy document from the MOE published in 2000 asserts that:

> The potential dominance of technology over culture and civilization will necessitate strenuous efforts to deepen the values of loyalty and belonging among Egyptian citizens, to affirm Egyptian identity and reinforce all which pertains to our civilization and cultural heritage; thus, we cannot discard ethical values such as appreciation of beauty, happiness, peace and stability originating from family life or noble human values such as friendship, respect for others. (cited in Baraka, 2008, pp. 46–47)

According to Baraka (2008), the same document also clarified the importance of extracurricular activities in achieving a comprehensive education reform strategy that supports students' application of democracy. In another document issued by the Ministry of Education in 2003, the characteristics of citizenship were highlighted in the purpose of education. Moreover, topics and areas of education for citizenship were identified to include: (1) "Civic Education" (duties and rights); (2) "Life Skills" (the ability to negotiate, to cooperate, to be tolerant with others, and to have diversity in opinions); (3) "Government System" (democracy, constitution, People's Council, elections, citizens' role in elections); (4) "Preserving Heritage" (Arab and Egyptian heritage, Islamic and Coptic heritage, Arab and Egyptian values and traditions); (5) "Egypt's Relations" with other countries (on the Arab, Islamic level, African, and the global levels); (6) "Non-Government Organizations" (conditions to establish NGOs, the role of NGOs); (7) "Arab Organizations and Institutions" (League of Arab States, Arab Common Market, Islamic Conference Organization, African Unity Organization); (8) "International Organizations and Institutions" (United Nations, World Health Organization, and International Labor Organization) (Baraka, 2008).

On the contrary, the most recent policy document published by MOE for pre-university education strategic plan 2014–2030 slightly touched on citizenship education principles as part of the general objective of grades 7, 8 and 9 (known in Egypt as the preparatory stage. Ironically, while in the post-revolution the Ministry of Education focused on developing and issuing new textbooks for citizenship education, its strategic plan for secondary education does not elaborate on the principles and purposes of citizenship education for students in secondary schools (Ministry of Education, 2014).

In their examination of citizenship education in Egypt, some scholars explain problems in the educational system and practice that affects citizenship education, making it a marginalized subject. Citizenship education is offered in Egyptian schools as a separate subject, which is obliged for all Egyptian students to take in all grade levels. Students are assessed through a final test and should pass this test in order to move to a higher-grade level. Nonetheless, the student test score is not counted as part of his/her accumulative, final score of all subjects. Taking into consideration what Qasim (2006) asserted about Egyptian students who tend to study only what would enable them to gain high score in their final exams, this explains the marginalization of citizenship education in Egypt as students would not give it the proper attention, thus will not locate or recall information about topics that are not counted towards their accumulative final exam score. Therefore, countering the marginalization of citizenship education could be by its integration in the school curricular and extracurricular activities rather than being offered as a separate, marginalized subject. Banks (2004) highlights the importance of school activities for teaching citizenship values focusing on co-curricular and extracurricular activities (i.e., students' associations). The interaction with school administration and teachers through discussing school's problems and assigning responsibilities to students, in addition to community services outside the school, would help build students' democratic values and civic personalities.

Further criticism on the teaching practice and knowledge-content of citizenship education at Egyptian schools is addressed from El-Naggar and Kurgly-Smolska's perspective (2009) that sheds light on *textbook content* as an element that weakens achieving the goals of citizenship education in Egypt. For them, the citizenship education curriculum in Egypt suffers at all stages from being a rhetoric information to a major lack of teaching aids and supporting materials and activities. For example, the content does not emphasize the concepts of liberty, equality, cooperation, responsibility, and critical thinking. These concepts are taught from a shallow perspective that would not enable achieving the desired objectives, learning outcomes, stated in textbooks. In addition, the values of citizenship are not better off on the cognitive and behavioral levels, as they are not clearly demonstrated in the school's culture and practice. They added that some studies showed curriculum deficiency in developing political literacy. In that, it does not clarify the political system, governance approach, and political parties, and has scarce information related to the formal and informal political institutions. Accordingly, citizenship education curriculum would not be able to achieve its main objective of preparing citizens for a democratic society, but also it would not encourage political participation, freedom of opinion, and opposition. On the contrary, it would promote values of compliance, subservience and obedience. Thus, "educational institutions in Egypt do not yet include the culture of civic society through the curricula" (El-Naggar & Krugly-Smolska, 2009, p. 47).

The criticism of citizenship education in Egypt prior to the January 25th, 2011 revolution raises the question of the extent citizenship education has changed after the revolution. This research addresses this question, yet it focuses only on the content of textbooks issued for secondary school students.

RESEARCH METHODS

Textbooks of Citizenship Education Issued after the Revolution

As mentioned earlier, this research critically analyzes the content of newly developed textbooks of citizenship education, termed in Egypt 'National Education.' During only four school years from 2011 to 2015, the Ministry of Education changed and issued six new textbooks of citizenship education for students (aged 14–17) in the secondary education stage (taught at grade 10, 11, or 12). The differences and changes of these textbooks were due to changes occurred in the political administration of Egypt during the aftermath of the revolution. This research focuses on the six newly developed textbooks. The textbooks under examination are classified below by its related political administration and grade level. They are labeled by alphabet letters (A through F) for differentiation and easy referencing.

First – During the rule of the Supreme Council of the Armed Forces (SCAF): Between the step down of President Mubarak in February 11, 2011 till the presidential election in June 2012, Egypt was governed by the Supreme Council of the Armed Forces (SCAF). This period included one newly developed textbook of citizenship education (Book A), taught in the school-year 2011–2012. Book A is titled 'National Education' for Grade 10.

Second – During the rule of Former President Mohammad Morsi: After the first presidential election following the revolution, two new textbooks of citizenship education were issued in the school-year 2012–2013, for grade 10 and grade 11 of secondary schools. These included Book B, titled 'National Education' for Grade 10, and Book C, titled 'Citizenship and Human Rights' for Grade 11.

Third – During the rule of Interim President Adly Mansour who was assigned to the position for another transitional period after the uprising of June 30th, 2013 that called for the step-down of President Morsi, Two new textbooks for the school-year 2013–2014 were issued and taught for grade 10 and grade 12 while the textbook for grade 11 was republished as a second edition, with minor modifications. In that, the new textbooks issued for this school-year included Book D, titled 'National Education: I'm the Egyptian' for Grade 10 and Book E, titled 'National Education' for Grade 12.

Fourth – During the rule of current President Abdel Fattah ElSisi who came to power through the presidential elections held after the June 30th, 2013 uprising: One textbook was newly issued and taught in the school year 2014–2015, Book F titled 'Citizenship and Human Rights' for Grade 11. During this school year, the same textbook issued in the previous year for grade 10 was republished as a second edition with minor revisions. As for the textbook for grade 12, the researcher could not find a new or a reissued copy at the Ministry of Education's online depository, thus cannot confirm if the citizenship education textbook for grade 12 in the school year 2014–2015 was a new version or the same textbook taught in the previous year.

Analysis Tool

The critical content analysis of the textbooks is conducted qualitatively. The text of each book was first reviewed for overall "consistency" and "repetition" (Collins & Levy, 2007). In addition, content analysis is used based on six criteria defined by Marsh and White, (2006) to include:

> (1) Coherence (the text has meaning, often established through relationships that may not be linguistically evident, and draws on frameworks within the recipient for understanding); (2) Intentionality (the writer or speaker of the text intends for it to convey meaning related to his attitude and purpose); (3) Acceptability (recipients of the message understand the text as a message they expect it to be useful or relevant); (4) Informatively (the text may contain new or expected information, allow for judgments about its quality of informing); (5) Situationality (the situation surrounding the text affects its production and determines what is appropriate for the situation and the culture); and (6) Intertextuality (the text is often related to what precedes and follows it, as in a conversation). (pp. 27–28)

The seven criteria have been adapted to accommodate the nature of the content analyzed as follows.

Table 1. Text analysis criteria

Text assessment criterion	Adaptation to text
Consistency and Repetition	Identifying the choice of words related to citizenship, their repetition as an educational context.
Coherence	Clarifying if the chapters' content and goals help students learn Citizenship Education.
Intentionality	The content relates to the goals of teaching citizenship in creating an active citizen who is aware of his rights and responsibilities on the political, economic, and social levels.
Acceptability	Recipients of the message understand the text as a message; they expect it to be useful or relevant.
Informatively	The content includes the dimensions of Citizenship Education (Active Citizenship – Public Interest – Community Service – Pluralism and diversity – Cultural Identity – Political literacy)
Situationality	The content relates to reality, addresses the current political and social conditions in Egypt.
Intertextuality	The information in the textbook is related to its context and is connected in sequence.

Source: Adapted from Collins and Levy (2007) and Marsh and White (2006).

The content of the textbooks was analyzed through the above-mentioned adapted criteria to assess to what extent the content is relevant to the goals and dimensions of citizenship education. These goals and dimensions are defined based on eight parameters mentioned in Baraka (2008) and Qasim (2006), which are adapted in this research as shown in Table 2.

Validity

The tool of this research is validated by what is defined in Kohlbacher (2006), *The Use of Qualitative Content Analysis*, to include "construct validity relates" and "sampling validity". "Construct validity relates" means using previous constructs, established models and theories, or representative interpretations, and "sampling validity" refers to the usual criteria for precise sampling (p. 16). The tool of this research is designed based on the adaptation of previous constructs and representative interpretations. In addition, the researcher carefully quoted text samples to provide evidences for each of the Citizenship Education parameters.

Table 2. Citizenship education parameters

Citizenship education assessment parameter	Citizenship education aspects
Civic Education (duties and rights)	Active Citizenship, defined as a sense of belonging to a state and performing the rights and duties identified by the state law and its constitution. Public Interest, focuses on developing citizens' perceptions and knowledge about public matter and political issues to be able to observe and demand rights for the common good.
Life Skills (ability to negotiate, to cooperate, tolerate with others, and to have diversity in opinions)	Pluralism and Diversity, seek the development of citizens who accept and respect multiculturalism and support pluralism to achieve coexistence, through discussions and evaluation of common values and ethics as well as through pedagogies for diverse learners.
Government System (democracy, constitution, People's Council, elections, citizens' role in elections)	Political Literacy, entails the required theoretical knowledge and interactional social capital that citizens should acquire to be able to engage in and pursue political participation.
Preserving Heritage (Arab and Egyptian heritage, Islamic and Coptic heritage, Arab and Egyptian values and traditions)	Cultural Identity, identifies the common heritage and characteristics of citizens in a given society based on shared customs, traditions, beliefs and history, as all these elements together constitute the nation's distinguished identity that presents and integrates its diverse citizens in the global society.
Egypt's Relations with Other Countries (as Arabs, on the Islamic, African, and the global levels)	
Non-Government Organizations (conditions to establish NGOs, the role of NGOs)	Community Service/Engagement, aims at not only engaging citizens in collaborative activities and services to enhance their social interaction skills, but also raising their awareness of the needs and rights of their local communities to prevent abuse of power by government officials.
Arab Organizations and Institutions (League of Arab States, Arab Common Market, Islamic Conference Organization, and African Unity Organization)	
International Organizations and Institutions (United Nations, World Health Organization, and International Labor Organization).	

Source: Adapted from Baraka (2008) and Qasim (2006).

CITIZENSHIP EDUCATION IN THE POST-REVOLUTION

In this section, I present the main findings of the content analysis of the six citizenship education textbooks and provide a general description of the most significant points in the content of each textbook using the criteria mentioned in Tables 1 and 2. Before presenting the content of each textbook, it is worth mentioning that the language and terminology used in the six textbooks is the simple, modern Arabic that can be easily understood by students in the targeted age range (14–17 years old). In addition, the organization of the text included a lot of information presented in specific points and bullets, which appears to be more convenient for the students to understand and follow. The colors and the pictures used and the overall design are all conceived. Yet, the textbooks are printed in a poor quality, which might be due to budget constraints.

Citizenship Education during the Rule of the Supreme Council of the Armed Forces (SCAF) – Book A (2011–2012)

Book A titled 'National Education' – Grade 10 – includes an introduction stating that national education aims at (a) promoting a sense of belonging and an understanding of the nation's history and the role of individuals in their modern society and (b) preserving human rights that will ultimately support democracy and 'Shura' (Advisory). These points are also presented as the objectives of this textbook. Out of the eight parameters used for analyzing the content of citizenship education, this book reflects on Preserving Heritage and Cultural Identity, mostly within its first and second chapters. The book also covers parameters such as, Life Skills, Pluralism, Diversity, and Active Citizenship though they are presented briefly in the third chapter without supporting examples from real life experiences.

The first chapter presents geographical and historical information about Egypt, mostly about after the 1952 "revolution." The most recent event mentioned in this chapter was in 1960 – Suez Canal nationalization. Furthermore, there might be an implicit meaning of Diversity in the first chapter, where it is asserted that "Christian minority is an unbreakable part of the Egyptian human body". Moreover, the chapter emphasized the importance of The Nile River, stating that; "The Nile River transformed Egypt and its society into a river community [all Egyptians reside around the Nile]. There is a need for enormous collective efforts to repair the Nile basin soil… the government established a central entity to regulate the relationship between the environment and the individuals" (p. 10).

With the same geo-historical approach, the second chapter addresses the history of Ancient and Islamic Egypt. Although parts of the lessons mention some political and social information like the role of the Egyptian rulers in Ancient and Islamic Egypt, it is questionable to what extent would this promote "Political Literacy" and "Active Citizenship" as all this information is obsolete. Yet, the content cannot be described as being subjective. On the other hand, the chapter content includes some aspects of the cultural heritage of Egypt during the Pharaohs era. Nonetheless, it misses other important aspects of Egyptian cultural heritage like the Coptic and Roman history in Egypt.

As for the third chapter, the content analysis reveals that it is the most informative part of this textbook as related to the citizenship dimensions of Cultural Diversity, Active Citizenship, Pluralism and Diversity and Public Interest. These dimensions are clearly demonstrated through the biography of male and female Egyptian role models like: Makram Ebied, Ahmad Lotfy ElSayed and Aaisha' AbdelRahman. As mentioned in the text, each figure had his/her own specialization that he/she contributed to the building of the Egyptian nation through remarkable achievements. Although all the chosen characters are deceased, I find the role model approach of teaching citizenship through real individuals' life journeys might make it easier for the students to embrace citizenship values and behaviors.

The content analysis of this textbook indicates that Egyptian citizenship is portrayed through geographical and historical approach, where nationalism is articulated in the context of the 1952 revolution and ancient heritage. In addition, national unity among diverse citizens is presented through the role model approach that took into consideration gender and religious diversity. Nonetheless, some aspects of the Egyptian cultural heritage that contribute to national identity were magnified (ancient and Islamic eras) on the expense of others (Roman and Coptic eras).

Citizenship Education during the Rule of Former President Mohammad Morsi – Book B and C (2012–2013)

Book B titled 'National Education' for Grade 10 was issued for general and vocational secondary schools. Thus, it is not surprising that one of the book's four chapters is devoted for work skills (such as management, communication …etc.). The first and third chapters of this book address conceptual knowledge about citizenship, such as the characteristics of a good citizen. These include topics on "Nationalism", "Identity", "Democracy", "Citizenship Values", and "National Unity". Although all these topics are directly related to the concept of citizenship, they provide cognitive knowledge while lack demonstrated examples or suggested activities that would enable students to gain the related values and skills of each topic. The other two chapters are about "Human Development" and "Work Skills". Both chapters focus on the importance of preparing citizens who are capable to participate in societal development. They highlight some of the 21st century skills such as collaboration, and communication skills. Hence, the book content offers basic information on the concept of citizenship and some of its related skills, which touches on the eight parameters identified for citizenship education. Yet, examples or activities that would demonstrate the conceptual knowledge in practice were absence.

Similarly, Book C titled 'Citizenship and Human Rights for Grade 11 includes four chapters. However, it differs in terms of approaching the four chapters in relation to political, economic, and social aspects when discussing specific topics of citizenship. As clear from its title, the entire book is informative on the "Political

Literacy" dimension. The first chapter covers the meaning of being a citizen and presents many rights and duties related to "Civic Education." The following two chapters clearly demonstrate some aspects of political awareness and civil society, which enliven the dimensions of "Active Citizenship" and "Public Interest". For example, it highlights the role of local community in promoting political awareness, stating that "active political awareness of the community enlightens citizens' insights of civil/legal rights, and constitutional obligations" (p. 20). The two chapters also provide knowledge about social, economic, and political opportunities for youth and the importance of their contribution to social changes and decision-making.

The final chapter focuses entirely on one society segment, that of women, which is needed in the Egyptian society to develop *Social Literacy*. The chapter gains its importance in the beginning when it mentions the custom distort perception about women's role and discrimination against. It also emphasizes equal rights for women, as stated "Women's right to citizenship, personal freedoms and the acceptance of free participation of all individuals as equal citizens are needed to lay the foundations of democracy" (p. 52). Furthermore, this chapter covers the dimensions of "Political Literacy", "Active Citizenship", "Diversity" and "Cultural Identity" as related to women's rights, trying to restore the image of women as equal citizens (one of the main citizenship values). I would recommend similar chapters on different minority and disadvantaged groups in Egypt.

It is worth mentioning that despite the objectivity and importance of the issues discussed in these two textbooks, there are very few sections in their text where the word Egypt or Egyptian was mentioned. I think that the use of such words should have been made more frequent as the content is addressed within the Egyptian context and for Egyptian students.

Citizenship Education during the Rule of Interim President Adly Mansour – Book D and E (2013–2014)

Book D, titled 'National Education: I'm the Egyptian' for Grade 10 and as stated in its text, is directed to youth and aims at developing their citizenship/national identity. The book content covers the dimensions of "Preserving Heritage" and "Cultural Identity". It starts with demonstrating the "Egyptian" character – this word choice makes the material more relevant to its context, as it describes the Egyptian individual (citizen) throughout the history till today, emphasizing "Diversity and Pluralism" by mentioning different races that lived in Egypt. However, some of the adjectives used tend to be a bit overstated. For example, the text describes the location of Egypt to be 'genius' (p. 14) and the Egyptian people to be 'religious' (p. 19). This contradicts the need to avoid exaggeration in the content of educational textbooks.

On another level, the first two chapters are informative on the "Political Literacy" level. Both introduce the three main authorities of the state (Legislature, Executive and Judiciary), which are essential in understanding the hierarchy and the structure of the government. This is in addition to introducing the "Islamic" perspective of state governance by describing what is called in Arabic 'Sahifat Al-Madina' – the first written constitution that was developed during the first Islamic century to govern the city of Madina in the Arabian Peninsula (Tahir-ul-Qadri, 2012) – which is further discussed in Book E. The second chapter addresses the basic concepts of citizenship in an informative approach that serves as an introduction for the preceding year's textbook. This chapter sheds light on citizenship values such as Equality and Identity. It states directly and clearly that "Citizenship is values and virtues; it is a culture that achieves social cohesion and establishes a common identity. It is the cornerstone of building the state because of it has profound effects on the attainment of national unity" (p. 29). In addition, the chapter covers the historical and regional (Arab) aspects of the Egyptian identity, showing how the different races and civilizations that lived in Egypt along the history affected and created the current Egyptian personality.

The final two chapters focus solely on Egyptian youth. They present youth as being the future investment for any nation. Then, the national policies for youth and their role in the society are discussed. In addition, examples of activities and contributions done by young Egyptian figures are introduced in the final part. This part demonstrates the means and images of Active Citizenship. Moreover, both chapters try to connect students to the concept of "Public Interest" by tackling policies offered by the state like mentioning the minimum age for running for the Parliament (35 years old) and for City Council (21 years old) as identified by the Egyptian Constitution. Finally, choosing young Egyptian role models and the frequent mention of the 2011 revolution, strengthen the relevance and connection of the material to the real-life experience of students, which in turn would achieves better results (learning outcomes) for citizenship education.

Book E titled 'National Education' for Grade 12 includes direct informative messages on clearly identified topics and aspects. The content's structure aligns with the goals and principles of education for citizenship in terms of creating a 'good citizen' through understanding how democracy relates to political, social, and economic conditions. The content thoroughly discusses four specific important topics; Democracy, Constitutions, Political Parties, and Human Rights. These four topics were being discussed and debated in the Egyptian society at the same time as this textbook was published. This book was published at the same time as the new 2013 constitution was being written. A referendum took place in January of the same year, which was followed by parliamentary elections. The civic knowledge offered in this textbook was thus aligned with the political transition occurred in this school-year which gave students who were over the age 16 and can vote, the opportunity to practice political participation as active citizens while they are studying about it. For example, the text explains that

> The parliament uses its authorities, including craft the public policy of the state, question the government ministers, and constitute commissions of inquiry and financial monitoring ... Also, it decides upon ministerial responsibility through a vote of confidence. The parliament has full authority regarding the issuance,

cancellation, or ratification of legislation and laws. In other words, it has the general right of final determination of the matters within its competence, as determined by the Constitution. (p. 6)

It is crucial for students to acquire this information, in order to be able seriously assess the political situation that Egypt was going through.

In addition, the chapters about "Democracy" and "Human Rights" include concepts on both, including how they are presented by religions, specifically Islam. Moreover, the last chapter is totally focused on revolutions, specially the very latest one in 2011. For example, it states that "A revolution is a holistic, sudden and drastic change of existing structures and intellectual notions of the political, social, and economic systems. It happens with means..., usually associated with violence and rage for achieving victory for the oppressed over the oppressor" (p. 76). However, including the 2011 revolution as part of this chapter would help in relating students to recent political transition and social unrest that they have been experiencing. This is a noteworthy and positive step from the Ministry of Education to devotes a chapter on revolutions in terms of the history and reasons in Egypt. This approach signals an official intention, guided by the current political will, to teach young citizens that vigorously opposing an unfair regime/government is an accepted attitude. On the same sequence, the final part of the book puts further focus on the 2011 revolution, its causes, demands, and results. This is regarded not only as documentation for a national significant recent dynamic that all Egyptians consider as a national historical event, but also it means a great appreciation of the active role of youth in this revolution, who are of the same age as the students studying this material. This is to say that this last part of the chapter about the 2011 revolution creates a direct link between the content and the students because it addresses an incident that they have already experienced. The overall content of this textbook succeeds in covering the citizenship education dimensions of Pluralism, Active Citizenship, Civic Education, Public Interest and informative on the Political Literacy level.

Citizenship Education during the Rule of Current President Abdel Fattah ElSisi – Book F (2014–2015)

This textbook titled 'Citizenship and Human Rights' for Grade 11 is newly developed, yet it includes some of the topics covered in previously published textbooks (Book C, Book D and Book E). The first two chapters focus on "Political Literacy" and provide information about citizenship values and citizens' rights and duties as well as human rights and related international agreements and organizations. The third chapter focuses solely on women. It discusses the development of women's social and political conditions throughout the Egyptian history and addresses the international agreements that aim to preserve women's rights. The final chapter is about "Civil Society and Volunteer Work." The content of this chapter touches on citizenship education dimensions of Active Citizenship, Public Interest and Community Service.

Most of the information in this textbook is theoretical content and definitions. For example, the text offers a description of volunteer work and its importance, stating that "Volunteer work became a basic pillar in building the community, spreading peace and social coherence, and that's because it offers different positive results on social, political and economic levels which in turn serves both the individuals and the community" (p. 42). This textbook does not include any information about revolutions or constitutions. This might be due to the inclusion of these issues in the textbook for Grade 12 issued in the previous year as discussed above.

Common Findings

As a general analysis, only five citizenship parameters were recognized in the six textbooks, which are Civic Education, Life Skills, Government System, Preserving Heritage and Non-Governmental Organizations. However, none of the following topics were mentioned: Egypt's relations with other countries (as Arabs, the Islamic, African, and global levels); Arab organizations and institutions (League of Arab States, Arab Common Market, Islamic Conference Organization, and African Unity Organization); and International organizations and institutions (United Nations, World Health Organization, and International Labor Organization).

DISCUSSION

I will begin with a personal note; the 2011 revolution was a dream come true, not only for me, but also for many Egyptians who participated in the 18-days sit-in in Tahrir square. It was the first time in Egypt that masses of people, from all walks of life and with different political views, could talk and discuss issues for hours and days without being scrutinized by security. The desire to remove a tyrannical regime that had always divided people was the driving force at that time. Unfortunately, after the first demand was met (which was the stepping down of Mubarak), we found ourselves unable to unite again for other similar causes. Egyptians, to a very large extent, are in urgent need for an education that promotes applicable understanding of coexistence, acceptance of diversity and respect for civic freedoms. Egyptians need to understand and learn more about Active Citizenship, in order for a cohesive democratic Egyptian society to emerge. This cannot be imposed on people. This is a glimpse of one of the reasons that motivated me to analyze the information that are being taught to youth after the revolution that aimed for building a democratic society. Citizens of my generation, who had not received an adequate level of citizenship education, participated in the 2011 revolution demanding a change in citizenship values, yet failed to reach a societal change towards these values. I believe if young generations receive better Citizenship Education now, they will be able to change the distorted values and perceptions into more democratic and just ones.

The findings of the content analysis clarify the picture of the progress made to citizenship education in Egypt after the 2011 revolution. It is obvious that the

Ministry of Education, guided by a political will, has given more attention to the content of citizenship education offered in secondary schools. After the revolution, Egyptians were discovering their potential as citizens in a new atmosphere, especially youth. Most of this potential could be invested to unite commonalities and respect differences between different segments of the population. It is the formal educational institutions (such as schools) that could influence direct citizens' perceptions and attitudes to achieve the revolution demands, social justice and freedom for all through better understanding of the meaning and practice of citizenship values.

The academic year 2013–2014 included three newly developed or reissued textbooks for grades 10, 11, and 12 (a newly developed textbook for Grade 10, a second edition textbook for Grade 11, and a newly developed textbook for Grade 12). The content of these altered textbooks, present a sequential body of information intends to acquire students with knowledge about citizenship. The two textbooks for grade 11 and 12 offer detailed information on Political Literacy and Active Citizenship through participation. Moreover, the content employs a role model approach to demonstrate the dimensions and values of citizenship as defined in literature. In many parts of these three textbooks, the concepts of citizens' rights, freedoms and duties are all defined and emphasized, in addition to the role of the government, civil society and the constitution in governing and securing them. It is very significant that the content also referrers to the Islamic thoughts and principles, and sheds light on human rights in the Islamic history but also in modern time as supported by international organizations and declarations.

The three textbooks portray the concepts and values of citizenship in relation to the current political, social, and economic conditions in Egypt, which is one of the goals of education for citizenship. Yet, this imposes questions such as, how far is the gap between the stated objective and theoretical content offered in the textbooks and the real-life experiences of students? How this gap affects the authenticity of the content of the textbooks? And how it affects students' reaction to the information presented in these textbooks? Such questions deserve to be examined by future research.

On the other hand, although understanding the principles of citizenship need theoretical knowledge, especially those related to Political Literacy and Civic Education, citizenship values are demonstrated by individual and collective behaviors and actions. According to literature, citizenship education is a humanistic discipline, which means that acquiring its related values and skills can hardly be measured by written exams. In this regard, the textbooks do include instructions for activities and problem-based exercises to help students embrace citizenship values and attitudes but are they practiced as instructed? Do students embrace or able to demonstrate citizenship values after studying these textbooks? Is there a different strategy rather than a written exam to assess whether students achieved the objectives mentioned in the textbooks and the extent to which these are demonstrated by their activities and actions?

On another level, some scholars described Egyptian education in general to be didactic and school subjects such as citizenship education to be marginalized, simply because they are not included in the total accumulative score (GPA). Hence, all the positive progress that has been made to the content of citizenship education textbooks can be jeopardized by intended neglect, as it continues to offered as a separate subject with a marginal – pass/fail – assessment. Nowadays, the Egyptian educational system, like many other systems, gives more attention to teaching applied sciences than to humanities and social sciences (Faour & Muasher, 2011). A new educational approach is needed to give humanities and social sciences their proper attention. The Egyptian political will and the Ministry of Education need to consider initiating a curriculum reform that would integrate citizenship education (National Education)in different school subjects and activities through pedagogies of interdisciplinary and active learning.

CONCLUSION

As I examined the content of citizenship education textbooks in the Egyptian secondary schools after the 2011 revolution. My research reveals the main concepts and topics discussed in these textbooks under the rule of four different political administrations. The content analysis of six textbooks was conducted using two adapted criteria for text assessment (Collins & Levy, 2007; Marsh & White, 2006) and content parameters (Baraka, 2008; Qasim, 2006). The findings showed noteworthy progress in the content, yet this research did not investigate the pedagogy used in teaching these textbooks, which needs further research. The Ministry of Education needs to sustain this improvement, which I consider one of the 2011 revolution gains as it demonstrates a 'positive change' that Egyptians have been struggling to achieve. Thus, there is a need for continuous improvement of textbook content but also to give more attention to pedagogical approaches and teaching methods through a long-term educational investment in building student characters and developing citizenship values that are demonstrated in students' behaviors and actions..Equally important, Egyptians as active citizens and educators as active professionals should contribute to and demand the integration of citizenship education across school subjects and activities along with the use of active learning pedagogy as a strategy towards a better quality of the Egyptian educational system.

REFERENCES

Banks, J. A. (2004). *Diversity and citizenship education: Global perspectives.* San Francisco, CA: Jossey-Bass.
Baraka, P. (2008). Citizenship education in Egyptian public schools: What values to teach and in which administrative and political contexts. *Journal of Education for International Development, 3*(3), 1–18.
Collins, W. M., & Levy, B. A. (2007). Text repetition and text integration. *Memory & Cognition, 35*(7), 1557–1566. doi:10.3758/BF03193490

Crick, B. R. (2001). *Citizens: Towards a citizenship culture*. Malden, MA: Blackwell Publishers.
Dewey, J. (1915). *The school and society*. Chicago, IL: The University of Chicago Press.
El-Bielawy, H. (2005). *Commentary* (pp. 1177–1182). The 17th Annual Conference of Political Research, Cairo University, Shorouk International Library, Cairo.
El-Naggar, A. M., & Krugly-Smolska, E. (2009). Citizenship education and liberal democratic change: The Egyptian case. *Canadian and International Education, 38*(2), 36–54.
Faour, M., & Muasher, M. (2011). *Education for citizenship in the Arab world key to the future*. Washington, DC: Carnegie Middle East Center.
Kassem, M. (2006). *Education and citizenship: The reality of civic education in the Egyptian school*. Cairo: Cairo Institute for Human Rights Studies.
Kjellin, M., Stier, J., Einarson, T., Davies, T., & Asunta, T. (2010). Pupils' voices about citizenship education: Comparative case studies in Finland, Sweden, and England. *European Journal of Teacher Education, 33*(2), 201–218.
Kohlbacher, F. (2006). The use of qualitative content analysis in case study research. *Forum: Qualitative Social Research, 7*(1), 1–23.
Lee, W. O., & Fouts, J. T. (2005). *Education for social citizenship: Perceptions of teachers in the USA, Australia, England, Russia, and China*. Hong Kong: Hong Kong University Press.
Marsh, E. E., & White, M. D. (2006). Content analysis: A flexible methodology. *Library Trends, 55*(1), 22–45. doi:10.1353/lib.2006.0053
Megahed, N. (2008). Toward improving the quality of education in Egypt: The implementation of national education standards. *Revista de Pedagogie (Romanian Journal of Pedagogy), 7*(12), 130–143.
Megahed, N., Ginsburg, M., Abdullah, A., & Zohry, A. (2012). The quest for educational quality in Egypt: Active-learning pedagogies as a reform initiative. In C. Acedo, D. Admas, & S. Popa (Eds.), *Quality and qualities: Tensions in education reforms* (pp. 41–68). Rotterdam, The Netherlands: Sense Publishers.
Ministry of Education. (2011/2012). *National education: Grade 10*. Cairo: Ministry of Education.
Ministry of Education. (2012/2013). *Citizenship and human rights: Grade 11*. Cairo: Ministry of Education.
Ministry of Education. (2012/2013). *Citizenship and human rights: Grade 11* (2nd ed.). Cairo: Ministry of Education.
Ministry of Education. (2012/2013). *National education: Grade 10*. Cairo: Ministry of Education.
Ministry of Education. (2012/2013). *National education: Grade 10* (2nd ed.). Cairo: Ministry of Education.
Ministry of Education. (2013/2014). *National education: Grade 12*. Cairo: Ministry of Education.
Ministry of Education. (2013/2014). *National education, I'm the Egyptian: Grade 10*. Cairo: Ministry of Education.
Ministry of Education. (2014/2015). *Citizenship and human rights: Grade 11*. Cairo: Ministry of Education.
Ministry of Education. (2014). *Strategic plan for pre-university education 2014–2030*. Cairo: Ministry of Education.
Qasim, M. (2006). *Education and citizenship: The status of civic-education in Egyptian schools*. Cairo: Markez El Kahera LeHuquq El-Insan (Cairo Center for Human Rights) publishers.
Rhoads, R. (1998). In the service of citizenship. *Journal of Higher Education, 69*(3), 277–297.
Rifai, Y., & Abuzyad, I. (2005). *Egyptian citizenship and the future of democracy*. Paper presented at the Annual Conference of the Center for Political Research and Studies, Cairo University, Giza.
Soutphommasane, T. (2011). Education, citizenship and democracy. *Ethos, 19*(1), 7–10.
Tahir-ul-Qadri, M. (2012). *Constitutional analysis of the constitution of medina*. London: Minhaj-ul-Quran Publications. Retrieved from http://www.academia.edu/2018309/The_Constitution_of_Medina_in_63_constitutional_articles

Soha Aly
Graduate School of Education
The American University in Cairo (AUC)

PART II

DIALECTICS OF EDUCATION FOR GLOBAL CITIZENSHIP AND WOMEN'S EMPOWERMENT

SHAIMAA MOSTAFA AWAD

5. GLOBAL CITIZENSHIP EDUCATION AND CIVIL SOCIETY IN EGYPT

A Case Study of a Character Education Program

INTRODUCTION

With the rise of globalization and the need to have a set of universal values respected by all humanity regardless of differences in cultures or religious beliefs, the importance of global citizenship education has emerged. All aspects of our lives, from our jobs to even the food we eat are connected and impacted by the global growth (Zahabioun, Yousefy, Yarmohammadian, & Keshtiaray, 2013). Therefore, it is becoming profoundly necessary to develop a generation of people who are fully aware of and able to meet the current (global) problems that confront humanity. It is greatly acknowledged that education plays an important role in transforming the lives of children and youth, and thus helps in developing their values, attitudes and personal behaviors. It is through the young people's capacity and positive contribution to their societies that individual, economic, and social lives can be improved (Education Above All, 2012). According to Oxfam (2006), education has the power to change the whole world, since it works on today's children who will be tomorrow's adults. The more people become aware of the interconnectedness and interdependence of the world, the more there is a need for having some universal values like tolerance, fairness, acceptance, compassion, and respect for diversity that help in stimulating a sense of universal belonging and oneness with the humanity. Therefore, these universal values of global interdependence have been constituted as basic values for global citizenship (Gibson & Landwehr-Brown, 2009).

The Egyptian context has gone through a lot of changes that resulted from the political unrest in the past few years especially after the January 25th 2011, revolution and the subsequent uprising of June 30th 2013, that led to a change in the Egyptian character in particular and society in general. There became a state of societal tensions and conflict between people and a tendency for revenge, aggression, disrespect and unacceptance for other's opinions. Throughout this period, Egyptians have been exposed to many new notions that they are not used to like democracy, freedom of expression and the privilege of having a voice that they can use freely to express their opinions and choices. In order to get the best out of this, the upcoming generations need to learn how to interact and deal with the new dynamics the Egyptian society is going through whether socially or politically; they need to learn how to respect the law and the rules of their country, to get their rights and fulfil their duties towards their society and to understand the true meaning of democracy, diversity and acceptance. This is in addition to the need to be provided with different social skills like cooperation, respect, responsibility, honesty and conflict resolution which would enhance and promote social cohesion in the Egyptian society.

All the previous factors highlight the importance of having a kind of education that prepares the Egyptian children to become well rounded and active citizens in a globalized world. In support of this belief, civil society organizations in Egypt thatact as volunteer and not-for-profit entities exert an effort and play an important role in providing support to the educational sector. In this research, I focus on a case study of a character-building initiative created by The Human Foundation, an Egyptian NGO through its character building program "*True Me: Focused, Free and Fulfilled*" that has been implemented in some Egyptian schools. Following a qualitative approach, I resorted to document review of the program and my fieldwork included individual, focus group interviews and a survey with open-ended questions with the program designer, trainers and public school representatives. In addition, observation of the program implementation was conducted in two different classrooms in one private school.

The study seeks to reveal the important role of civil society in supporting education in Egypt during the post-revolution time by examining the character building program developed and offered by the Human Foundation. It investigates the extent to which the values promoted through this program provides an introduction for ideas connected to global citizenship and the discourses on global citizenship education. The case study is conceptualized in the international and national discourses on global citizenship education which would enable a better understanding of the challenges this NGO confronted and the opportunities of implementing similar character building programs for promoting global citizenship values on a wider scale in the Egyptian schools.

INTERNATIONAL DISCOURSE ON GLOBAL CITIZENSHIP

"Global Citizenship" seems to be a term that lacks consent on its definition. It might give the meaning of surpassing ethnic, religious, or racial differences (Zahabioun et al., 2013). According to UNESCO (2013), global citizenship has been called by some as "citizenship beyond borders" or "citizenship beyond the nation state." Others suggested that the term "cosmopolitanism" might act as a broader term. There is also a suggestion for calling it "planetary citizenship" as it strongly relates to preserving the planet Earth (UNESCO, 2013).

Global citizenship emerged as a new way to define rights and responsibilities and above all a sense of social belonging to the whole world (Zahabioun et al., 2013); it does not refer to a legal state; however, it is more related to:

> A sense of belonging to the global community and common humanity, with its presumed members experiencing solidarity and collective identity among

themselves and collective responsibility at the global level. Global citizenship can be seen as an ethos/metaphor rather than a formal membership. (UNESCO, 2013, p. 3)

Due to the rapid and dramatic global changes that have been taking place on the social, cultural, economic, and technological levels, there is a significant need for developing a universal code of ethics, in which the world becomes a moral concept (Zahabioun et al., 2013). Accordingly, people should feel their moral or ethical responsibilities towards others (Feature Report on citizenship, 2008). As the term "global citizenship" is strongly connected and linked to ethics, it might constitute an implication for an ethically motivated action on global problems (Feature Report on citizenship, 2008).

On another level, the new technological facilities of the 21st century contributed to the development of the ordinary citizens and transformed them into "global citizens" through creating virtual spaces and changing the way they communicate with each other and thus, affecting their sense of belonging to the community both nationally and globally (Gibson & Landwehr-Brown, 2009). As a member in the global community, a "global citizen" needs to receive an education that would help him/her to develop a sense of responsibility and connectivity towards others not only on the local level but on the global level as well; an education that would help them acquire all the necessary values, skills, and knowledge to enable him/her to deal with a world of diverse religions, nationalities, ideologies, races and to qualifies him/her to deal with the challenges that they might confront (Zahabioun et al., 2013).

In support of this belief, "The Global Education First Initiative" that was launched by the UN Secretary-General in 2012 has global citizenship education as its third priority, in addition to putting every child in school and improving the quality of learning as its first two priorities (UNESCO, 2013). According to UNICEF (2013), good quality education is supposed to equip people with the skills, knowledge, and attitudes needed to enable them to learn to live together as active citizens both on the national and the global levels. Most of the consultations done by the UNICEF highlighted the need for an education agenda, which would help in preparing children, youth and even adults to become active citizens who would participate and engage in transforming their societies and the whole world at large. This point affirms the goals of the UN Secretary General's Education First Initiative (UNICEF, 2013). Education for global citizenship "means embracing a more holistic view of what kind of skills and attitudes are needed in our world today. While skills for jobs are important, so are skills for living together" (Carolyn Medel-Anonuevo, participant in online consultations on Education as quoted in UNICEF, 2013, p. 26). In a recent report, UNESCO defined global citizenship education as "a framing paradigm which encapsulates how education can develop the knowledge, skills, values and attitudes learners need for securing a world which is more just, peaceful, tolerant, inclusive, secure and sustainable" (UNESCO, 2014, p. 9).The goal behind citizenship education has been observed as to prepare students to play active roles in their schools, families, and societies as well as on the global level. This is in addition to their active participation and responsibility towards other human beings and the planet Earth at large (Education above All, 2012). However, the goal behind global citizenship education is to empower learners to engage actively, playing active roles on both the local and global levels in order to participate in solving the global challenges and to succeed in having a more just, tolerant, and inclusive world (UNESCO, 2013, 2014). According to Oxfam (2006), "Education for Global Citizenship" enables children to think critically about global matters and qualifies them with the abilities to express their own values while listening to and respecting others' views.

Furthermore, there are numerous and different approaches and programs through which global citizenship can be promoted, such as those offered by civil society (UNICEF, 2013). Global citizenship education can be delivered either in formal, non-formal, or informal education modes and venues. However, if it is delivered in a formal system, it still needs to be complemented by both non-formal and informal systems (UNESCO, 2013). A curriculum for global citizenship needs to stress the following goals and learning objectives: to develop global citizens in relation to culture, language and learning to live together, and to instill and develop in students a set of universal values (Zahabioun et al., 2013). As advised in Education Above All (2012), there are various ways through which education for global citizenship can be inserted into the school program, both explicitly and implicitly. For example, the active engagement and participation of students throughout the learning experience is highly encouraged. In order for this "compound learning" process to take place there are some activities that can be used like a "stimulus activity," which engages the student personally and is then followed by discussion to link the activity to the key values and behavioral learning objectives (Education above All, 2012). These stimulus activities can be in the form of stories, games and role playing, or through expressive activities like art, drama, creative writing, music, and dance which stimulate students' emotions and involve their personal identities. It also encounters the psychological needs of students and helps them to freely express their feelings and emotions (Education above All, 2012).

There are many ways in which we can divide the approaches to global citizenship education. Among which is the distinction between "soft" and "critical" global citizenship education. In the 'soft' approach, morals act as the starting point for global citizenship education and it is centered on the moral and ethical notion of the oneness of humanity and the need for universal ethics (Tawil, 2013). On the other hand, the 'critical' approach has to deal more with the concepts of social justice and human rights. This study focuses on the 'soft' approach as it emphasizes the importance of morals and values and the role they play in developing the characters of citizens. Accordingly, character education can play a pivotal role in constructing and developing students' characters. In a study that was conducted by Althof and Berkowitz (2006) the interrelations between the roles of educating for character, including moral and character education, and educating for citizenship, including civic education and citizenship skills and dispositions, were explored. The study also highlights the role of schools in developing students' characters to become moral citizens in democratic societies and this necessitates a great focus on moral development, character development, and the teaching of civics and citizenship skills. The researchers conclude that integrating these kinds of education are very important to have a liberal democratic society. According to Althof and Berkowitz (2006), both character education and citizenship education share many dispositions of personality traits, values and motives, such as: "social justice, honesty, personal and social responsibility, equality… Of course, there are some character dispositions that are less central to citizenship and vice versa, but the overall set has great overlap" (pp. 512–513). This overlap between character education and citizenship education lead us to describe a "civic character." Boston (2005) describes a civic character as "responsible moral action that serves the common good" (p. 5).

However, global citizenship education is facing many tensions and challenges among which is that of the human resources and how to develop a strong cadre of teachers who are capable of transmitting the values of global citizenship and are not affected to the traditional ideas and methods of teaching and are not open-minded (Education Above All, 2012). Another major challenge is the tension between the national and the global identities; this is a main issue especially in the countries where identity is a very sensitive issue and attaining the national identity itself is a problem and considered a challenge (UNESCO, 2013). The problem in many nations when developing curricula for citizenship education is that they work only on developing citizens who can function within the nation borders and not globally. However, the fact is that "globalization and nationalism are contradictory but coexisting trends and forces in the world today" (Banks, 2004, p. 6). It is acknowledged that "the increasing importance of cross-border flows and networks undermines the principles of the nation-state as the predominant site for organizing economic, political, cultural, and social life" (Banks, 2004, p. 18). That's why there is an essential need to develop a kind of civic education that enables students to live and act within their national context as well as abroad. According to Banks (2004), citizenship education has to strengthen students' relation and sense of belonging to their cultural attachments as well as their ability to praise and respect other cultures and identities. It also has to qualify them to be able to live in other cultural communities through helping them develop the needed skills and attitudes. Banks (2004) believed that individuals can endorse "multiple identifications and attachments, including attachments to their cultural community, their nation, and to (the world and humanity in general)" (Banks, 2004, p. 8).

THE NATION-STATE AND THE "EGYPTIAN IDENTITY": SETTING-UP THE CONTEXT

Identity is about belonging; it is about what one has in common with some and what distinguishes oneself from other people. Identity is about relationships and involvements with one's forefathers, which in modern societies are very complex; it is about contradictions and values we share with others. At its best, identity gives us a sense of personal location, a sense of a stable core to one's individuality. On a societal level, the notion of identity is a key for social integration. It holds a society together or tears it apart (Taha, 2011, p. 2). The Egyptian identity is believed to have been affected after the revolution of 1952 and under the rule of President Gamal Abdel Nasser who believed in the unity of the Arab States and Arab nationalism. This is a time when "Egypt's official name became the Arab Republic of Egypt-as opposed to simply the Republic of Egypt... [This] was a short push to an Islamic identity" (Ibrahim, 2011, p. 1). For years, the Muslim Brotherhood tried to impact the Egyptian society with their beliefs and conservative values. Thus, it was their chance after Egypt's second revolution in 2011, and electing one of their leaders, Former President Mohamed Morsi, the first elected president for Egypt in the post-revolution when they officially started to impose their social values on society. This was clear through the constitution that was passed by the fundamentalists, which contained many restrictions on freedom of faith and expression. They also used education to impose the same conservative values using the appointed Brotherhood members who worked in the Ministry of Education. Those members tried to change and remove sections from the national curricula which described their violent history (Nawara, 2013).

It was obvious that "the Muslim Brotherhood ideology didn't acknowledge the concept of the nation-state and calls instead for a monolithic Islamic nation [Al Ummah Al-Islamiya] that ignores national borders" (Nawara, 2013, p. 2). Accordingly, Egyptians rose up against Morsi and his government in June 30th revolution as they felt the threat that might affect Egypt's future as a nation and their identity as Egyptians. Many people (Muslims and non-Muslims) were very angry and protective of their culture and their way of living that they refused to change. So, "if the January 25th revolution was about freedom, justice and dignity, the protests of June 30th were about Egyptians salvaging their Egyptian identity" (Nawara, 2013, p. 2).

However, it is becoming currently difficult to identify the values that characterize the Egyptian identity. The Egyptian society is becoming more contradictory than ever as it is claimed to be religious and conservative while at the same time sexual harassment and violence are prevailing. Unfortunately, it is obvious that there is deterioration of values and that "Egypt has experienced a major setback in some of the moral values that used to constitute an integral part of society, such as honour, dignity, trust, and respect." (Nosseir, 2014, p. 3). Moreover, identity, as stated by Nosseir (2014), "should reflect the behavior of mainstream Egyptians, habits and traditions that they have been practicing for centuries and that will serve to unite society, instead of discriminating among its members or polarizing them" (p. 4).

How the "Egyptian identity" is perceived by young Egyptians is another main point. In a study that was conducted on young Egyptians to find their perceptions about what being an Egyptian means to them, there were a variety of responses. Some of them believed that being Egyptian included different dimensions as Egyptian, African, Arab, and Muslim. On the other hand, some identified themselves as being Muslims as they see that one's identification with his/her religion is superior than being Egyptian. This perception was not restricted to religious people only but with others who are not religiously committed too. Another group identified themselves as Egyptians and expressed that they are proud to be. They related this to the fact that they were "born, raised, educated, and having their families and their friends in the country" (Taha, 2011, p. 6). One of the participants believed that "the Egyptian identity is older and more developed than the Arab, Muslim, or other related identities" (Taha, 2011, p. 6). One of the most interesting findings in this study is that a big portion of the sample identified themselves as being "human and belonging to humanity." But this mostly related to the fact that they were unsatisfied with the political and socioeconomic conditions in Egypt.

In the same study, young Egyptians were asked about the relationship between identity and belonging. The findings showed that "there are degrees of loyalty to Egypt among Egyptian youth" (Taha, 2011, p. 8). There are those who, out of their love for Egypt are willing to work so hard in order to help improve the country's situation and others have been critical but out of their concern on wishing to see the country in a better position. On the other hand, there were those whose sense of belonging have weakened and they have blamed this on the deteriorating political and socioeconomic conditions that caused Egypt to retreat into a degraded position among other countries. This resulted in Egyptians being treated in a disrespectful manner by others (Taha, 2011).

As a consequence, "preserving the national identity" of Egyptians has been the focus of attention in the Egyptian society especially after the one-year rule of the Muslim Brotherhood and their trials to transform the Egyptian identity (Makar, 2013). Thus, it was very important to include it in the amended constitution under the main aim behind education which can be achieved through building the Egyptian character.

> Article (19) Every citizen has the right to education. The goals of education are to build the Egyptian character, preserve the national identity, root the scientific method of thinking, develop talents and promote innovation, establish cultural and spiritual values, and found the concepts of citizenship, tolerance and non-discrimination. The State shall observe the goals of education in the educational curricula and methods, and provide education in accordance with international quality standards. (Amended Constitution, 2014)

The higher purpose of education in this constitution is to "build the Egyptian character (and to) preserve the national identity" and this is what makes the aim behind education in this constitution really unique and distinguished from the previous constitutions that only stated that education was a right for all Egyptians. Developing 21st century skills like creativity and innovation, in addition to values of citizenship, tolerance, and non-discrimination were also highlighted and prioritized as they were given special significance in the same article.

Accordingly, the Ministry of Education (MOE) in this transitional period reinforced the urgent need for change in order to confront the social challenges and fulfill the demands of the revolution. Thus, education has to play an important role in this critical period through developing the political awareness, building the capabilities of citizens for political participation, and enhancing the values of democracy, freedom, citizenship, tolerance, and acceptance of others (MOE, 2014). According to the Ministry of Education (2014), the Egyptian society has suffered lately from many social transformations that drastically affected its culture and values. This created problems and challenges for social institutions such as the family, the school and the whole education system. Examples of these challenges and problems include the weakening of the impact of education on culture and the collapse of moral and ethical values (MOE, 2014). Currently, the Egyptian society and its culture are described to be suffering from losing its unity and national identity. This is caused through the weakness that hit its political and social institutions due to the uprisings and social unrest. In addition, it is worth mentioning that during the previous years, the political systems didn't pay much attention to strengthening and preserving the societal values and culture. In addition, the Ministry of Education (2014) highlights that among the reasons of Egypt's cultural crisis is the lagging behind from the contemporary world's needs and demands.

In the above-mentioned context, the Ministry of Education set a new strategic plan for pre-university education (2014–2030) while taking into consideration the different contexts that affect and are affected by education such as the national and the global contexts as well as the economic, cultural and political contexts, which are the most relevant for the focus of this research. According to the Ministry of Education (2014), culture plays a major role in determining the future and the societal interactions between people in any country. It is believed that the contemporary world goes through radical transformations that constitute a Cultural Revolution, which has long-term effects on societies, and cause a deep gap between what has been achieved through technology and the cultural beliefs in some conservative communities. The progress in technology and means of communication eliminated distances between people globally and put the future in the hands of the more developed countries, which through these communication means can export their knowledge, culture, and values. The Ministry of Education believes that this constitutes a huge challenge that Egypt has to confront through education (MOE, 2014). It is believed that if the culture of the society in the receiving country is strong enough, it can easily absorb these intruding cultural aspects without being affected itself and without losing its identity. However, if the culture is weak, it will be affected by whatever it receives (MOE, 2014).

From here emerges the importance of "citizenship education" in supporting the vision of the government in the previously mentioned documents by working on developing the Egyptian character and conserving their local identity as Egyptians, while at the same time helping them become more tolerant, open-minded and accepting to differences and diversity in a globalized world.

CITIZENSHIP EDUCATION AND CIVIL SOCIETY IN EGYPT

The main concern about citizenship education implemented in public schools in Egypt is that it is basically theoretical depending on textbooks and thus lacks the practical and experiential part. In a study that was conducted to get the perceptions about citizenship education, participants were asked about the appropriate approach for teaching citizenship and the suggested topics they think are important to be taught. The participants were divided into four categories: students, parents, teachers, and school administrators, and education activists (Omar, 2012). Most of the respondents articulated that teaching citizenship education has to be "skill-based." Teachers and administrators believed that non-formal and informal approach is the most suitable and successful one but they expressed that it needs readiness and skills from the teachers, thus they preferred the formal approach that they are familiar to. However, teachers showed interest in learning about the non-formal approach (Omar, 2012).

When asked about the topics that need to be included in the curriculum of citizenship education, almost all the respondents stressed the importance of focusing on morals as a basis for citizenship. Students emphasized that "they need to learn how to build their personality... (and that) no one can be a good citizen unless he is a balanced, confident person" (Omar, 2012, p. 22). Parents also suggested teaching morals as conscience and honesty. Teachers' support for teaching morals is highlighted by one of the study's respondents, who said that "morals is prior to citizenship. Morals are the main motivator for citizenship." They also emphasized that "building a confident personality of students is prior to citizenship education" (Omar, 2012, p. 24). Last but not least, education activists believed that "building self-esteem of the students is also prior to constructing citizenship" (Omar, 2012, p. 27).

Civil Society Organizations (CSOs)

Civil society organizations are "autonomous, voluntary, not-for-profit associations that have a structured governance and organizational framework. They operate within boundaries defined by legislation and defend the public interest outside of the political realm" (Egypt Human Development Report, 2008, p. 5). They include "non-state and non-market bodies" and they vary according to their "purpose, philosophy, expertise and scope of activities." They comprise of organizations with "a philanthropic or services orientation, community associations, associations reflecting special interests such as business, advocacy groups to defend the 'collective benefit' and professional groups such as syndicates" (EHDR, 2008, p. 5). There are a variety of factors and conditions that affect the nature of a society and thus the nature of CSOs such as political values, privatization, the percentage of women's participation in the labor force, young population, and globalization (EHDR, 2008).

Civil Society's Support to Education in Egypt

A brief history of NGOs in Egypt: Since their establishment in Egypt, NGOs played a great role in providing many services in the fields of health care, social assistance, and educational services. Continually, in the past three decades, they paid attention to local development, women's and children's issues and problems, human rights, and protecting the environment. They also had many projects through which they tried to contribute in solving problems like combating poverty and unemployment (Ministry of Education Portal). They also had projects that supported both formal and informal education.

The role of NGOs in supporting education in Egypt: Based on the vision of the Ministry of Education, the community participation is one of the main themes of the pre-university education and NGOs working in the domain of education is one of the main means for achieving this. The activities of those NGOs vary but they have to be in accordance with the policy and the strategic plan of the Ministry. The role of NGOs and civil society institutions is illustrated through projects that support the educational process through three main domains. Firstly, to support educational function like raising the efficiency of the educational process, technological support, environmental services, literacy, community schools, one classroom schools and child-friendly schools. Secondly, to support education profession through offering seminars, lectures and conferences, caring for special needs and stressing the idea of inclusion. Thirdly, to support the link between school and family through tackling the problem of leakage; spreading social, cultural, health and environmental awareness, and offering social assistance (Ministry of Education Portal).

Table 1. Number of Egyptian NGOs and their funding, target audience, and projects

Theme	Funding	Target audience	No. of projects	No. of NGOs
Support the Learning function of school	368	851	2183985	86029360
Support the educational function of school	192	445	469353	37456849
Support school-community relationship	293	571	560016	27767441
Total	853	1867	3213354	151253650

Source: Ministry of Education Portal, accessed 15 December 2014

On the other hand, the Ministry of Youth (MOY) is the one responsible for offering citizenship education through forming partnerships with different NGOs and CSOs. This is done in the form of extra-curricular activities and camps and is mainly targeting youth aged (18–35). However, in this study, I focus on the effort of an NGO which is The Human Foundation in offering a character building program for young children in some Egyptian public and private schools in order to provide them with the needed values and skills to help them develop their characters and become well-rounded citizens.

THE HUMAN FOUNDATION ORGANIZATION

The Human Foundation, is a non-profit Egyptian organization that was founded and registered with the Ministry of Social Solidarity in 2011. The vision of the organization is to have "a Society where citizens have an equal opportunity to bring forth their human potential by contributing positively to their human and natural environments". Their main mission is to "work to foster human values that cherish freedom, maintain equality and justice, respect diversities, cultivate gender balance, and secure human rights… [they] are guided by the belief that such values are intrinsically related to fulfillment of human potential" (Human Foundation, n.d.). The organization contributes to the development of the social life in Egypt through offering different services and carrying out different projects that help in establishing and founding the concept of knowledge based society. Among the organization's programs is the "Be Yourself" program which is a group of personal growth programs that are built on one philosophical background based on the belief that the life of every individual is valuable and that it is through our consciousness and the connection to the innate divine spark inside us that we can discover the higher value of our lives. According to the program's philosophy, "to 'be oneself' is to manifest all one's potentials; spiritual, emotional, mental and physical." Accordingly, this collective consciousness of the higher value of life would lead a whole society to reach spiritual, psychological and physical balance (Be Yourself Program Presentation, n.d.).

The "True Me: Focused, Free and Fulfilled" is one of these sub-programs and it is the main focus of this study. This program is designed for children and it is implemented either in Arabic or in English. The program is mainly a moral development and a character building program with the aim of fulfilling the following mission:

> To raise young souls who are conscious of the honour of being human, and work for making our planet a safe environment for all to realize that high state of being-ness." The program vision is founded on how to cultivate "each child's unique character that s/he was born with.

Tools and course duration: There are diverse tools used through the implementation of this program. They can be divided into four categories, the first of which is mind mastery, which is done using silence exercises like concentration, relaxation, stillness; or through movement exercises like stretching, dancing or walking. The healing storytelling uses stories in the form of fiction, real situations or about great figures. Stories are used because they are believed to cause fun, help in communication and self-discovery. It exposes the students to high values, help them understand the world around them and thus enrich their experience. The self-expression activities are in the form drawing and painting, role playing and games. Last but not least is the group singing where the children stand in a circle and start singing together in a circle of love (Be Yourself Program Proposal).

As for the course duration, it is normally done in sixteen sessions. Each session lasts for 90 minutes. The number of children per session is preferred not to exceed twelve children. The environment or the setting where the session is being taken has to be quiet whether outdoors or indoors (Be Yourself Program Proposal).

RESEARCH METHODS

To conduct my research, I adopted a qualitative research approach; it is a case study that focuses on the contribution of The Human Foundation Organization and the effect of its program, "True ME: Focused, Free & Fulfilled" on building the Egyptian children's characters. The research depends mainly on document review of the organization and the program, individual and focus group interviews and a survey with open-ended questions with the program designer, trainers and public school representatives. In addition, observation of the program implementation was conducted in two classrooms in a private school which would enable the "triangulation" and the validation of the research findings (Patton, 2002).

The research sample is a purposeful sample that included a total of 19 participants: the program designer, 12 program trainers, 3 social counselors who work in three public schools and attended the program as observers and evaluators of its implementation, 3 trainers whom the researcher observed during the implementation of the program in two classrooms, each classroom included 15 students in grade one.

The research instruments and fieldwork included interviews that were conducted to get in-depth data from the participants in order to understand their perceptions, experiences, and feelings about the program. The interviews consisted of a one-time session with the participants who were interviewed individually. The interview questions were in the form of open-ended questions (Gay, Mills, & Airasian, 2009). There was also a focus group discussion that was conducted with the program trainers, all 12 of them, in order to get a deeper understanding of their shared perspectives about the program. This is in addition to an online survey with open-ended questions that was sent to a group of the participants. Document review was also undertaken to allow for knowing the required information about the organization, its foundation history and the different services it offers. I also conducted a non-participant observation of the program implementation where I was not involved in the situation that is being observed. An observation guide was used, which helped in taking field notes and thus organizing and categorizing the data (Gay, Mills, & Airasian, 2009). Last but not least, I resorted to taking some field notes that included both descriptive and reflective information which record the researcher's personal reactions, thoughts and experiences during the observation.

Data Analysis

Interview and focus group data were transcribed and developed in Arabic then translated into English. Thematic analysis was conducted to the survey responses along with the qualitative transcript. Most powerful, expressive and representative quotes were identified then integrated in the research findings. Field notes were reviewed and organized systematically in alignment with the qualitative data thematic analysis. The findings of observation were used to support and validate other collected data. Triangulation was ensured based on using several tools for data collection (interviews, focus group, survey with open-ended questions, and observation). In addition, participants in the study included the program designer, trainers and social counselors, in addition to observation of the implementation of the program inside classrooms helped the validation of research findings.

FINDINGS

The Program Impact on Building a Cadre of Trainers

The very first step towards becoming a trainer for the "True Me" program is to undergo training in another training course which is "Awakening Our Inner Child" that is another sub-program of the "Be Yourself" program to enable the trainers to learn how to deal with the problems that confront them and how to heal them in order to get prepared to deal with the children they will later on teach. This training helps building a cadre of trainers capable of delivering the values of the program among Egyptian children; the theoretical part it is complemented by practice through their teaching the children's program, "True Me: Focused, Free and Fulfilled".

Almost all the trainers agreed that the program had a very deep impact on their characters and personalities and caused a drastic change in the way they see, react, and behave towards different issues in their lives. They mentioned that the program had a healing effect on their characters. For example, respondents believed it cured their feeling of fear of committing a mistake and made them confront their flaws and shortages in their characters, making them able to express their feelings more than before. They asserted that the program provided them with the tools to deal with their inner problems and solve them in order to be able to deal with the children and their problems. After going through this process, they became more self-confident, more accepting of themselves and others, and more aware of their needs whether emotional or spiritual. They became more capable of dealing with their negative feelings and develop them to give them power to decide on their goals and decisions.

One of the trainers mentioned that "the journey to self-healing and self-actualization starts with acceptance and love...Yes, we all make mistakes, yet we never deserve to be unloved or de-humanized for those mistakes." This sense of acceptance was the way that led them to "start a journey towards happiness." They agreed that happiness comes from within oneself when one is more accepting of her/his flaws and those of others. This developed another very important trait in the trainers' characters, which is that of not being judgmental towards other people's characters or reactions. This is obvious in one of the trainer's words, who "learned to criticize people's ideas and not the people themselves." They learned to see what's behind the actions and see things from other people's perspectives.

Another important impact of the program on the trainers' personalities is that it helped them to develop a sense of inner peace and to get rid of the wrong beliefs and traditions. From their perspective, this sense of inner peace is automatically reflected upon their relationships with others and thus the whole society. Quoting one of the trainers: "I believe that inner peace is a first step towards changing the whole society."

The Program Impact on Developing the Children's Characters

Values promoted through the program: The participants stressed the point the program is mainly a moral program that focuses on the implantation of some very important moral values, which are not imposed on the children; however, the children get to grasp the moral message and the intended value after listening to the story and after doing the activities. From the respondents' perspective, the program helps the children know that "the value of a human being lies inside his/her soul and in the abilities that God bestowed him with," which when discovered leads him/her to happiness. They also added:

> The values in this program are not imposed on the children from outside but they are rather implanted in their hearts and they just acquire the skill of how to discriminate between right and wrong.

They stressed the point that the trainers do not impose their opinion on the child but only provide their experience in an indirect way. The children get to know that they are not followers and thus cannot be deceived by any fake or superficial religious, social, or cultural factors. They also emphasized that the program enables the child to know the deep meanings of forgiveness, acceptance, honesty, self-confidence, self-appreciation, respect for diversity and freedom. One of the participants mentioned that "the program promotes for the uniqueness of every individual, but at the same time it pushes them to seek integration and cooperation with others."

As for the effect on the children's characters, the trainers expressed that the children developed a sense of self-appreciation and self-confidence by being provided with the tools that helped them discover their own potentials and capabilities. The children also developed a sense of control over their nerves and aggression. Through the use of stories, they identified with the characters and were able to learn how to act and react in different situations. They learned to control their outbursts and think carefully before reacting to any situation as one of the trainers responded:

The children got to understand that they can impact the quality of their lives by simply choosing to react and act differently towards daily events...they discover that they can have a say in their happiness and their lives.

Thus, the children develop a sense of acceptance of their flaws and they love themselves for what they are and they find the light and goodness and right decisions from deep inside. This is not imposed on them through certain direct values that are stressed but rather the moral message is delivered through the different stories and the various activities of the program that help the children develop this moral obligation towards themselves and in their different relationships with others. Instead of being very rude at the beginning and they refused to listen to the trainers as they were used to always listen and not being listened to, they developed an ability to listen to others and accept their opinions. They became less aggressive and they developed the skill of peacefully resolving their conflicts and problems.

The same effect and changes were also stressed by the social counsellors (public school representatives) who when asked about the impact of the program on the children answered that it had a great impact on controlling the children's nerves and reactions. One of them explained that "there was a spirit of forgiveness and acceptance among the children; even brothers, but unfortunately this had changed after the program had stopped." Another social counsellor who works in another school said that the program helped in knowing students' tendencies, beliefs and thoughts and that it also helped in behavior regulation and taught the students how to freely express themselves and their views. The third social counsellor mentioned that the program affected the students' relationships with their colleagues and with their teachers. It also affected the relationship of the child with his/her parents. All the previous affected the whole school atmosphere.

Safe and free environment: The program also proposes that the core of education is to create a safe and free environment through which the child is encouraged to discover his/her full potential and the world around them where they can freely express their fears, feelings, and problems. This was one of the most recurrent privileges of the program that was highly stressed by most of the trainers. It also provides the tools by which they can discover their hidden potentials. This safe environment in addition to the needed tools allow for a space where the children become themselves; to become more creative and to discover their inner beauty which is automatically reflected on their outer character. One of the trainers said:

> The child feels that he is a human being who deserves to be loved and respected and that he has got all the abilities that he needs to reach his goals and dreams.

Another trainer confirmed:

> Through the program, the child finds a safe environment where there are no threats, no fear and no humiliation where s/he is able to express her/himself and create.

In that way, the child feels his/her own value, which is considered as the key towards any other change without being obligated to follow a certain role model or being molded into a certain form. As mentioned by one of the trainers, the children at the beginning of the program "would copy each other's answers in any discussion; they would even copy each other's drawings and they drew with a ruler." However, after a while this had changed and they were able to talk freely and to be creative in their drawings as they were encouraged by the trainer who met anything they did with great appreciation and admiration which gave them a high sense of self-confidence.

Challenges and Constraints of the Program Implementation

The participants were asked about the challenges and constraints that confronted them while implementing the program and the possibility of implementing it on the whole school level. In their responses, they stated some of the different obstacles that they faced. In addition, their views varied upon the possibility of implementing it on the whole school level.

As for the challenges and constraints, they expressed that the main obstacles are the culture and the traditional mentality of some officials in schools, some teachers and parents. From the designer's point of view that the main challenge is:

> The culture of parents and teachers and the whole community because children are taught something and then they go home and are confronted with a completely opposite culture and attitude; they are maltreated by their parents at home and the same with their teachers in schools; I believe that when children are treated with love and respect, they respond positively.

Other respondents asserted the previous point by saying that many teachers in schools are neither helpful nor cooperative as they are not convinced with the importance of the program. But this changes if it happened that the teachers go through training or a workshop that would help them treat the children in a different way and find alternatives for the traditional punishment/reward method.

Other obstacles that were mentioned by the respondents were the failure to provide a suitable place for the trainers to work in with the children especially in public schools. Furthermore, another obstacle is having some children amongst the group who have a complex background due to being exposed to abuse or aggression, which is reflected on their behaviour and relationships with others. Those children need special treatment and a longer time to respond as they need first to feel that they are accepted and to be provided with love and kind feelings. This might affect the rest of the group in an indirect way.

Another challenge that came up through the responses was that in public schools there is no desire for transformation or change. In addition to the previous point, they added that the fact that teachers are overloaded with workloads strengthens this rejection for the idea of the program. The respondents perceive the importance of the teachers taking the training as a cornerstone for maintaining the sustainability of the program's effect on students.

When the participants were asked about the possibility of implementing the program on the whole-school level, most of them emphasized the importance of having a kind of partnership with the Ministry of Education in order for this to be possible, especially in public schools. This partnership would help most of the constraints met during the implementation as providing a suitable place, trying to take off some of the workloads of the teachers who are attending the training. One of the respondents talked about a previous experience of training some teachers, but unfortunately it failed because "of the workloads and the harshness of their schedules as the number of teachers was fewer compared to the number of classes and periods." She added that "even through the summer vacation, they go through professional development trainings." It is also through the Ministry of Education that teachers can be given incentives in order for them to feel that their contribution is appreciated.

Alignment with the International Discourse on "Global Citizenship"

The definition and traits of a "Global Citizen." When the participants were asked about the definition of a global citizen and the traits that s/he needs to possess, their responses showed a great consensus and alignment with the international discourse on defining a "global citizen."As for the definition of a "global citizen", the respondents' answers varied according to how they perceived the meaning of a "global citizen" and how they understood his/her qualities and responsibilities should be. As defined by the program designer:

> A global citizen is the one who knows or whose objective in life is to be human in the deeper sense of the word; to be growing spiritually and manifesting this development in the concept of being in service. On another level, s/he is the one who is open to knowledge and to new experiences; who can integrate and not compete with others; who can embrace differences and be able to see the oneness beyond it; who seeks knowledge forever; who respects scientific methods and who has the moral values which are part of being human.

Another respondent added that:

> A global citizen is the one who knows her/his value and capabilities as an individual, but at the same time can integrate and cooperate with others in having one unified goal, which is building a new civilization. S/He accepts diversity and appreciates the value of life and respects the environment. S/He has the ability of accepting her/his own mistakes in order to be able to accept and forgive others and thus spreads the peace inside her/his soul, which is reflected on her/his relationships with others.

Among the traits that they agreed upon were acceptance of self and others, tolerance, respect for diversity, to be non-judgmental, to respect science and scientific methods and be creative, to be self-confident, to accept criticism, to know how to deal with the feelings of both anger and joy in a balanced way, to think positively and be able to deal with whoever contravenes his/her ideas and beliefs, to appreciate the value of a human being and feel the sense of belonging to humanity at large, to be aware and caring of what goes on and happens all around the world and to be a servant for humanity. They also added that a global citizen must be non-discriminative of race, skin color, religion, and culture.

According to the participants, a global citizen needs also to be responsible for making the world a better place and s/he is the one in whom the meaning of humanity is achieved. They also added that a global citizen is the one who is open to the world and who knows that his views and perspectives are not sacred; but can be changed if there is a better view. S/he is the one who appreciates his/her cultural heritage but is open to other cultures and accepts and learns from them. They believe that a global citizen is the one who carries love and peace in his/her heart and who tries to find common things with others to cooperate and build a future that encompasses all humans. One of the respondents expressed that:

> Global feels like belonging to the world and the world is my home and home is the self; when we reach the point of belonging to our own selves that is the point where we are really united with the globe and the whole universe.

Teaching Strategies of "Global Citizenship Education"

According to the document review and the interviews with the trainers about the session plan and its sequence, the session starts with exercises for concentration, visualization and mindfulness. They are done through silence and movement and help children get rid of their distracting thoughts and communicate with their inner part where all the values exist. The second thing is the storytelling and discussion where stories are used because of the healing effect they have. They help children reflect upon their own experiences when they unify the story characters. The after-story discussions enrich the students' experience and help them grasp the moral message behind the story. There are different types of stories like those about birds and animals, daily life situations, biographies of famous figures from diverse cultures, scientific fiction, traditional fables and myths that include universal wisdom, and other stories about different Messengers and Prophets of God. Moreover, there are activities; which help students to express themselves in an artistic way and help develop their creativity. Activities include: Free drawing, role playing, games, and coloring. Last but not least, children sing in a Circle of Love and this is done at the beginning of the session and at the end where students stand in a circle in a state of harmony. The song shall represent the theme or the value conveyed during the session.

The Importance of This Program and Similar Ones to Egypt

According to the participants, the program provides children with the tools and the methodology by which they can achieve their full potentials so that the social and cultural factors and influences might not hinder the development of their characters. The children acquire different psychological and behavioural skills that enable them to serve their society and be creative; rather than becoming an imitator or a follower, they become able to set their own goals and take the responsibility of achieving them. Children also acquire the skills of conflict resolution and team-work. Participants also believe that the program helps the children to develop and build their character and not to be molded by others' thoughts and society's requirements, where the children recognize their uniqueness and at the same time not to become discriminative or judgmental towards others.

The participants were asked about the importance of and the need for such programs in Egypt and how they would help in constructing the characters of Egyptian citizens. The responses made it clear that Egypt deeply needs such programs especially in such a transitional period where people are moving from the state of being for long governed by an authoritarian rule into a democratic one. This transition led to a state of chaos as people used to obey the rules out of fear and not out of the desire of being good and conscious. One of the participants, a trainer, said:

> There is a great need as people have become very fixed in their ideas and intolerant of anything and anyone who is different. Moral behaviour is not something that stems from inside them; they do it out of fear or out of keeping up appearances.

They agreed that such programs are needed as they would help in constructing a new generation who can unify around one ethical goal, which is building a civilization with humans at its core. This civilization will be based on moral values like acceptance, forgiveness, and respect for diversity and others. They believe that when those children are equipped with the right tools and a safe environment where they can act, interact, and freely express themselves and their views, they can get rid of the mistaken and superficial traditions and beliefs and thus be able to act in the right way consciously and not out of fear. From the respondents' point of view, another striking phenomenon that started to prevail among Egyptians especially after the January 25th revolution is aggression and a misconception of the true meaning of freedom. So, such programs would help in adjusting people's wrong behaviours and attitudes.

These programs would also work on adjusting the attitudes of the parents who abuse their children. They also agreed that the program helps the children discover their points of strengths and how to become decision makers. They learn how to peacefully resolve their problems and to accept constructive criticism. According to almost all the respondents, the program also helps the children to become creative and unique, something which is not highly stressed by the Egyptian education system and curricula, making such programs important. As mentioned by one of the trainers:

In Egypt, the education system doesn't address all levels of thinking within the students. It only focuses on memorization. However, creativity which is the highest thinking level is rarely addressed. That's why such programs that address imagination and creativity within children are highly needed to compensate for the deficiency within the education system.

Another participant confirmed the previous view saying:

The Egyptian curricula focus on theories and passive learning. The "Be Yourself" program is about active interaction and a lot of reflective questions which gives the child the opportunity to tune into his own creativity and be himself.

Global versus Local Identities

When asked about how the program develops a sense of belonging to Egypt, they replied that the program helps the children to develop a sense of belonging to human moral values in general, which they consider a way to feel the sense of belonging to homeland and the whole universe. They believe that it is through the program that the child learns to value everything in her/his life and thus learns to value the meaning of her/his homeland and the whole world. They also added that the program works on developing the individual's sense of her/himself and hence of her/his country and the world as it helps the individual to accept her/himself and those around him. A respondent replied:

The program has some shared values among all humans, no matter what their religions are; it is only by being aware of their value as human beings and developing a sense of belonging to humanity.

According to the participants, the program helps the human being to discover his/her unique individual capabilities and talents which allow him/her to cooperate and integrate with other members in his/her society. This would help in constructing well-rounded characters that can appreciate everything in life and thus appreciate the value of homeland. One of the participants said:

All the values and techniques, the eye-openers that the program offers help in constructing a healthy human being who can function positively and in a balanced way and thus becomes a productive part of society.

The main aim behind the program is to build a "stable well-rounded person who is accepting of himself and others and who can reach his full potential." The designer of the program mentioned that there is nothing special in the program that addresses strengthening the sense of belonging to Egypt in specific, but she believes that the child connects to the light inside him/her, a part which is free from bias, superiority, jealousy, rigidity and other things that differentiate people. She said:

The main idea of the program is that the child by nature possesses all the good values and when this part is vivid inside him/her, s/he has no inclination or cultural molding and barriers.

In their responses, the participants emphasized a main effect of the program that can deeply help Egyptians become "global citizens" which is that of acceptance and celebrating differences. One respondent said:

Acceptance and celebration of differences and diversity are values that the program promotes and which help children and adults who participate in the program realize through the constant self-reflection, exposure to stories and activities that we are all different and see how that is a blessing...diversity is a divine law encrypted in the DNA of this universe.

They also added that the program helps children to be positive, interactive and accepting of other cultures but at the same time proud of their identity and heritage and to become a well-rounded person and this is what the world needs.

As for the part of how the program can help spreading peace and harmony in the Egyptian society and the world, the participants believed that the seed of peace lies inside every individual, so when the human being develops this sense of inner peace it is reflected on his/her outer relationships with others. They emphasized that the program helps in healing the spiritual side of the human being and helps him/her to reach a sense of safety and that this safety comes only from God. This is how the sense of inner peace is achieved through solving the inner struggle and developing a better understanding of the person's inner feelings, the person gets to know his/her "True Me." One of the respondents said:

The program trains the child to use different tools that would enable her/him to transform all the challenges s/he meets into opportunities for moral and personal development and growth. This helps in building a well-rounded character who can live in peace and harmony with her/himself and spread it in her/his relationships with members of his little family in Egypt and those of his bigger family in the whole world.

The participants believed that when both adults and children are helped to discover the moral values in themselves, there will be no conflict, no discrimination which help in eliminating the power of struggle amongst people and even governments. Another respondent explained that, "outer peace can never be achieved unless inner peace is achieved. This program's main target is to help all individuals achieve inner peace and thus happiness in their lives."

DISCUSSION

This study was initially conducted to explore the efforts of civil society in support to education as represented in the initiative undertaken by the "The Human Foundation" in order to implement a character building and moral development program in Egyptian schools. Moreover, it sought to explore to what extent character education can help in constructing the characters of Egyptian students thus helping them to develop into well-rounded characters who acquire the global values of citizenship.

Results from the participants' responses about common features and stressed values of the program showed much consensus to the international discourse on the values stressed through global citizenship education. From the perspective of the trainers, their responses showed that the program had deep impact on both the trainers and the students. It helped to change the way they value themselves and life around them. It helped them develop many skills and morals and be able to manifest them in their relationships with other people. They asserted that they became more tolerant and accepting of others' diversities. They also emphasized that they gained a set of universal moral values that would help them develop a sense of cooperation and feeling for others. According to the program designer the core of the program is to enhance the sense of belonging to humanity. All the aforementioned qualities reflect the international discourse for global citizenship and the required skills and values that need to be stressed in order to promote for global citizenship. This aligns with what has been mentioned in (Zahabioun et al., 2013) about global citizenship as being belonging to a global community and the world social family. It also aligns with the UNESCO's definition of global citizenship education as "belonging to the global community and common humanity" (UNESCO, 2013, p. 3).

Participants' responses reflected a deep sense of awareness of the definition and the traits of a "global citizen." The definition that was given by the program designer echoed her deep belief in the concept of a "global citizen." Through her definition, she highlighted some of the traits that a "global citizen" should have like to feel the deep sense of being a human, to love being in service to others, to be open to knowledge and embrace differences and diversities. This aligns with the definition of a global citizen as having a state of open-mindedness and to develop a sense of belonging to the bigger community (Zahabioun et al., 2013).

The program goals and pedagogies also showed similarity with those suggested for global citizenship education in the sense that both stress the importance of developing the ability of learning to live together and instilling in students a set of universal values (Zahabioun et al., 2013). There are also the methods of teaching like using "stimulus activity" that engage the student personally and is then followed by discussion to link the activity to the key values and behavioral learning objectives (Education Above All, 2012). These stimulus activities vary between using stories, game-like, role-playing, expressive activities, and cultural and religious references (Education Above All, 2012). The program uses almost the same teaching methods and stimulus activities.

Although the literature on the conflict between local and global identities support having a kind of citizenship education that would work on developing both the national attachment and the global sense of belonging (Banks, 2004), when asked about whether the program enrich the Egyptians' sense of belonging to Egypt, most of the responses were in favour of belonging to morals which would reflect on one's character and thus reflect on society in general. The designer responded that there is no special part in the program that tackles this point in specif. According to the literature reviewed this doesn't support the higher purpose of education as set in the amended constitution in article (19) which is that of "building the Egyptian character... [and to] preserve the national identity."

As for the challenges and the possibility of implementation in schools, findings showed that the program implementation met many challenges like high group capacity, providing a suitable setting for the sessions. Moreover, the teachers' traditional mentality and culture caused a great resistance to the idea of the program and its goals. It was also mentioned by one of the respondents that those teachers had many workloads, which prevent them from accepting any new ideas or approaches. According to the participants' perspectives, the previously mentioned challenges might affect the implementation process. This aligns with the challenges and constraints for implementing global citizenship education stated in the "Education Above All" (2012).

CONCLUSION

My study intended to reveal the important role of civil society in supporting education in Egypt during the post-revolution time by examining the character building program developed and offered by the Human Foundation. It investigated the extent to which the values promoted through this program provide an introduction for ideas connected to global citizenship and the discourses on global citizenship education. The case study is conceptualized in the international and national discourses on global citizenship education which would enable a better understanding of the challenges this NGO confronted and the opportunities of implementing similar character building programs for promoting global citizenship values on a wider scale in the Egyptian schools.

The program's importance to Egypt lies in the fact that Egypt is experiencing many changes on both the political and the social levels in this transitional period. Thus, the Egyptian children are in a need for similar character building programs to help them develop into well-rounded characters, capable of preserving their local identities, while at same time possess the values of tolerance, respect and acceptance to diversity that would enable them to fit in the global world. This can be done through encouraging more partnerships and cooperation between the Ministry of Education and similar NGOs that can provide similar programs. Such programs can act as a complementary part to the theoretical curriculum of national citizenship education, where it can compensate for the practical and interactive part that is missing from the national curriculum.

Thus, this study acts as a first step towards introducing the notion of "Global Citizenship" through a character building program and calls for its implementation on a wider scale in the Egyptian schools.

NOTE

[1] Some public schools function in the form of shifts, for example a "morning shift" and an "afternoon shift," where different groups of students attend school in different times of the day; this is to overcome the high capacity in those schools.

REFERENCES

Althof, W., & Berkowitz, M. W. (2006). Moral education and character education: Their relationship and roles in citizenship education. *Journal of Moral Education, 35*(4), 495–518.
Amended Constitution of the Arab Republic of Egypt. (2014). Retrieved December 15, 2014, from http://www.sis.gov.eg/Newvr/Dustor-en001.pdf
Arthur, J., Davies, I., & Hahn, C. (Eds.). (2008). *The Sage handbook of education for citizenship and democracy*. London: Sage Publications.
Banks, J. A. (Ed.). (2004). *Diversity and citizenship education: Global perspectives*. San Francisco, CA: Jossey-Bass.
Be Yourself Program Presentation. (n.d.). *The human foundation document*.
Be Yourself Program Proposal. (n.d.). *The human foundation document*.
Boston, B. O. (2005). *Restoring the balance between academics and civic engagement*. Washington, DC: American Youth Policy Forum.
Dewey, J. (1899). *Lectures in the philosophy of education*. New York, NY: Random House, Inc.
Education Above All. (2012). *Education for global citizenship*. Doha: Education Above All. Retrieved from http://www.ineesite.org/uploads/files/resources/EAA_Education_for_Global_Citizenship.pdf
EHDR. (2008, January 1). *Egypt's social contract: The role of civil society*. Retrieved from http://www.eg.undp.org/content/egypt/en/home/library/human_development/publication_3
Gay, L. R., Mills, G. E., & Airasian, P. (2009). *Educational research: Competencies for analysis and application*. Upper Saddle River, NJ: Pearson.
Gibson, K. L., & Landwehr-Brown, M. (2009). Moral development in preparing gifted students for global citizenship. In D. Ambrose & T. Cross (Eds.), *Morality, ethics, and gifted minds* (pp. 301–312). New York, NY: Springer.
Human Foundation. (n.d.). Retrieved from http://www.hfegypt.org
Ibrahim, R. (2011, February 14). *Egypt's identity crisis*. Retrieved from http://www.meforum.org/2832/egypt-identity-crisis
Makar, F. (2013, December 19). *Education with a higher goal*. Retrieved January 9, 2015, from http://www.madamasr.com/opinion/politics/education-higher-goal
Ministry of Education Portal. Retrieved from December 15, 2014, from http://portal.moe.gov.eg/AboutMinistry/Departments/cabe/dep-centers/dep-centers/Pages/Default.aspx
MOE. (2014). *National strategic plan for pre-university education 2014–2030*. Retrieved December 10, 2014, from http://portal.moe.gov.eg/AboutMinistry/Pages/plan2014.aspx
Nawara, W. (2013, July 1). *It's the Egyptian identity, stupid*. Retrieved January 9, 2015, from http://www.al-monitor.com
Nosseir, M. (2014, August 30). *Egypt's identity: Hovering between love and rule of law*. Retrieved January 9, 2015, from http://www.dailynewsegypt.com
Omar, F. M. (2012). *Perceptions of citizenship education in Egypt: A case study of a public middle school* (Doctoral dissertation). University of Birmingham, Birmingham.
Oxfam, C. H. (2006). *Education for global citizenship. A guide for schools*. Oxford: Oxfam.
Oxfam, G. M. (2006). *Education for global citizenship: A guide for schools*. London: Oxfam Development Education Programme.
Patton, M. Q. (2002). *Qualitative research and evaluation methods*. Thousand Oaks, CA: Sage Publications.
Taha, Y. (2011). *Identity in Egypt: Snapshots of Egyptian youth*. The International RC21 conference 2011, Lecture conducted from Amsterdam, Amsterdam.

Tawil, S. (2013). *Education for 'global citizenship': A framework for discussion* (UNESCO Education Research and Foresight (ERF) working papers series 7). Paris: UNESCO.

UNESCO. (2013). *Global citizenship education: An emerging perspective* (Outcome document of the technical consultation on global citizenship education). Paris: UNESCO.

UNESCO. (2014). *Global citizenship education: Preparing learners for the challenges of the twenty-first century.* Paris: UNESCO. Retrieved from http://unesdoc.unesco.org/images/0022/002277/227729E.pdf

UNICEF. (2013). *Making education a priority in the post-2015 development agenda: Report of the global thematic consultation on education in the post-2015 development agenda.* New York, NY: UNICEF. Retrieved from http://www.unicef.org/education/files/Education_Thematic_Report_FINAL_v7_EN.pdf

Zahabioun, S., Yousefy, A., Yarmohammadian, M. H., & Keshtiaray, N. (2013). Global citizenship education and its implications for curriculum goals at the age of globalization. *International Education Studies, 6*(1), 195–206.

Shaimaa Mostafa Awad
Graduate School of Education
The American University in Cairo (AUC)

OLA HOSNY

6. YOUNG RURAL WOMEN'S PERSPECTIVES ON THE IMPACT OF EDUCATION SUPPORTED DEVELOPMENT PROJECTS

INTRODUCTION

Prior to the January 25th, 2011 revolution, there was a proved negligence of social and ethical responsibility and ignorance of the rightful interests of Egyptians (Rennick, 2015). The overall persistent high level of poverty in Egypt suggests that poverty is primarily the consequence of the way society is organized and resources are used, both of which promote inequality (Verme et al., 2014). Causes of poverty and approached actions to hinder its repercussions were areas of interest for many studies. Yet, the results show that the poverty issue was never handled holistically (Mossallem, 2013). The level of improved outcomes compared to the exerted inputs revealed clear absence of consistent strides to deal with poverty from its grassroot. Sustainable plans to secure the attained improvements were missed between scattered efforts by the private sector and different governmental interests (Kassem, 2013). Ultimately, the high risk the poor lived in showed meager progress on all levels, with no premium solid actions (Mossallem, 2013).

Post-revolution, Egypt gained political awareness. Millions spoke-up and a force of public dialogue was initiated which was never seen before, with a strong wave of anti-authoritarian engagements toward social rectification (Kassem, 2013). The majority of Egyptians, from different socio-economic backgrounds, gained the experience of articulating their problems and the courage of drawing attention to different unacceptable living, working and economic conditions. Eventually, the voice of Egyptians became an issue of consideration for the government (Abdou & ZaaZou, 2013).

The Egyptian uprising and the call for social justice invited the researcher to examine young rural women's perspectives on the impact of educational supported development projects on their lives post the January 25th, 2011 revolution. It was important to gauge women's views on the extent to which the efforts exerted to lift up their lives had sounding effect or not. It was also important to measure the level of impact of education-supported development projects on rural women's surrounding environment, and articulate the effect of the Egyptian alarm to adopt new philosophies that allow the private as well the public sectors to support the improvement of the poor on multiple levels.

Contextually, Egypt used to have around twenty-five percent of the population under the poverty line (Central Agency for Public Mobilization and Statistics, 2011), i.e., an income of less than $1.25/day (United Nations, 2009). The poor are mostly located in rural areas in Upper Egypt governorates as shown in Figure 1 (Central Agency for Public Mobilization and Statistics, 2011). They stand at a critical point; failure in facing different social, cultural, economic and financial barriers deprive them from accessing the education, employment, and health services in their country (The Global Monitoring Report Team, 2010).

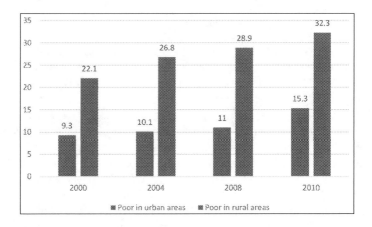

Figure 1. Percentage of poor in Egypt, by location and years (2000–2010)

Among the poor, as mentioned in the Population Council's (2010) report, "young people are important catalysts for development and change…investment in this crucial group provides an unprecedented opportunity to accelerate growth and reduce poverty" (p. 1). To help young people improve their social efficiency and economically contribute to their societies they need to be either educated and/ or trained to fit certain jobs and act as active members inside their communities (Labaree, 1997).

Unfortunately, public schools in Egypt lack the capacity to make young people's fulfillment possible (Hurn, 1985). Low quality education has been dominating many public schools particularly in low-income areas (Assaad & Barsoum, 2007). Advantaged families were able, to an extent, overcome the gap of equal opportunities for educational quality; however, the poor remain trapped by the deficiencies of the system and became in most cases socially excluded (Assaad & Barsoum, 2007). Since 1970s, non-formal education in Egypt was born to fulfill the formal education gap and support the poor on the social, financial or cultural levels (Loveluck, 2012; Sabri, 2007; The Global Monitoring Report Team, 2010). Thus far, despite the efforts exerted in helping the young poor in rural areas to improve their living conditions, not all segments were well served (Sabri, 2007).

As illustrated in the 2006 Egyptian census, there is a remarkable increase in young rural women's illiterate and unemployment rates in comparison to young rural men. Young rural women, as shown in Figure 2 proved to be the most deprived segment of the education services in Egypt, and the second highest deprived segment from entering the labor market force as shown in Figure 3 (EBRD, 2012; Assaad, 2007).

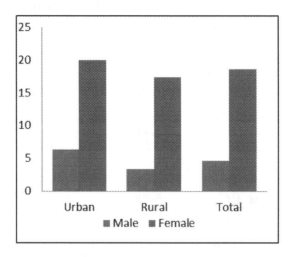

Figure 2. Education status aged 15–64 by location and gender (Census, 2006)

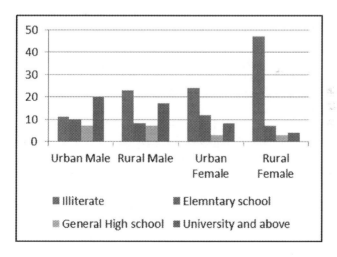

Figure 3. Unemployment rates aged 15–64 by location and gender (Census, 2006)

Other than domestic and field work, these young rural women have virtually no opportunities for mobility, inspiration, or participation in their community's activities. Despite the fact that many of them work in farms, they are considered to be part of the informal economy, defined to be economic activities that do not meet the formal arrangements, which are not yet properly covered in Egypt's statistical data (International Labor Organization, 2012). Ultimately, a helpful approach for this deprived segment might be to create a new blend of already-existing developmental strategies to attempt to compensate for the defects of certain models, and to ameliorate the outcomes of others.

Why Rural Women in Egypt?

Young rural women's vulnerability to the social and economic conditions became recently the focus of literature concerning development (El Laithy, n.d.). Current studies show that women's capacities to participate in the development processes of their communities have been jammed with unequal gender, socio-economic, and power relations (Kabeer, 2012). The Millennium Development Goals have lately integrated new goal concerning women's right to have decent jobs (Kabeer, 2012), urging the necessity of developing programs that can reach women from different socio-economic backgrounds, specifically those in deprived areas, educate or train them, build their capacities, and prepare them for the labor market.

In recent times, several development projects in Egypt have been directing much of their funds and efforts towards achieving the above-mentioned goal (USAID, 2013). Nonetheless, while most projects' reports show satisfaction of projects' results (Center for Development Services, 2005), it was evident that there is dearth of data on beneficiaries' perspectives and the articulation of their experiences towards such projects. Hence, this research contributes to fill such gap in literature by addressing the following main question: what are young rural women's perspectives of the impact of the education supported development projects implemented in Upper Egypt governorates on their lives?

The objective of this study is to critically examine the perspectives of young rural women (in Upper Egypt governorates) on the impact of the education supported development projects on their lives post the revolution, and update the state of knowledge of the effect of development projects on specific areas such as: women empowerment, gender equity, civil society enhancement, and the integration of social stratification in such underprivileged communities. The study captures young rural women's perspectives using the OECD/DAC projects' assessment criteria, which will be further explained (Chianca, 2008). It intends to address young rural women's projected needs that would enhance their economic, social, and cultural contribution within their societies. In addition, it seeks to promote a better understanding of development projects, especially those devoted to enhance young rural women's skills and serve their needs, and to identify proposed modifications in the current designs and policies that better address the needs of young women in local communities.

Education and Development Projects

In the context of educational development projects, Klosters (2014) explains that anticipated outcomes, staff capacity, and learning environments are crucial factors for any project's success. In addition to, the importance of the monitoring and evaluation role in supporting any project's implementation process (Kabeer, 2012).

In the past years, the majority of development projects' outcomes focused on "Universal Youth Literacy" (UYL), which worked on increasing literacy rates among youth (UNESCO-UIS/Brookings Institution, 2013). The UYL movement as seen by most countries allowed better chances of preparing qualified candidates for their vital role in development in different sectors, in an attempt to make crucial changes to their economic and social status. Brazil, China, Indonesia, Iran, and Mexico were successfully able to reach near 100% literacy rates (UNESCO Institute for Statistics, 2012); evidencing the fact that improving the education sector is a channel for improving other sectors in any country.

However, given diversified contexts of different countries, there was a global transformation from 'universal youth literacy' to the 'universal youth learning' (Youth Led Development Agency, 2012), updating the targeted aim from just reading and writing to being trained to act and participate (UNESCO-UIS/Brookings Institution, 2013). Universal youth learning enrapt the engagement of every citizen into the building of their country's economy, being the infinite action for success (Youth Led Development Agency, 2012). Consequently, general tendencies took place for local initiatives, aided programs, and government movements to support the underserved youth to play different roles inside their communities. These initiatives aimed to provide youth with quality learning, making them visible to the community, and involving them in sustaining their countries' economic growth. Most importantly, these initiatives worked on shrinking any possibilities of losing youth's energy towards efficiently and effectively utilizing countries' resources, while preparing them to be civic actors (EQUIP2, 2004).

Nevertheless, as argued by Hammond, Austin, Orcutt and Rosso (2001), it is not only about designing education initiatives activities, it is also about contextualizing these activities to consider beneficiaries' nurturing, parenting, and social and economic conditions, contributing to beneficiaries' learning capacities. An important perspective to be deliberated is the rarefied application of relevant components, activities and anticipated outcomes to the intervened communities (EQUIP2, 2004). Recent studies indicate immense admonition towards beneficiaries' needs, communities' challenges and the contextual frameworks to make good sense of relevant needed outcomes.

Emphasizing on individual accountability and ingenuity, student-centered became the dominating learning scheme (The 21st Century Learning Initiative, 1997). To adopt this new learning scheme, projects' designers and implementers revealed their need to walk their beneficiaries through consequential stages in order to support them in developing themselves and appraising their beliefs and thoughts

(International Institute for Educational Planning, 2006). The core idea of these stages is 'skills' transformation', through which beneficiaries are inspired to discover new experiences, witness them, think thoroughly of them, and finally update their state of knowledge and action (Passarelli & Kolb, 2011). Beneficiaries' transferable skills help them get engaged from interdisciplinary perspectives, deepen their understandings, and make quality of links and reasons to the knowledge they gain, rather than making no use of the quantity of knowledge they have (The 21st Century Learning Initiative, 1997; Martin, 1981). Arguably, provoking beneficiaries' skills evolve the relationship between theirnature and nurture, placing learning as an ongoing process. Perceptibly, the success of this transformation cycle depends much on many factors, among which is the existence of trained teachers or promoters, the latter refers to selected individuals who are usually the highest educated in the intervention areas who would be trained and hired to act as teachers in development projects (International Institute for Educational Planning, 2006).

Lessons from rural projects in India and Mexico show that teachers/promoters' understanding of community needs, intention of resolving problems, and ability to engage everyone in a participatory approach help significantly in providing a quality learning environment (Fox & Gershman, 2001). Ultimately, as argued by Prendiville (2008), teachers'/promoters' styles of facilitation have great impact on the quality of outcomes of any project.

Facilitation is not an easy process, given the tendency of people who associate their achievements to their capacities and failure to outside conditions (Jordan, Carlile & Stack, 2008; Prendiville, 2008). In non-formal education development projects, blame of students' failures are mostly directed towards teachers/promoters' lack of capacities (VSO, 2009). In fact, big percentage of teachers/promoters lack many cognitive skills (Church Educational System, 2001), yet they are still seen as role models. Subsequently, to resolve this contradictory setting, the international interventions supplemented their projects with promoters' professional development trainings as an essential component, whereas no intervention could start without the completion of such activities to intensify the likelihood of reaching the quality of learning planned (Jordan, Carlile & Stack, 2008).

Leadership, critical thinking, and life skills are on the top priorities for building promoters' professional competencies, helping them to understand students' determinations and visions (European Union, 2011; Goetzman, 2012). As proved in many studies focusing on promoters' performances; promoters who act as leaders inside their classes can easily ingrain real changes to their students by doing the right action through the right rational (Teach for America, 2011; Freire, 1998). This understanding was endorsed by the global context where educational reforms worked on the improvement of promoters' standards rather than the improvement of the aims of teaching (Zhou, n.d.). The impact of such reforms, as shown in China, encouraged education's adjustments, and strengthened promoters' abilities to stimulate students' attention (Zhou, n.d.). Yet, promoters' level of power remained an issue for urgent consideration.

While giving attention to building promoters' leadership, critical thinking, and life skills, it is very important to pay good attention to the sense of power promoters may have over their students. Since education is seen as the process of building an end product, it was essential for projects' designers to determine promoters' level of power inside class, and make sure that it does not go beyond acceptable borders (Martin, 1981). Through development projects, students' characters are shaped, values are added, and students start developing their own personal plans. Accordingly, promoters' level of power inside the class needed to be well monitored to promote for building dynamic rather than fruitless community members. Eventually, power became one of the important issues that need to be considered while building promoters' competencies to further advance an active learning environment.

Projects' learning environments also play an essential role in promoting the quality of their outcomes. Dewey, the well-known education philosopher, defined education as a social practice that should magnify the integration of students' capacities into a meaningful output (as cited in Hammond et al., 2001). Notwithstanding to the social, economic, behavioral, physical, and mental conditions, the educational global transformation assured the right of all students to socially practice education (Banks, 2004). Yet, Labaree (1997) argued that failure to make students' social practice of learning possible refers to projects' political deficiencies, which is the lack of devising clear projects' goals and outcomes, and/or, the deprived methods used in developing such goals, which apparently build detrimental learning environment. Evidently, development projects became in a long-lasting assessment status, where methods of building productive and proactive learning environments needed to be invincible, supporting students to be unparalleled to others (Herrara & Torres, 2006).

The association between social cohesiveness and building active learning environment is worrisome given the evidence that an active learning environment is associated with the existence of universal goals and values, an issue that is not guaranteed in underprivileged communities where complexities are widely diversified (Friedkin, 2004). Schunk (2012) argued that locating long-term goals inside any learning environment, developed by students and schools/projects' staff cooperatively, enhance both groups' self-efficacies, increase their level of commitment to achieve such goals, and to some extent build the learning environment attempted. However, Prendiville (2008) believed that projects' cohesiveness is vulnerable to many conditions. Alteration in factors such as; teaching methodologies, staff's structure, project's components, and others factors may force cohesive group members to change their beliefs, with no guaranteed performances or reactions. Durkheim, being the first sociologist calling for social cohesion, reasoned this transitory action to defects in shared dispositions i.e. values, commitments and challenges, increasing disparities, and weakening social bonds that may have already been established among groups' members (Berger-Schmitt, 2000). Hence, social cohesion is an essential aspect for mounting stakeholders' inputs towards desired outputs and intended outcomes.

In the context of the above discussion, this study seeks to capturing perceptions that reflect and update the existing knowledge of the effect of the education-supported development projects on young rural women's lives in Egypt. Perceptions are categorized according to the OECD/DAC assessment criteria (Chianca, 2008), which are defined as:

> Relevance: measure of the extent to which the aid activity is suited to the priorities and policies of the target group i.e., beneficiaries…Efficiency: measure of the outputs—qualitative and quantitative—versus the inputs… Effectiveness: measure of the extent to which an aid activity attains its objectives…Impact: measure of the positive and negative changes produced by a development intervention, directly or indirectly, intended or unintended… Sustainability: measure of the extent to which the benefits of an activity are likely to continue after donor funding has been withdrawn. (p. 43)

METHODS AND DATA ANALYSIS

Research Design and Tools

The study drew its sample from three development projects in the Sohag governorate (seven villages), and Qena governorate (three villages); both are located in south of Egypt, known as Upper Egypt governorates. Sohag governorate is considered to be one of the poorest governorates in Upper Egypt (World Food Programme, 2013), while Qena is the most conservative (Brady et al., 2007). Both governorates, according to the 2010 Egypt Human Development Report, are ranked to be among the bottom five governorates of the human development indicators (UNDP, 2010), comprising the poorest villages in Egypt (UNDP, 2010). Several development projects have been undertaken in these two governorates. For the purpose of this study, the perceptions of rural women were examined in relation to three development projects that intend to empower Egyptian women in rural areas.

First, the Population Council's project, "Successful Transition to Work", known on the ground, in Arabic as *Neqdar Nesharek*, aimed at empowering young rural Egyptian women economically through the provision of trainings in business, vocational, and life skills. The trainings were planned to support and enable young women to either joining an existing business or starting their own business. It targeted four thousand and five hundred (4,500) young rural women aged 16–29 in thirty villages in Sohag, Qena and Fayoum governorates (Population Council, 2013). Second, the CARE's project, "Banking on Change", known among Egyptian participants as *Idkhar*. This project aimed to economically empower young rural women and men in Upper Egypt by teaching them the savings' techniques, guiding them to build their funds, and accomplish their personal goals. Through implanting the saving skill into the communities, people were able to group in an average of 15–25 members and build their own fund, decide on their shares of savings, set their fund's regulations, manage their funds and sustain their accomplishments. According to the 2014 project plan, the project focuses on increasing beneficiaries' awareness, contributing to their empowerment and supporting their solidarity. And third, the Misr El-Kheir's (an Egyptian NGO) project, "Community Schools", is an expansion of the UNICEF's initiative of community schools. The project is built on the idea of introducing active learning in primary and preparatory schools. The project is implemented in Sohag, Assuit, Aswan and Qena governorates. In collaboration with the Ministry of Education, the project works on providing quality educational opportunities for children, especially girls, who have not been enrolled in primary education or who have dropped out, in the age group of 6 to 14 years in disadvantaged areas. Age bracket is expanded to 18 years to ensure full inclusion of marginalized girls. The project targets thirteen thousand five hundred girls. It is important to clarify that while focusing on young women's perceptions of and experiences with these three projects, the evaluation of the overall quality and outcomes of the selected projects is beyond the scope and purpose of this study.

The researcher employed mixed research methods, relying primarily on a qualitative tool supplemented by a quantitative questionnaire. Qualitative data was collected through in-depth interviews (IDI) and focus group discussions (FGD). The interview guide aimed to gauge projects beneficiaries' views and identify their perceptions on the projects of this study in terms of the five main themes used. In addition, it measured the barriers beneficiaries faced during intervention, and major outcomes they possessed. The interview guide also allowed beneficiaries to provide their vision on projects' management schemes, influential projects' components, and social and economic contributions these projects affected on their lives. As for the quantitative data, it was collected through a questionnaire with three main sections; personal information, educational background, and perceptions of development projects. This quantitative research aimed to provide an account of community members' and non-project young rural women's perceptions on development projects in terms of relevance, efficiency, effectiveness, impact, and sustainability.

It is worth noting that the researcher is a former staff of one of the projects of this study. Thus, to preserve work ethics and keep the same level of accessibility equal in all three projects, the researcher used only public accessible documents for the projects under examination.

Research Sample

A purposive sample was used to select 101 interviewees for the qualitative data, while a snowball strategy was employed to select 156 respondents for the quantitative data.

The qualitative sample is divided into five targeted groups as follows:

- Thirty-one (31) young rural women project's beneficiaries
- Twenty (20) young rural women projects' promoters/facilitators

- Eight (8) community development associations' project staff
- Eleven (11) beneficiaries' mothers
- Thirty-one (31) male guardians (10 fathers, 11 community leaders and 10 religious leaders)

As for the quantitative sample, it included the following groups who represented the surrounding community of beneficiaries:

- Thirty-seven (37) women over 45 years old
- Thirty-seven (37) Men over 45 years old
- Thirty-seven (37) Male youth aged 18–29 years old
- Thirty-seven (37) Non-projects young rural women aged 18–29 year old

Research Tools

The qualitative interview guide aimed to gauge projects beneficiaries' views and identify their perceptions regarding: barriers they face during intervention, major outcomes they possess, management schemes they see effective, influential projects' components, and social and economic contributions these projects affect. Same interview guide was used for all groups, after tailoring the language to specific needs. The quantitative questionnaire aimed to provide an account of community members' and non-project young rural women's perceptions of development projects and the extent to which they shape the surrounding environment.

Research Data Analysis

Using the thematic analysis, data was categorized under the OECD/DAC assessment criteria. From an ontology paradigm lens, the research methods were designed to gather data from different angles. The thematic analysis method best suited the analysis process, allowing a wide spectrum of details and interpretations (Braun & Clarke, 2006). By comparing the similarities and differences among perceptions, data was synthesized under new captured sub-themes, articulating the key content of each theme in terms of its significance to the research questions.

The following discussions and interpretations connect the findings to the context and concepts examined earlier in order to fulfill the purpose of this research. Under this mandate, the researcher will answer the main research question and its sub-questions, highlighting proposed/identified needs, and necessarily requirements of development projects. Then based on this discussion, recommendations will be offered in the concluding section. The findings will be categorized under the five main themes of the OECD/DAC criteria. Perceptions of interviewees and respondents are displayed revealing their perspectives and experiences with development projects in rural areas during the transitional time in Egypt, and the extent to which some areas are needed to be improved.

FINDINGS AND DISCUSSIONS

Perceived Relevance

Data revealed that a crucial aspect to accomplish relevancy of any project is the consideration of the contribution of communities' members in developing the learning goals of any project, which in turn would increase their commitment to accomplish the intended results, and raise the potential of affecting necessary changes. Among the interviewed sample, views confirmed lack of 'social accountability', which is defined to be the action of setting an atmosphere that enables stakeholders to have a strong say in: planning and managing interventions they are exposed to, making sure that any proposed intervention is drawn upon their needs, and deploying all available resources inside their communities (World Bank Group, 2012). Findings of this study marked that the examined development projects under this research did not fully address young rural women's life-related activities that respond to their direct needs.

A factor affecting young rural women's perceptions is the lack of being convinced to change. This lack of conviction is a result of the scarce links beneficiaries can build between the kind of services offered by the development projects and the kind of beneficiaries' uprising needs (Schunk, 2012). Exemplifications can be seen in the following quotes; "We need moral support from our community members. So, I hope the project could have addressed this issue with the community" (IDI, a beneficiary, 20 years old, vocational diploma, N*eqdar Nesharek*, Sohag). Another perception mentioned that, "If the project really wants to serve us, they should have included male youth as well in the program, because they deserve to make use of these services, and we need to get married to qualified husbands" (IDI, a beneficiary, 18 years old, preparatory education, *Neqdar Nesharek*, Sohag).

In addition, findings showed that secondary beneficiaries of any project are more likely to see the relevance of these projects to their needs than primary beneficiaries. For example, male guardians and in some cases mothers were more likely to admit the 'relevancy' of the project they are related to, more than the beneficiaries themselves. The findings of this research clarified the deviation in projects' level of relevancy admitted by different stakeholders by the level of expectations each has drawn prior to implementation. Accordingly, the culture and the social needs play pivotal role in shaping these expectations. For example, a father expressed his opinion by saying, "If religiously accepted, which is something I'm not sure of yet, I would look to *Idkhar* as a good project that resolves the community's problems from its grassroots, providing acknowledged community support to its members", (FGD, a father, 72 years old, primary education, *Idkhar*, Sohag).

Furthermore, although the magnitude of using outside experts exists, the findings of this research revealed that people may still consider an insider, with less information, as an expert, as long as he/she can add to their knowledge, even if it is a minor addition, and provide on-going mentoring to community members. From young rural women's perceptions, two privileges are seen for an insider. First, he/she is an existing body inside the village, which means that his/her handiness and readiness are higher than any outsider. Second, deploying an existing caliber inside the intervened village gives the ownership of the project to community members. In addition, using existing caliber means investing in improving community members' capacities and increasing the probability of transferring the capacities the insider has to younger generations. This finding is best expressed in the following quote, "We all agree that the technical support is a basic requirement for any project's success, however, we believe that the efficiency of such technicians would be much higher if they were selected from within the same intervened villages or its neighbours. If done, this technician will be familiar with the contexts of the intervened villages and would better deal with hidden complications in the community that cannot be explained but has to be felt" (FGD comprising; a father, 72 years old, primary education, a community leader, 44 years old, diploma in teaching and a religious leader, 53 years old, illiterate, *Idkhar* Sohag).

As indicated from the field work of this study, strengthening civil society and integrating social stratification into the underprivileged communities are associated with extending services to the wider possible spectrum of stakeholders, contributing to the deployment of any possible opportunities existing inside these communities. Table 1 offers a brief on the perceived relevance of the examined development projects in Egypt.

Table 1. Brief findings of perceived relevance of development projects

Theme	Qualitative data		Quantitative data
	Sub-themes	Brief description	
Relevance	Prioritized areas for improvement	• Age range, • Inclusion of male youth, • Specialized teachers, • Financial support, • Community members' acceptance, • Bridging with actual job opportunities, • Extending services to larger number of beneficiaries	• Only 16% (n = 25) of the respondents participated in any community assessment surveys, • Around 93% (n = 145) of the whole respondents agreed that the development projects responded to community needs • Almost 94.5% (n = 147) believed in development projects.
	Pro-poor social capital	• Poor usage of parents' experiences • Poor consideration of previous projects' achievements • Poor usage of local villages' resources	
	Technical expertise and support	• Introducing technical expertise is a must • Supporting beneficiaries with job coaching is a must.	

Perceived Efficiency

This research built a correlation between the provision of holistic approaches and the accomplishment of efficiency. Women's perceptions under this theme called development projects for the provision of an inclusive package of services that may ensure for them a smooth transition from discriminated situations to privileged situations. Eventually, quotes extracted shed light on the importance of having 'social resilience' inside their intervened communities, which is the capacity of coping, collaborating, and connecting inside the intervened communities. Ultimately, it was evident that building individuals' competencies and/or stakeholders' capacities to be able to seek any possible interdisciplinary opportunities among different projects or initiatives is the key for success.

Young rural women's perceptions shed light on the importance of providing complementary components under any area of focus of each project, drawing clear milestones of improvement to beneficiaries and supporting them through till the end. An expressed opinion said, "The provision of seed money was essential for this project to make it of real benefit for us, or if it is a matter of distrust, the project staff could have given us instead sewing machines to start our projects" (IDI, a beneficiary, 29 years old, illiterate, *Idkhar*, Sohag).

As for the kind of adaption needed for current projects' purposes, policies, actions, activities, decisions, or resource allocations, the focus of young rural women's perceptions poured in one bowl; the quick need of identifying and introducing any communities' opportunities from different lenses in an intersectional structure. Each lens should be addressing certain project's strength that when grouped together present a meaningful life-related opportunity for beneficiaries, making diverged opportunities meet together at a converged point that articulates specific outcomes. An exemplification of this opinion can be seen in the following opinion, "Because I'm a beneficiary of both *Neqdar Nesharek* and *Idkhar* projects, I expect to gain from both projects; *Neqdar* will teach me a skill, and *Idkhar* will help me generate funds, so I will be well served on two different levels; education and employment", (IDI, a beneficiary, 29 years old, illiterate, *Neqdar Nehsarek* and *Idkhar* projects, Sohag).

At the same time, young rural women's perspectives revealed that to implement a successful project, the contextual framework needs to be inviting. That being said, women highlighted the essentiality of considering other projects' achievements prior to deciding a certain new project idea. Not just other projects' achievements, but also other contextual considerations, marketing possibilities, capital responsibilities, etc., before raising beneficiaries' hopes without paving the road for them to move forward. Table 2 offers a brief on the perceived efficiency of the examined development projects in Egypt.

Table 2. Brief findings of perceived efficiency of development projects

Theme	Qualitative data		Quantitative data
	Sub-themes	Brief description	
Efficiency	Seed money	• Essential to support beneficiaries in starting their business • Better be supported by technical assistance • Build trust in beneficiaries • Must connect beneficiaries to different funding opportunities	• Almost 100% (n = 99) measure efficiency as an aspect of any project's success.
	Dual interventions	• Allow holistic opportunities • Make use of each other's strengths • Strengthen beneficiaries	
	Trust and social bonds	• Being transparent re-projects' resources during launching events is a must • Planning realistic outcomes is a must • Gaining community's trust is a perceived as urgently needed.	

Perceived Effectiveness

From the analysis, it was seen that the arch ing objectives of any development project are building the capacity of the intervened communities, working with different groups, and focusing on different areas of competence. Quote of beneficiary said, "I felt the change the life skills component made to my personality, now I'm capable of understanding people, dealing with them, and discussing any concerns they have on women's work in a way that suits their mentalities" (IDI, a beneficiary, 28 years old, holder of diploma of commerce, *Neqdar Nesharek*, Qena). Accordingly, data publicized 'scaffolding' as means of effecting change. Based on Qu et al. 1991 (as cited in Zhou, n.d., p. 8) scaffolding is to, "teach people how to teach." In brief, the finding under this theme yields to the reality that every person can affect another, or scaffolds others. What differs is how this effect is shaped, directed, and applied. Scaffolding is best expressed in one of the beneficiary's opinion who said, "I dream of being a promoter to help my community members to make savings and achieve their plans. I also dream of changing the community's perceptions of the old norms regarding women engagement" (IDI, a beneficiary, 18 years old, secondary vocational education, *Idkhar*, Sohag).

This research revealed that beneficiaries can hardly detect their shortages and/or characters' deficiencies unless they are enrolled in a heavy detailed training. That is why projects' implementers reached an evidential need of using the experiential learning method to support the development of self-motivated beneficiaries, through a trust-worthy mutual learning relationship. An exemplification of this evidence can be seen in the following quote, "The girls watched the efforts we, the promoters, exerted and the results achieved, so I believe each girl has the wish now to go through the same experience and be useful to others" (a promoter, 28 years old, diploma in computer, *Neqdar Nesharek*, Qena) noting the dreams of girls of being promoters.

The kind of adaptation suggested by young rural women in the three projects were: adding more activities on narrowing the beliefs gaps, and increasing the acceptance of others' decisions and opinions. Harmony among community members was a contextual issue that found to be a cause of lot of challenges. Thus, as discussed in earlier themes, including wider spectrum of population in the project's mandate is expected by interviewees to narrow the negative effect of the social norms and open new opportunities for beneficiaries to positively get engaged, as evident by one of the beneficiaries, "Success of any project depends on the parents' level of education. Illiterate people can hardly think, and thus they are not convinced of projects and they excel to create obstacles for their daughters. However, well educated people endorse development projects and their related activities all through. Thus, it is important to include everyone in your projects" (IDI, a beneficiary, 20 years old, holder of diploma of commerce, *Neqdar Nesharek*, Qena). Table 3 provides a brief summary of the perceived effectiveness of the examined development projects.

Perceived Impact

The findings of this study exhibited that the norms and beliefs of local communities affect the extent of any projects' impact. Voices of young rural women highlighted the vicious cycle between the impact of projects' successions and inherited beliefs, although it is unclear of which affects the other more. Women's perceptions indicated a kind of 'ideological debate' inside the intervened communities, which is defined by Skinner in 1999 as a debate on, "definitions and uses of concepts" (as cited in Haapanen, 2011, p. 102). The Human Development Report indicated that on ground, ideological debates in most cases lead to depression which is initially attributed to, "the vast difference in services and opportunities for youth in rural and urban areas" (UNDP, 2010, pp. 185–186), this can be displayed in the following quote, "I don't care about people's perceptions and disappointing comments, because most of them have blocked minds and if I follow them I'll never develop" (IDI, a beneficiary, 29 years old, illiterate, *Neqdar Nehsarek* and *Idkhar* projects, Sohag). This puts into question the extent to which the ideological debate emerged between the participating women in development projects and other members of their communities was taken into consideration in the strategic planning and management of these projects.

While the majority of interviewed young rural women perceived the development projects as contributing in developing their ideology and understanding of their roles, they confirmed that the projects didn't address the wide spectrum of different

Table 3. Brief findings of perceived effectiveness of development projects

Themes	Qualitative data		Quantitative data
	Sub-themes	Brief description	
Effectiveness	Life skills component	• Supports the building of beneficiaries' personalities • Awakens beneficiaries' desire of learning • Strengthens beneficiaries' critical thinking skills	• Around 47% (n = 73) thought that any project's main aim is to help its beneficiaries to generate income • Almost 44% (n = 68) thought that projects should heavily contribute to the well-fair of the society • Around 33% (n = 52) thought that projects should help beneficiaries get educated • And 29.5% (n = 46) thought that projects are designed to help beneficiaries start their business
	Intergenerational problem	• Urgency of initiating community dialogue about old norms and beliefs • Urgency of narrowing the gap between the old and the new generations	
	Parental education	• Is a significant determinant of the likelihood of beneficiaries continuing their education • Build confusion between formal and non-formal education	
	Promoters as role models	• Are catalysts of change inside the community • Occupy very special social positions • Are actual projects' implementers on the ground • Lucky to have suitable jobs • Change community's perceptions of women engagement • Successful in facing different financial, social and cultural barriers.	
	Knowledge transfer	• Beneficiaries' capacities of knowledge transfer heavily relies on their level of conviction of their knowledge • Successful knowledge transfer is more common among younger generations	

social and economic concepts that are inherited into the local communities. A representation of such opinion signposted that, "This village has around 10,000 populations; the project serves only 150 girls out of them, so how would we say that the project served our community while it did not even serve 50% of them! To make real change, the project needs to reach more people and provide more services" (FGD comprising; a father, 56 years old, diploma in teaching, a religious leader, 34 years old, BA in social services, and a community leader, 48 years old, diploma in teaching, *Neqdar Nesharek*, Qena).

An important finding of this research exposed the reality that a young rural woman's ideological debate can be treated through matching the new beneficiary's ideology with the interests of her surrounding community. For example, male guardians revealed their complete acceptance to young rural women's participation, as long as their participation has direct positive impact on male guardians' lives. That being said, if young rural women's needs intersect with the needs and demands of their households, the existence of an ideological debate is likely to diminish. An expressive representation of this opinion can be seen in the following quote, "The religion belief says 'work is worship'. So, if our girls and wives contribute to the increase of our families' income through these projects, we wouldn't mind their participation. In addition, when women work, they better realize how hard it is to collect money, and thus they become more careful in their consumptions" (FGD comprising; a father, 72 years old, primary education, a community leader, 44 years old, diploma in teaching and a religious leader, 53 years old, illiterate, *Idkhar*, Sohag).

The above findings reprove the need for a monitoring and evaluation system of project activities with flexible action plans that would enable to take into consideration the emerging needs of stakeholders as related to the projects' indicators. In addition, including community members and engaging them, along with the project's targeted beneficiaries, in joint activities would help in achieving a higher positive impact in their community. Furthermore, the inclusion of community members would allow for their participation in combating any type of resistance or violence that may occur, and in endorsing civic harmony and peace building inside their communities. Table 4 offers a brief on the perceived impact of the examined development projects in Egypt.

Perceived Sustainability

The core discovery of this section relies on the extent and level of existence of 'social cohesion' inside intervened communities. As mentioned by Friedkin (2004), "a cohesive group is one in which there is a uniformly high positive level of individual membership attitudes and behaviors" (p. 414). Social cohesion is built on sustaining individuals' membership within a community, and building long-lasting descent relation that provides a person with the sense of responsibility towards a group (Fearon, 1999; Kennedy & Nilson, 2008). This aspect is essential for the

Table 4. Brief findings of perceived impact of development projects

Theme	Qualitative data		Quantitative data
	Sub-themes	Brief description	
Impact	On-ground results	• Maintain community awareness and conviction of develop. Projects • Grab the interests of beneficiaries • Are well acknowledged if they meet communities' personal needs.	• Around 51% (n= 80) saw literacy as the main impact • Around 42% (n=66) saw vocational training as the main impact • Around 38% (n=59) saw SMEs as the main impact • Around 28% (n=44) saw Employability as the main impact • Around 23% (n=36) saw Entrepreneurship as the main impact • Around 21% (n=34) saw Public Awareness as the main impact • Around 56% (n=88) still have gender issues, underestimating women's roles. • 82% (n=128) of respondents indicated that women should not stay at home • 83% (n=130) confirmed their approval of women's work. • Around 95% (n=149) confirmed that projects leave positive impact after they terminate, • An average of 91% (n=142) reported that projects equip women with various skills
	Early marriage	• Grants the authority of women's engagement to husbands • Preventing it provides time for young women to get engaged	
	Critical gaps	• Lack of engagement of community members in developing projects' objectives • Lack of clear explanation of projects' outcomes • Projects work in isolated islands focusing on very specific areas with no consideration to other areas • Projects address very limited percentages of population, leaving the majority with no services	
	Participants' potential barriers	• Women's male guardians, mothers-in-law and grandmothers are the main motivators behind keeping women away from education and work • Domestic work remains the main barrier behind high drop-out rates • Fears are still existing from wasting time in the classes	

sustainability of development projects' activities in local communities beyond the life of the projects. It was evident from the findings that social cohesion exists in the participated communities, yet the extent to which these projects helped beneficiaries to culturally assimilate, unfolding inquiries on the expected level of sustainability of the projects remains questionable. However, the findings of this study indicate that social cohesion and its main determinant of culture assimilation need to be fostered inside intervened villages in order secure sustainability and make use of available intakes, while strengthening the outtakes. An expressed opinion said, "I can see some girls dividing responsibilities and roles between each other to run the classes

Table 5. Brief findings of perceived sustainability of development projects

Themes	Qualitative data		Quantitative data
	Sub-themes	Brief description	
Sustainability	Volunteerism	• Is a common ground aspect in development projects • Is suggested to be an obligation for projects' graduates in an attempt to foster knowledge transfer • Can be a channel to sustain projects and keep faith in them • Need to be systemized	• Around 80% (n = 125) were interested in working for development projects to serve the community.
	Partnerships	• Beneficiaries have disquiets and uncertainties when it comes to financial peer-to-peer partnership • Beneficiaries are supportive and welcoming when it comes to knowledge peer-to-peer partnership • Value chain partnerships are needed • The know-how of establishing 'safe' partnership is needed • Partnering with governmental bodies is needed for the purpose of institutionalization • Expected contribution by local partners needs to be more clear	
	CDAs' strengthened status	• See themselves as administrators rather than implementers • Lack the capacities of sustaining any project i.e. need to learn how to make projects that generates income to cover at least their running costs, in order to secure their existence • Those with wide network can better survive and serve the community	

(*Continued*)

Table 5. (Continued)

Themes	Qualitative data		Quantitative data
	Sub-themes	Brief description	
	Dissemination and outreach	• Lack of well disseminated project's results, and accordingly lack of, sustainability • Need to be tailored to address community leaders who can incubate the projects after termination	
	Implanting desired changes	• Projects must be community-based • Projects must work on narrowing the social gap between community members • Community members must be involved at an early stage in designing the activities • Data evidenced an intertwining relation between impact and sustainability	

after the project termination, and in my opinion this is a good sign that they can cooperate in the future" (IDI, a promoter, 21 years old, technical vocational diploma, *Neqdar Nesharek*, Qena).

Young rural women's perceptions proved that beneficiaries and promoters have a strong intention for sustaining their improved living conditions, and supporting others. As examples of these intentions were volunteering the delivery of extra classes, suggesting ways of maintaining the existence of Community Development Associations (CDAs), and disseminating results to solicit the support of more leaders to the projects. Nevertheless, data proved that individual efforts that are scattered with no governing system can hardly achieve the desired level of sustainability. Thus, preparing young rural women to act as role models inside their communities should be treated as a top priority action plan for all further projects.

CONCLUSION

Over the past years prior to the 2011 revolution in Egypt, young rural women's capacities to participate in the development processes of their communities have been faced with hurdles of unequal gender, socio-economic, and power relations. During the post-revolution, in response to the urgent need of empowering young rural women and fostering their rights to live and participate, many development projects were designed and implemented to prepare women to join the labor market and contribute to the well-being of their communities.

The extent of designing development projects in the context of targeted communities is a key factor for affecting real changes. The views of young women of the development projects' impact on their lives indicated the need for engaging local community members in the change process while empowering women. As discussed in the findings of this study, the change process referred to establishing social accountability, building social resilience, effecting scaffolding, resolving ideological debates, and integrating projects' social cohesion inside the intervened communities. Accomplishment of these five suggested changes is expected to better organize the communities' engagement and the use of their resources.

The study revealed the emergent need of applying the 'change management' which call for deploying the projects' mechanisms to support community members with smooth transition of "adoption and realization of change" (Creasey, 2007, p. 3). In other words, for improving the outcomes of development projects, priority should be given to engaging community members and stakeholders through stimulating and supporting their desire and ability of effecting change, then align the 'activities and tools' of the project itself to best suit community members' needs (Creasey, 2007; McCarthy & Eastman, 2010).

It is recommended for educators, policy makers and practitioners to set strategic and management plans that are based on prioritized areas determined through community or stakeholder's analysis. In addition, developing constructive policy for cooperation between institutions working in the same area would provide possibilities of collaboration and drive projects' beneficiaries to the maximum possible benefits. More importantly, policies for young rural women that are demand-driven with key aspects that are relevant to their lives are needed. Developing strategies (i.e., community-based initiatives) that inspire young rural women to share their innovative suggested changes with the governmental and non-governmental institutions could be a channel to develop a joint venture strategy that directs different efforts towards the desired changes.

In the post-revolution Egypt, the engagement of youth in policy making became more acceptable. Initiating dialogues with youth became a common practice to identify their needs. Strengthening the managerial capacity of development projects through the involvement of young rural women in the projects' planning and policy formulation would help in developing demand-driven projects. Empowering and encouraging young rural women to integrate valuable intakes and introduce new norms and beliefs into their communities would pave the road for the whole intervening community to change. The inclusion of diverse community members, along with targeted beneficiaries of development projects, would help significantly in creating supportive atmosphere, especially in projects that support disadvantaged groups such as young women in rural communities.

REFERENCES

Abdou, D., & ZaaZou, Z. (2013). The Egyptian revolution and post socio-economic impact. *Topics in Middle Eastern and African Economies, 15*(1), 92–115. Retrieved from http://www.luc.edu/orgs/meea/volume15/pdfs/The-Egyptian-Revolution-and-Post-Socioeconomic-Impact.pdf

Assaad, R., & Barsoum, G. (2007). *Youth xclusion in Egypt: In search of "Second Chances"* (The Middle East Youth Initiative Working Paper No. 2, pp. 37–47). Washington, DC: Wolfensohn Center for Development & Dubai School of Government. Retrieved from http://ddp-ext.worldbank.org/EdStats/EGYpub07.pdf

Banks, J. A. (2004). *Diversity and citizenship education: Global perspectives* (1st ed., pp. 3-427). San Francisco, CA: The Jossey-Bass education series.

Berger-Schmitt, R. (2000). *Social cohesion as an aspect of the quality of societies: Concept and measurement* (EuReporting Working Paper No. 14). Mannheim: Centre for Survey Research and Methodology. Retrieved from http://www.gesis.org/fileadmin/upload/dienstleistung/daten/soz_indikatoren/eusi/paper14.pdf

Brady, M., Assaad, R., Ibrahim, B., Salem, A., Salem, R., & Zibani, N. (2007). *Providing new opportunities to adolescent girls in socially conservative settings: The ishraq program in rural Upper Egypt.* Cairo: The Population Council.

Braun, V., & Clarke, V. (2006). Using thematic analysis in psychology. *Qualitative Research in Psychology, 3*(2), 77–101.

Center for Development Services. (2005). *Asset-based development: Success stories from Egyptian communities.* Cairo: The Center for Development Services. Retrieved from http://coady.stfx.ca/tinroom/assets/file/CDS_manual(1).pdf

Central Agency for Public Mobilization and Statistics. (2011). *Living standards and poverty.* Retrieved from http://www.capmas.gov.eg/pages_ar.aspx?pageid=728

Chianca, T. (2008). The OECD/DAC criteria for international development evaluations: An assessment and ideas for improvement. *Journal of Multidisciplinary Evaluation, 5*(9), 41–51.

Chinese Ministry of Education. (2011). *Outline of China's national plan for medium and long term education and development (2010–2020).* Beijing: Chinese Ministry of Education. Retrieved from https://www.aei.gov.au/news/newsarchive/2010/documents/china_education_reform_pdf.pdf

Church Educational System. (2001). *Principles of leadership teacher manual.* Salt Lake City, UT: Intellectual Reserve. Retrieved from http://institute.lds.org/bc/content/institute/materials/english/teacher-resources/religion-180r-principles-of-leadership-teacher-manualeng.pdf

Creasey, T. (2007). *Defining change management.* Loveland, CO: Prosci and the Change Management Learning Center. Retrieved from http://www.change-management.com/prosci-defining-change-management.pdf

El Laithy, H. (n.d.). *The gender dimensions of poverty in Egypt* (ERF Working Paper Series No. 0127). Cairo: ERF. Retrieved from http://www.erf.org.eg/CMS/uploads/pdf/0127_Elleithy.pdf

EQUIP2. (2004). *The challenge of achieving education for all: Quality basic education for underserved children.* Washington, DC: EQUIP2. Retrieved from http://www.equip123.net/docs/e2-ChallengeEFA_IssuesBrief.pdf

European Commission. (2015). *Erasmus programme guide.* Brussels: European Commission. Retrieved from http://ec.europa.eu/programmes/erasmus-plus/documents/erasmus-plus-programme-guide_en.pdf

European Union. (2011). *Entrepreneurship education: Enabling teachers as a critical success factor.* Frankfurt: European Union.

Fearon, J. D. (1999). *What is identity (as we now use the word)?* Stanford, CA: Stanford University. Retrieved from https://web.stanford.edu/group/fearon-research/cgi-bin/wordpress/wp-content/uploads/2013/10/What-is-Identity-As-we-now-use-the-word-.pdf

Fox, J. A., & Gershman, J. (2001). The World Bank and social capital: Lessons from ten rural development projects in the Philippines and Mexico. *Policy Sciences, 33*(3), 399–419. Retrieved from https://escholarship.org/uc/item/1vj8v86j?query=development projects

Freire, P. (1998). There is no teaching without learning. *Pedagogy of freedom: Ethics, democracy, and civic courage* (pp. 29–48). Lanham, MD: Rowman & Littlefield Publishers.

Friedkin, N. E. (2004). Social cohesion. *The Annual Review of Sociology, 30*, 409–425. doi:10.1146/annurev.soc.30.012703.110625

Global Monitoring Report. (2010). *Reaching the marginalized*. Paris: UNESCO. Retrieved from http://www.uis.unesco.org/Library/Documents/gmr10-en.pdf

Goetzman, D. M. (2012). *Dialogue education: Step by step*. New York, NY: Global Learning Partners.

Haapanen, J. (2011). Language, time and the may fourth movement. *Graduate Journal of Asia-Pacific Studies, 7*(2), 99–116. Retrieved from https://cdn.auckland.ac.nz/assets/arts/Departments/asian-studies/gjaps/docs-vol7-no2/Language,%20Time%20and%20the%20May%20Fourth%20Movement.pdf

Hammond, L., Austin, K., Orcutt, S., & Rosso, J. (2001). *How people learn: Introduction to learning theories*. Stanford, CA: Stanford University School of Education.

Herrara, L., & Torres, C. (2006). Introduction: Possibilities for critical education in the Arab world. In L. Herrara & C. A. Torres (Eds.), *Cultures of Arab schooling: Critical ethnographies from Egypt* (pp. 1–21). Albany, NY: State University of New York Press.

Hurn, C. (1985). *The limits and possibilities of schooling: An introduction to the sociology of education*. Boston, MA: Allyn & Bacon, Inc.

International Institute for Educational Planning. (2006). *Non-formal education. Guidebook for planning education in emergencies and reconstruction*. Paris: UNESCO. Retrieved from http://www.iiep.unesco.org/fileadmin/user_upload/Research_Highlights_Emergencies/Chapter12.pdf

International Labor Organization. (2012). *Statistical update on employment in the informal economy*. Geneva: International Labor Organization. Retrieved from http://laborsta.ilo.org/applv8/data/INFORMAL_ECONOMY/2012-06-Statistical%20update%20-%20v2.pdf

Jordan, A., Carlile, O., & Stack, A. (2008). *Approaches to learning: A guide for teachers*. New York, NY: Open University Stress. Retrieved from https://archive.org/details/ApproachesToLearningAGuideForTeachers

Kabeer, N. (2012). *Women's economic empowerment and inclusive growth: Labor markets and enterprise development* (SIG Working Paper 2012/1). Ottawa: IDRC and DFID. Retrieved from http://www.idrc.ca/EN/Documents/NK-WEE-Concept-Paper.pdf

Kassem, T. (2013). Post- january revolution Egypt: Is it a potential LICUS state? A political- economic perspective. *International Journal of Humanities and Social Sciences, 2*(4), 43–60.

Kennedy, F. A., & Nilson, L. B. (2008). *Successful strategies for teams*. Clemson, SC: Clemson University. Retrieved from http://www.clemson.edu/OTEI/documents/teamwork-handbook.pdf

Klosters, D. (2014). *Matching skills and labor market needs*. Geneva: World Economic Forum. Retrieved from http://www3.weforum.org/docs/GAC/2014/WEF_GAC_Employment_MatchingSkillsLabourMarket_Report_2014.pdf

Labaree, D. F. (1997). Public goods, private goods: The American struggle over educational goals. *American Educational Research Journal, 34*(1), 39–81.

Loveluck, L. (2012). *Education in Egypt: Key challenges*. London: Chatham House. Retrieved from http://www.chathamhouse.org/sites/default/files/public/Research/MiddleEast/0312egyptedu_background.pdf

Martin, J. R. (1981). The ideal of the educated person. *Educational Theory, 13*(2), 97–109.

McCarthy, C., & Eastman, D. (2010). *Change management strategies for an effective implementation*. New York, NY: Healthcare Information and Management Systems Society. Retrieved from http://himss.files.cms-plus.com/himssorg/content/files/changemanagement.pdf

Mossallem, M. (2013). *The illusion dispelled*. Cairo: The Egyptian Initiative for Personal Rights. Retrieved from http://eipr.org/sites/default/files/pressreleases/pdf/egypts_economic_crisis_e.pdf

NCCM. (2008). *Girls education initiative*. Retrieved from http://www.nccm-egypt.org/e11/e3151/index_eng.html

Passarelli, A., & Kolb, D. (2011). *Using experiential learning theory to promote student learning and development in programs of education abroad*. Cleveland, OH: Case Western Reserve University.

Population Council. (2010). *Survey of young people in Egypt*. Cairo: The Population Council.

Prendiville, P. (2008). *Developing facilitation skills*. Dublin: Combat Poverty Agency. Retrieved from http://www.combatpoverty.ie/publications/DevelopingFacilitationSkills_2008.pdf

Rennick, S. A. (2015). *The practice of politics and revolution: Egypt's revolutionary youth social movement*. Lund: Lund University.

Sabri, A. (2007). *Country profile commissioned for the EFA global monitoring report 2008, education for all by 2015: Will we make it?* Retrieved from http://ddp-ext.worldbank.org/EdStats/EGYgmrpro07.pdf

Schunk, D. (2012). *Learning theories: An educational perspective* (6th ed.). Boston, MA: Pearson Education, Inc.

Teach for America. (2011). *Classroom management & culture.* New York, NY: Teach for America.

The 21st Century Learning Initiative. (1997). *A policy paper: The strategic and resource implications of a new model of learning.* London: The 21st Century Learning Initiative. Retrieved from http://www.21learn.org/wp-content/uploads/PP.pdf

World Bank Group. (2012). *Monitoring through beneficiary feedback.* Washington, DC: The World Bank Group. Retrieved from http://www.worldfishcenter.org/sites/default/files/Stocktaking-Monitoring-through-Beneficiary-Feedback.pdf

UNDP. (2010). *Egypt human development report 2010.* Cairo: UNDP and The Institute of National Planning.

UNESCO-UIS Brookings Institution. (2013). *Toward universal learning.* Paris: UNESCO-UIS/ Brookings Institution. Retrieved from http://www.uis.unesco.org/Education/Documents/lmtf-summary-rpt-en.pdf

USAID. (2013). *Audit of USAID-Egypt's education support program.* Retrieved from http://oig.usaid.gov/sites/default/files/audit-reports/6-263-13-008-p.pdf

Verme, P., Milanovic, B., Al-Shawarby, S., El Tawila, S., Gadallah, M., & El-Majeed, E. A. (2014). *Inside inequality in the Arab republic of Egypt: Facts and perceptions across people, time, and space.* Washington, DC: The World Bank.

World Food Programme. (2013). *The status of poverty and food security in Egypt: Analysis and policy recommendations.* Cairo: World Food Programme. Retrieved from http://documents.wfp.org/stellent/groups/public/documents/ena/wfp257467.pdf

Youth Led Development Agency. (2012). *Youth in Tanzania today: Report 2012–2013.* Stockholm: Swedish Cooperation. Retrieved from http://restlessdevelopment.org/file/youth-report-201213-englishlowresonline-pdf

Zhou, H. (n.d.). *The spread and impact of deweyan educational philosophy in China.* Wuhan, China: Education College of Central China Normal University. Retrieved from http://citeseerx.ist.psu.edu/viewdoc/download?doi=10.1.1.564.1723&rep=rep1&type=pdf

Ola Hosny
Graduate School of Education
The American University in Cairo (AUC)

PART III

DIALECTICS OF TEACHER PROFESSIONAL DEVELOPMENT AND EDUCATIONAL QUALITY

AMIRA ABDOU

7. SCHOOL-BASED TEACHER PROFESSIONAL DEVELOPMENT

Examining Policy and Practice in the Egyptian Context

INTRODUCTION

At this momentous time in Egypt's history, it becomes imperative for the state to embark on a range of state-wide as well as institutionalized reform initiatives. At the heart of these reform initiatives comes educational reform with education being the corner stone of all societal reforms. Since 2007, and with the launching of its National Strategy for Education Reform, Egypt has realized the pressing need to shift from the centralized educational system towards a decentralized educational model. School-based reform, thus, becomes one of the adopted approaches for reforming education in Egypt. Therefore, this study focuses on school-based teacher professional development at policy and practice levels towards improving teacher performance and the quality of education.

The study examines the discourse and practice of school-based teacher professional development in Egyptian public schools during the aftermath of the 2011 revolution. It explores teachers' perceptions and identify the extent to which school-based teacher professional development approach has been implemented in Egyptian public schools. Field work was conducted in three national, language urban schools that is known as experimental schools and include elementary, middle, and high school levels. The study follows a qualitative approach that includes document review and conducting individual and focus group interviews, using semi-structured open-ended questions in addition to the researcher's observation during the school's field visits. The paper intends to identify the gaps between the policy discourse and the practice of teachers at school level in order to come up with recommendation for bridging the gap. I begin by presenting some of the main concepts of teacher professional development and the significance of the school-based approach. This will be followed by the research design including research setting, sampling strategy, and data collecting tools, then the perceptions of teachers will be presented and discussed.

CONCEPTUAL FRAMEWORK

In the age of rapid social and political changes, calls on school reform are echoed across the world. The focus on schooling institutions as the cornerstone of education reform is continuously growing. Effective teaching is primarily dependent on high-quality teachers who are competent enough to prepare students to be life-long and self-directed learners (OECD, 2005). Parents, along with education experts consider teachers as one of the most determinant factors of students' academic performance. In their rigorous study of 28 such factors, Wei, Darling-Hammond, Andree, Richardson, and Orphanos (2009) found that the two most prominent factors were directly related to teachers. Hence, teachers, being the front liners, are key instruments in transforming their schools into effective learning communities. Building teachers' capacity, therefore, drives our attention to the importance of providing effective school-based professional development for teachers being the link between standards input-driven movement and student achievement output-driven movement (Wei et al., 2009).

To understand clearly the crucial role of effective school-based professional development for teachers at the school level, we must first define effective professional development. In their report published by The National Staff Development Council (NSDC), Wei et al. (2009) define effective professional development as "that which results in teachers' knowledge and instructional practice, as well as, improve student-learning outcomes." In this respect, professional development does not only positively affect students' learning outcomes, but also reinforces the new role assigned to teachers as active learners and reflective practitioners at their own schools, which could be the first building block towards a community of learners where teachers become generators of knowledge for professional practice.

The last two decades have witnessed a paradigm shift in the research concerned with professional development. The new paradigm focuses on distinguishing between high-quality or effective professional development, which aims at offering active opportunities for teachers' learning, and traditional professional development that is criticized in literature for being ineffective (Opfer & Pedder, 2011). The most common forms of traditional professional development are workshops, conferences, courses, and institutes. School-based teacher professional development or "reform" activities of effective professional development take the forms of coaching, mentoring, peer observation, and study groups (Garet, Porter, Desimone, Birman, & Yoon, 2001; Wei et al., 2009). Glickman, Gordon, and Ross-Gordon (2010) list other alternative formats of professional development such as action research, partnerships between schools and teachers' universities, teachers' networks, where teachers from different schools have access to shared information on concerns and accomplishments, and where teachers can engage in active learning through computer links, newsletters, etc. Teachers' networks could also facilitate the arrangement of teachers' seminars and conferences. Such seminars could be held at "teachers' centers", which represent another alternative format for professional development. Teachers' centers enable teachers from various school contexts to participate in constructive dialogue and develop new skills in their profession.

Research on effective teacher professional development places emphasis on significant common characteristics of reformed, or rather, school-based professional development activities. These features include collective participation, coherence, content-based, and time-sustained activities, which could be implemented when adopting school-based approach (Fishman, Marx, Best, & Tal, 2003; Garet et al., 2001; Opfer & Pedder, 2011; Wei et al., 2009).

Literature on effective professional development has reached a consensus that collegial and collective participation of teachers—in the on-going process of professional development—have strong positive impacts on students' achievements, teachers' teaching practices, in addition to teachers' beliefs and attitudes (Opfer & Pedder, 2011). As highlighted by many researchers, collective participation of teachers within the context of their own school enables teachers to rely on one another and to engage in professional dialogue and rigorous processes of both self and students' assessment. This kind of interdependency of teachers motivates teachers to carry their practices to a public level, hence, forming a community of active learners. Teachers then get the opportunity to be generators of knowledge, rather than being passive recipients of it. In this respect, the school also fulfils its role as a learning community (Wei et al., 2009).

The duration period and intensity of professional development activities have also been determinants of whether these activities are effective or not with respect to teachers' learning and students' achievements. Research findings on time sustained and more intensive professional and learning development activities, suggest that teachers are more likely to implement these well-absorbed and reflected-upon activities into their own daily teaching practices (Garet et al., 2001; Opfer & Pedder, 2011; Wei et al., 2009). Thus, the time-sustained professional development activities prove to be more effective than the "flavor of the month" or the one-shot workshop whose impact is minimal on teachers' learning and students' achievements (Garet et al., 2001).

Effective professional development requires activities that are content-based and job-embedded as well, in order to be of high-quality. The literature divides the content-based activities into two main categories; the first category is the knowledge-based content, which includes knowledge of the subject matter taught and the tools and skills related to deliver that knowledge. The second category is pedagogical competences that include teaching strategies, classroom management, and assessment (Fishman et al., 2003). Effective professional development needs to be rich in both categories in order to be meaningful to teachers. This will guarantee continuous and consistent implementation as well.

Coherence of teacher professional development is a key component to its success. Effective professional development aims at activities that are carried out in coherence within the school context and in alignment with the school's endeavors toward reform, rather than patched or fragmented activities that are done in isolation of the school context (Wei et al., 2009). Coherence of effective school-based professional development practices calls for collaboration of school leadership and teaching faculty. In this respect, promoting the concept of distributed leadership becomes imperative and strongly related to effective teacher professional development. Coherence, as a concept, could also be expanded to embrace teachers' individual goals for growth in addition to the school-wide goals, where each of these two sets of goals support and reinforce one another (Glickmanet al., 2010). Lambert (2000) adds a further dimension to school leadership with respect to effective teacher professional development when she suggests that school leadership should not be reduced only the post of school principal; she states that leadership is derived from synergy and collaboration of all those who want to join the wave and construct collective meaning and knowledge. Consequently, all stakeholders need to develop a shared sense of community and work toward achieving collective goals and promoting their school as a center for knowledge and empowerment. Hence; school leaders become orchestral leaders who are "skilled in helping large teams produce a coherent sound, while encouraging soloists to shine" (The Wallace Foundation, 2013, p. 22).

The above discussion on effective teacher professional development suggests that school-based teacher professional development approach could render better results in terms of teacher professional learning because it encompasses all the components of collective participation, coherence, common moral purpose, and time sustainability. More importantly, school-based teacher professional development could be regarded as a perfect provision for teachers to examine their perceptions, attitudes, values, beliefs, and culture that underline their accustomed teaching approaches, giving teachers the invaluable chance to unlearn and relearn (Butler & Leahy, 2003).

Implementation of effective school-based professional development mandates efforts on the policy level to reach the domains of pre-service training, in-service induction, and on-going school-based teacher professional development activities and practices. Teachers' colleges and institutions should collaborate with schools where teacher candidates' educators collaborate with practicing teachers in devising teaching practices, content-based and pedagogy-based knowledge, and curricula that are compatible with global standards and in alignment to the school-wide goals and vision for reform. Such partnership must also be sensitive to the specificity of school context and school culture as well. Veteran and effectively experienced teachers could be of great help to novice teachers in induction programs through mentoring. To sum up, effective school-based professional development is an on-going process, rather than an episode, that can contribute to transforming teachers to the model of teachers as active learners, decision makers, problem-solvers, and active agents of change.

INTERNATIONAL DISCOURSE OF SCHOOL-BASED PROFESSIONAL DEVELOPMENT

The Global Monitoring Report (GMR), 2013–2014, states that more children are gaining access to schools than ever. International education policies, since the Dakar World Education Forum held in Senegal in 2000, have been geared toward providing universal primary education access, which also represents the Second Millennium Development Goal. In post-2015 global framework, the proposed shift in focus towards quality learning and teaching becomes a necessity. According to the GMR (2013–2014) this could be attributed to the fact that 130 million students out of 250 million still exhibit the need for better learning opportunities even though they spent "at least four years" in formal schooling (p. 191). The shift in emphasis coupled with the immaterialized learning opportunities for enrolled students suggest that policy discourse and implementation have been preoccupied with quantity over quality. The GMR (2013–2014) states that national education policies must prioritize quality learning and teaching; a goal that cannot be achieved without well-trained quality teachers.

Quality teachers' features are commonly identified through significant indicators such as: qualifications, experience, teacher knowledge-base content, and pedagogical knowledge. Nevertheless, there are other equally significant indictors to teacher quality that are strongly related to quality learning and harder to capture such as: the ability to create effective environment for all types of learners, nourish productive teacher-student relationship, last but not least, the ability to work effectively and collaboratively with colleagues and parents (Stronge et al., 2012). Research on constituents of a quality teacher demonstrates common characteristics of professionalism, passion for teaching, reflective and analytical thinking, and respect for others (Scwille et al., 2007).

This trend has been examined by OECD since 2005 till present; the OECD (2005) country background notes indicate that "school-based professional development activities involving the entire staff, or significant groups of teachers are becoming more common, and teacher-initiated personal development probably less so" (p. 77). In parallel, Feiman-Nemser (2001), suggests that establishment of a continuing and systemized structure for school-based teacher professional development, where teachers can "talk" about their teaching practice p. 107. Teacher "talk" in this context is identified more different than the casual informal or personal teacher talk; rather, it is a professional dialogue that tackles all pertaining issues of the teaching and learning processes inside the school including: teaching practices and instructional approaches, and evaluation methods, with the aim of on-going refinement of the end product, which is enhancing students' learning outcomes to the fullest potentials.

Teacher policies play a pivotal role in establishing effective school-based teacher professional development. OECD (2005) encourages the inclusion of teachers in the design and implementation of policies by which teachers can become empowered to fulfill their role as active and life-long learners. In this respect, teachers gain ownership over their learning and teaching. Furthermore, the same report reinforces the significance of teachers being supported by policy to form "professional learning communities" within their schools, as well as, beyond (p. 6). This would enable teachers to analyze their teaching practice according to professional benchmarks and standards, in addition to, analyzing their students' learning performance in light of the student learning standards.

But, teachers cannot shoulder this immense task alone, they need the help, guidance and support of an enlightened school leadership. It should be noted that the term "school leadership" does not necessarily refer solely to school principal;

it is an expandable expression that is school-culture embedded and community-nurtured. School leadership is a shared vision and goals that encompasses all forms of leaderships within the school: teacher leadership teams, heads of subject departments, and individual teacher leaders (Lambert, 2000). OECD (2008) report "Improving School Leadership: Policy and Practice" indicates that school leadership is a key playing actor in improving the whole school outcomes including students' learning outcomes and teacher quality through influencing the school culture and learning environment, in addition to motivating teachers to build their capacities. The report suggests "redefining" the roles assignments to school leadership to foster school-based teacher professional development in relevance to school's local context. Furthermore, school leadership is responsible for promoting team work among teachers (OECD, 2008, p. 8).

SCHOOL-BASED TEACHER PROFESSIONAL DEVELOPMENT IN REGIONAL POLICY

As an integral member of the international community, the League of Arab States (LAS) endorses the view that education must be prioritized among all development endeavors. Hence, a report that included purpose and direction of how education can be incorporated into all development processes in all areas in the Arab world was presented to the Arab Summit in Riyadh in March 2007. This report was followed by the "Plan for Development of Education in the Arab World," which was adopted in the Damascus Arab Summit in 2008. The two documents, the report and the plan, place great emphasis on the role of Arab teachers in the academic, social, and political education of Arab generations, in addition to helping them acquire foundations of "citizenship and a civilization-based identity."

In this respect, the Arab states recognize that they are part of the global system. Therefore, efforts should be geared towards navigating through the challenges and opportunities imposed in the increasingly globalized world. The Arab states, thus, responded to the five most recent and significant initiatives that direct efforts for education development:

1. The Millennium Development Goals document that sets eight MDG to be reached by 2015;
2. The Education for All Initiative launched during Dakar Conference in 2000 with six goals to be achieved in 2015;
3. The declaration of Literacy Decade (2003–2013) under the UN umbrella;
4. The UN "Education for Sustainable Development Decade Initiative" (2005–2014);
5. The Declaration of the Plan of Education in the Arab World in 2008 (LAS-UNICEF, 2010).

Committed to the cause of educational reform and providing quality teaching and learning that is learner-centered, LAS joined with international partners—the

United Nations Children's Fund (UNICEF), Unified Nations Education, Science and Culture Organization, along with Arab Education Science and Culture Organization (AESCO) and Arab Bureau of Education for Gulf States (ABEGS)—to launch the *Guiding Framework of the Performance Standards for Arab Teachers* in 2010. The Guiding Framework is primarily concerned with developing the capacities of Arab teachers in the areas of teacher education, teacher preparation, and on-going teacher professional development. The Guiding Framework also targets the professionalization of teachers where teachers are empowered to issue and solve practice-related challenges based on decision making processes. This requires quality teachers who possess professional competencies and constantly work on improving their performance levels (LAS-UNICEF, 2010).

To achieve this goal, The Guiding Framework introduced an "Integrated Model" for Arab teachers. This "Integrated Model" acknowledges the necessity of teacher professional development, yet, within its humanitarian framework. The "Integrated Model" rests on major pillars that are aligned with the international policy discourse with respect to providing quality teaching and learning in addition to placing teachers at the heart of school-based reform. For example, pillar one recognized teachers as allies in the education reform process and merely agents of change. It emphasizes the importance of teacher relations within the school that could enable teachers to "forge" collaborative activities and form collegial school culture that fosters teamwork among teachers. Furthermore; pillars four and five advocate the development of schools as institutional contexts and a space for professional activity and dialogue where schools practice autonomy in "school-based professional development for teachers" (LAS-UNICEF, 2010, pp. 34–35).

The Guiding Framework proposes a bundle of projects and programs that represent "A Policy Framework for Teachers' Professional Development." One of the proposed projects is Project 6, titled "Professional Development Units in Schools," which reinforces the principle of "school-based reform" through the implementation of school-based professional development for teachers. The project identifies the effective school system as the system where professional decisions on professional development are made by those who encounter challenges and recognize opportunities based on their daily experience in that place, within that system. Project 6 suggests that school-based professional development units will reinforce the professional and social interaction of teachers helping them to identify the gaps in the teaching and learning processes in addition to implementing professional development programs that address teachers' as well as students' leaning needs. In conclusion, Project 6 as proposed by the Guiding Framework aims at providing a school context that is conducive to professional development for teachers, monitoring and evaluating teachers' learning and teaching practices in action on the ground with the aim of developing teachers' performance levels, and on-going development for teacher professional development programs in light of teachers' performance (LAS-UNICEF, 2010, pp. 69–70).

THE EGYPTIAN CASE STUDY

Egypt is the most populous state in the Arab world. According to the 2012 census, official figures released by the Central Agency for Public Mobilization and Statistics (CAPMAS) indicate that Egypt's population has reached 92 million living on just 5.3% of the country's area. The noticeable feature in the demographics of Egypt is its huge youth bulge, where 34% of the population is under the age of 15. Around 98% of the population is crowded around the narrow stripes of the Nile valley. These demographic features place significant value on the role played by the human capital in Egypt in the process of educational reform. Investment and development of the human capital, represented in Egyptian teachers, form one of the most critical challenges that educational reform must deal with in Egypt.

In 2007, Egypt launched its five-year National Strategic Plan for Pre University Education Reform that marks a paradigm shift in achieving quality education in Egypt. The plan aimed at achieving three main goals: (1) Higher quality of education; (2) Enhanced system efficiency, institutionalized decentralization, and community participation; and (3) Equitable access to education. One of the major pillars in the five-year plan (2007/2008–2011/2012) is "School-Based Reform," which rests on enabling schools to practice autonomy and develop school improvement plans and quality management systems. In addition, the plan sets the strategy of "building sustainable professional development systems based on the cascade training model to provide professional development for teachers at the school level, in addition to building the capacity of leaders at all levels: district, governorate, and central level" (National Strategic Plan, 2007, p. 130). The plan further reinforces the same concept of, the significance of sustainable school-based professional development for teachers, in the chapter titled "Human Resources and Professional Development." In this chapter, the plan acknowledges the dire need for teachers to participate in school-based professional development programs (National Strategic Plan, 2007, p. 140).

Despite the 2011 revolution and its aftermath, there has not been a radical shift in the national planning of education. Egypt's National Strategic Plan for pre-university education (2014–2030) builds on its predecessor with respect to school-based Professional development for teachers. The plan rests on three main pillars: (1) Access; (2) Quality; and (3) Education Management system. The plan identifies professional development as crucial in the process of achieving "school-based reform." Furthermore, it suggests establishing new and innovative mechanisms for continuous monitoring and evaluation of teachers' performance from the perspective of building teachers' capacities and enhancing the teaching and learning competencies of teachers as well as of students.

The establishment of the National Authority for Quality Assurance and Accreditation, (NAQAAE) in 2007 and the Professional Academy for Teachers (PAT) (year) came in response to meeting the national needs for the development and reform of education in Egypt.

THE NATIONAL AUTHORITY FOR QUALITY ASSURANCE AND ACCREDITATION (NAQAAE)

The National Authority for Quality Assurance and Accreditation (NAQAAE) is responsible for disseminating the culture of quality in educational institutions in Egypt, in addition to developing the national standards in alignment with their international equivalents. It aims at restructuring educational institutions through internal and external review systems that would enable these institutions to develop better quality outcomes. To fulfill its designated role, NAQAAE relies on the two main domains of: institutional capacities and educational effectiveness. The first domain comprises five standards: Vision and Mission; Governance and Leadership; Human and Financial resources; Community Participation; and Quality Assurance and Accountability. The second domain constitutes four standards, which are: Learner; Achievements; Teacher Qualifications; Academic Curriculum; and Educational Environment.

The fourth standard "Quality Assurance and Accountability" mandates the enactment of a school-based "Training and Quality Unit" to enhance teachers' performance levels. The school-based Training & Quality Unit is entirely devoted to the design and implementation of "school-based professional development" for teachers based on the on-site teachers' needs and challenges. One of the recommended mechanisms to achieve that goal, as set by NAQAAE, is conducting needs assessment to identify the gaps encountered in the daily practices of teachers. The unit is also encouraged to include teachers' input and vision to bridge the identified gaps in a systemized school-based structure that rests on teachers' collaboration and collegial endeavors. The school-based "Training and Quality Unit" coordinates with the corresponding offices on the district and governorate levels.

The school-based "Training and Quality Unit" is headed by the school deputy for quality and professional development, sometimes also known as "Internal quality assurance analyst." The job description and responsibilities of that position extend over the domains of: leadership and institutional supervision, teaching and learning processes, quality assurance and accreditation, professional development, and community participation.

It is worth mentioning that the core of this position's responsibilities lies in the enactment of the school-based quality units through designing on-going professional programs and plans that address the needs of the local school community. The role additionally extends to providing guidance, support, and continuous constructive feedback within a framework of supportive school culture that encourages teachers to experiment new modes of teaching and learning. Furthermore, the position holder's responsibilities extend beyond the school walls with neighboring school clusters to furnish the exchange of expertise and wider-scope professional dialogue among teachers of different schools. Finally, the position holder supervises the school-based accreditation action teams and acts as the liaison between NAQAAE and his/her school.

THE PROFESSIONAL ACADEMY FOR TEACHERS (PAT)

The Professional Academy for Teachers (PAT) was established in 2008 as part of Egypt's education reform plan. Envisioned to become a regional center of excellence, the PAT has set several goals to build teachers' capacities and support teachers' empowerment. The goals of PAT include setting standards for teachers' promotion, setting standards for teachers' professional development, accrediting teachers' certification, granting teachers' licensures, and supporting educational research studies

The PAT was able to achieve accomplishments, in partnership with some donors, in the field of Egyptian education. Some Examples of PAT's achievements are (El Kharashy, 2010): The strategic plan for The Professional Academy for Teachers (PAT); The promotion matrix for teachers; Job description for teachers' cards; Teachers' performance evaluation tools; Teachers' skills and knowledge matrix; Human resources management system; and a proposed framework for the professional development of school leadership.

It is worth mentioning that one of the main objectives of The National Reform Strategy, launched by the Egyptian government in 2007, and of The Professional Academy for Teachers (PAT), is to enhance and ensure all-inclusive professional development plans for all Egyptian teachers working in the public sector (MENA-OECD, 2010). Nevertheless, the existing professional development strategy is fragmented. It is currently implemented on small scale, rather than covering the whole public teaching force. One of the attributes of this situation might be that education reform hasn't been among the priorities of Egypt's former regime. Another attribute is that endeavors that have taken place so far are the results of small-scale initiatives that are done on the part of donors of worldwide organizations such as the World Bank and the United Nations Development Program (UNDP), in cooperation with the Ministry of Education in Egypt (MENA-OECD, 2010).

Some assessment reports claim that PAT has many gaps to fill in the field of implementing formative professional development strategy and procedures with respect to initial teaching training, induction programs for veteran teachers, which are primarily aimed at teacher empowerment and teacher involvement in decision-making as well as policy-making.

El Kharashy's (2010) assessment report summarizes the gaps that PAT need to fill. He states that PAT has accomplished many achievements. However, it still faces some challenges. Some of the gaps that PAT needs to fill are insufficiency of qualified human resources and lack of assessment tools to evaluate them, absence of internal quality system that ensures ongoing performance self-evaluation, and absence of data base for local and regional professional development needs. Finally, the report emphasizes the need for PAT to reinforce communication with professional educators across the Arab region, in addition to, promoting its programs, mission and vision through various mechanisms locally, regionally, and internationally.

The review of policy discourse on the international, regional, and national level reflects the emphasis on school-based professional development for teachers. It also provides the contextual framework for examining school-based professional development as perceived by teachers in public experimental schools in the Cairo governorate.

RESEARCH METHODS AND DESIGN

The study follows a qualitative approach that includes document review and conducting individual and focus group interviews using semi-structured open-ended questions in addition to the researcher's observation during the school's field visits. A purposive sampling strategy was employed. Male and female teachers from different disciplines, years of experience, and school stages, primary, lower secondary, and high secondary, were sampled. A total of 32 participant teachers who fulfilled these characteristics were nominated by the key informant (school principal), who introduced me to the nominated teacher participants at their work place.

Semi-structured open-ended questions were used to collect data that explored teachers' perceptions and experiences with school-based teacher professional development in their work place.

Interviews were conducted in Arabic then transcribed and translated. I used thematic analysis where I read the interview transcript, my field notes, and personal memos several times to extract themes that both represent and reflect participants' responses. During the process of thematic analysis, I recurrently referred to participants for clarifying some emergent ambiguous points, and/or validating my analysis of their responses.

SCHOOL PROFILE

School X is a compound school that is located in one of Cairo's middle class neighborhoods. It comprises three schools: kindergarten & primary school, preparatory school, and secondary school. Each school has a deputy principal that reports to the general principal of all three schools. The compound of school buildings was founded in 2004 as a donation from one of the Gulf countries' monarchs to act as a model language experimental public school compound. Among the 528 language experimental schools in Cairo governorate, school X is considered among the top schools in terms of its facilities, infrastructure, and teachers' academic caliber. School X currently houses 1708 students placed in 55 classes and 145 teachers, in addition to 13 personnel and two custodians. Most of the teachers have more than 10 years of teaching experience and about half of the teachers have been appointed at the school since its foundation.

The school facilities include a language lab that is equipped to serve 28 students, a multimedia room, library, large theatre, traffic city in the kindergarten building, large dining room, kitchen, cafeteria, clinic and two well equipped lecture halls. It is worth noting that the theatre, cafeteria, dining room and lecture halls appear to be in need for some maintenance and renovation because, according to the teachers, those facilities serve not only the school, but also all other public schools located in the same educational zone.

When the school was founded and for several years after, it was considered a privilege to join the school either as a student (for his/her parents) or as a teacher. For parents the school offered good education with affordable fees for the middleclass families through experienced and well prepared teachers that could compete with those of private language schools. Furthermore, the teacher: student ratio was 1:25, which is quite less than the ratio at other public schools that could reach 1:75 (School Key Informant). Teachers at the school were privileged because they received 200% bonus over their basic salaries, which as per the Egyptian education law, is the highest among all state public schools. Teachers were appointed after screening through interviews and written English test. Likewise, students were admitted after their parents were successfully interviewed. While not abiding to the geographical zone regulation set by the Ministry of Education, the school would accept students from any part of Cairo if they are qualified for admission. Since 2011, the school started accepting a larger number of students, increasing the class capacity to 33, after a considerable decrease in the school fees, a procedure that wasn't positively received by the teachers as they thought that this was leading to a decline in the quality of the service they are providing.

As with the rest of most of the experimental language schools in Egypt, school leadership in School X was chosen from the English Language department; except for the last two years when the school leadership was appointed from the Math department.

FINDINGS AND DISCUSSION

The overall findings show teachers' perceptions of their roles and responsibilities and their experiences with school-based teacher professional development inside their schools.

Teachers' Roles and Responsibilities

Teachers as leaders. The majority of participant teachers identify themselves as leaders but only on the classrooms level. They identify their roles as teachers who deliver lesson plans, instruct and assess students' academic performance, proctor and grade exams, attend weekly department meetings, in addition to, carrying out some super visional duties in the school playgrounds during break time and on the school corridors during classes.

During the focus group interviews, I noticed that most teachers refrain from leadership roles, that are either voluntarily or mandatory, because they think leadership roles would make them more accountable before the principal, or more liable to receive blame and criticism from both the principal and their colleagues, which they completely reject and did not want to experience .

More importantly, participant teachers view leadership roles as more responsibility and work load that "will not be appreciated", the head of the English department says. He adds that he has around five teachers in his department, plus himself, that hold the Professional Educator Diploma in educational leadership from the American University in Cairo which is perceived as "one of the best educational institutions in Egypt", he proudly states. Nevertheless, he is struggling to implement some of the knowledge and techniques that he learnt because the school leadership doesn't favor implementing new ideas or initiatives and prefer to "adhere to the known and experimented, rather than fostering innovative approaches."

Despite all the above mentioned challenges, the head of the English department has managed to implement delegation among early career teachers e since "it is always easier to coach a young group especially if they are homogeneous." He adds that teachers in the primary school are more responsive to change and implementing new approaches in instruction than teachers in the middle or high school. However, he appreciated having a mixed age group that includes able experienced teachers as well as novice teachers, the latter for him represents "new blood and thirst for learning." When I interviewed this group of teachers, they described themselves as a family that helps one another. They don't know how it began, as the most experienced teacher says, "but it was always the culture here to volunteer to help one another and to support any new teacher joins, s/he catches on and starts behaving the same." Another supporting factor is that those teachers refused and do not give private lessons, accordingly there exists no rivalry that would negatively affect their work as a team. In spite of the fact that those teachers are, to some extent, fulfilling their roles as teacher leaders, they were reluctant to identify themselves as leaders. From their perspective, they are "unqualified" to become leaders and that they are not "equipped" enough to benefit and support one another professionally as they would want. They believe that they need an off-site school expert and coach to teach them new trends and techniques in teaching and learning, help them grow professionally, and motivate them to perform their best. The ideal case, as described by one of them, is to have "professional development that is balanced between an off-site coach and a school based professional development coordinator because we can't do it alone."

Teachers as decision makers. The majority of participant teachers' responses state that teachers have no role in the decision making process inside the school whether or not it pertains to school-based professional development for teachers. The majority of responses suggest that none of the teachers were involved in the design or delivery of any workshops or sessions targeting teacher professional development. Many of the respondent teachers, especially in the foundation and primary stages, did not know the name of the person in charge of the school-based training unit. It should be noted that School X as accredited school, similar to all accredited schools in

Egypt, must have a school-based Quality and Training unit that is responsible for school-based teacher professional development activities and that is also linked to the Quality and Training head office in the Directorate of Education.

Two identified exceptions among the interviewees are a high school Arabic teacher and another high school English teacher. The Arabic high school teacher states that he has once designed a 30-minute power point presentation for the Arabic language department. In this context, the Arabic teacher explains that he volunteered to do the presentation because he had been working for seven years in an American school in Saudi Arabia where teachers used to do these type of activities for knowledge sharing periodically. Thus, he wanted to transfer this experience to the school in Egypt as he found it to be beneficial for teachers. The teacher adds that he was never approached by his head of department or the head of the school based training unit to design or deliver any professional development sessions afterwards. Similarly, the high school English teacher says he has designed a comprehensive teacher professional development program for the entire high school. He then adds that the program was never implemented on the grounds but rather it was designed to fulfill the accreditation dossier requirement set by NAQAAE. Moreover, the vast majority of respondents have not participated in any "needs assessment" conducted in their schools. However, most of the participants exhibited knowledge of needs assessment as a requirement for school accreditation by NAQAAE. A middle school English teacher describes the Needs Assessment as "perfectly set in the school accreditation dossier."

Teachers agreed of their role as "passive recipients of the decisions taken by the school leadership," as described by a female primary school Arabic teacher. To elaborate more on this point, participant teachers said that during the past year of the revolution aftermath, the school leadership decided to use surveillance cameras that were placed in the school playground, gates, and corridors. None of the teachers were consulted by the school leadership before taking this action. In fact, teachers did not learn about the cameras until they were actually fixed in their places, even though there is a teacher representative on the school-board. In this respect, it is worth mentioning that nearly only the English department teachers knew the name of the elected teacher representative on the school-board because he was their head of department, whereas the majority of teachers from other disciplines did not know who their representative on the school-board was. Cameras were purchased by the parents through the parents' council. The school leadership introduced the idea to the parents who regarded the idea as a safety measure given the security conditions the country was going through.

Lack of professional dialogue. Participant teachers say, they are burdened with substitute periods almost on a daily basis due to the relatively high-rate of other colleague teachers' absence. As a primary school teacher of sciences says, "there is no time for conducting professional dialogue or discussing any academic problem." She adds that the weekly department meetings are mostly devoted to informing teachers about new decisions or instructions that have been issued by the school leadership or the educational district. A high school math teacher adds that he and colleagues face a challenge in that they cannot attend weekly department meetings since they are usually teaching primary or middle school at that time to cover the shortage in teachers at the school. In this respect, teachers are also absent because they are busy with private lessons and must leave their school during the school day to deliver private tutoring—a huge source of income especially among teachers of math, Arabic, English, and sciences in the middle and high school stages. When I asked how the school leadership deals with this, as it seems that it was a well-known information across the whole school, some participant teachers said that those things could always be worked out or as a geography middle school teacher puts it, "things are to go smoothly if you are on good terms with the principal, or if you are a math teacher because the principal used to be the head of the math department and he treats the math teachers with nepotism." The other reason behind teachers' absence is that some teachers work in more than one school within the same educational district because of the shortage in the number of teachers teaching certain subjects, mostly English, math and sciences.

Teachers' Perceptions on School-Based Professional Development

School leadership as a support base. The majority of participant teachers do not feel they are supported by the school leadership to fulfill their role as teachers. They don't see the school leadership playing an effective role in the professional growth of teachers. The vast majority suggests that the role of the school leadership is "managerial more than anything else." As a high school math teacher puts it, "they [school administration] all are, our principal is no exception." The majority of participant teachers say that the principal is responsible for all administrative issues that concern teacher attendance, punctuality, and classroom management among other managerial tasks. With respect to teacher professional development, it is the responsibility of the district supervisor and the school-based head-of-department or senior teacher of the subject matter. Most of the teachers don't think it would be beneficial if the principal acts as an instructional leader. Only the teachers who hold a diploma in educational leadership expressed that the school leadership could help all teachers develop professionally if it adopts the transformational leadership model. However, all participant teachers agree that the school leadership is not fulfilling its role in fostering a culture that promotes professional dialogue and exchange of experience. A primary school French teacher says that she heard about teachers at the school who hold a professional diploma; although she wants to learn from them how to develop herself as a teacher and learn about new trend in education, there is no time devoted to do, thus she holds the school leadership responsible for this matter. Holders of the same diploma express similar feelings, for example, a middle school teacher of sciences says, he would appreciate if the school allocates time for teachers by rotation to exchange knowledge and experience with their fellows and allow them to implement the gained knowledge and techniques. "It is very frustrating to look at my diploma hanging on the wall when I can't implement what I have learnt even on my department's level," a high school math teacher says.

Nepotism is one of the factors that most of participant teachers identify as hindering the school leadership to act as a support base for school-based teacher professional development. Participant teachers, from disciplines other than math, think that the school leadership favors math teachers over other teachers. In this context, it is interesting to mention that some math teachers stated that English teachers used to be favored by the previous school principal who used to be an English teacher.

Lack of a structured system for school-based teacher professional development. The majority of participant teachers expressed that they lack a systemized structure for school-based teacher professional development, as mentioned earlier by one of the high school teachers. Participant teachers, who have participated in preparing the school dossier for accreditation, say that such structured system exists but only on paper. A high school French teacher says that he doesn't believe that the head of the School-based Training and Quality Unit (STQU) could help him become a better teacher. He adds, "that person [head of STQU] was chosen for this position not because she is competent or qualified, but because she had the least packed schedule as she teaches an elective subject." This comment represents a shared view among many participant teachers who expressed the need for a monitoring and evaluating process that is transparent in order to ensure that what's documented is implemented in practice. It should be mentioned that the Ministry of Education has set a criterion for the position of the head of STQU that also includes the job description and responsibilities, nevertheless, participants believed that the announced criterion was not followed or implemented.

Dominance of the centralized system. Despite the fact that the education system in Egypt has been trying to shift from the centralized system towards more decentralized approaches, which is clearly reflected in Egypt strategic plan for education reform 2005 and the draft issued in 2014, the majority of participant teachers' responses suggest that the centralized administering system is still domineering over new trends of delegation and distributed leadership that aim at building teachers' capacities. A middle school science teacher says that "it is futile to initiate change or development in teachers' capacities when our seniors or those in positions hold the same centralized mindsets."

The majority of participant teachers did not know that the PAT provides professional development sessions and training for teachers. The few teachers that exhibited knowledge stated that PAT used to provide the service free of charge, however, at the present time, teachers who wish to register for professional development training must pay for it. Teacher professional development is currently managed by the district supervision. Professional development workshops are designed by the district supervisor that gathers teachers of the same subject matter for training, but according to the majority of participant teachers, this happens once or twice at the most throughout the entire academic year.

IMPLICATIONS FOR POLICY AND PRACTICE

> An education system is good as its teachers. Unlocking their potentials is essential to enhancing the quality of learning. Education quality improves when teachers are supported- it deteriorates if they are not. (GMR, 2013/2014, p. i)

This study aimed at examining the policy discourse on school-based professional development for teachers to identify to what extent the government has adopted school-based professional development for teachers as an approach. In addition, it intended to identify the extent to which public schools in Egypt implement this approach through the examination of teachers' experiences and perceptions on school-based professional development for teachers in a public language school that offers elementary and secondary education. The purpose was to better understand if there is a gap between the policy discourse and the actual practice at school level as perceived by participant teachers and to uncover the reasons behind this gap.

The results of the study reveal that there exists a gap between policy discourse and practice at school level with respect to school-based professional development for teachers. Participant teachers' responses identify the main impediments that stand between realizing the policy discourse into practice. School leaders play a key role in improving school outcomes by influencing the motivations and capacities of teachers, as well as the school climate and environment, while the policy discourse in Egypt emphasizes the significant role of the autonomous school leader that can communicate a vision of shared goals that ultimately improve the learning outcomes of learners. From the perspective of interviewed teachers, the school leadership does not support their professional growth or nurture a school culture that is cooperative, collegial, and conducive to teacher life-long learning. The deeply rooted bureaucratic system is still dominating school leadership practice that is supposed to be autonomous. Participant teachers say that the school leadership is burdened with administrative tasks that are extremely time consuming leaving very little or no time at all to building their teachers' capacities in terms of fostering school-based teacher professional development. Nevertheless, participant teachers state that they have had three previous individual female school leaders that were initiators, proactive, innovative, and transformational in their leadership style. In light of this, school leadership is proposed to be subject to individual differences among school principals which should not be the case as all school principals should be practicing through a guiding framework that considers each school's individual culture and environment. In this context, the sample responses point blame at the process of preparing, monitoring, and evaluating the capabilities and leadership practices of school leaders. They recommend an air-tight selection process for school leaders that is based on competency.

Examining the policy discourse, it was found that there are screening tools for the selection process of school leaders. After potential school leaders have been accepted as qualified, they receive training and preparation courses, however, most of the training is devoted to managerial, administrative, and fiscal issues with quite minor focus on leadership skills and styles in a way that should enable those leaders to be the catalyst for change at their own schools.

Dominance of the centralized system is also another factor that is hindering schools to adopt and implement school-based professional development for teachers. While the school-based Training and Quality unit is responsible for, among other responsibilities, school-based professional development for teachers, we find that the district supervision is also primarily responsible for the professional development for teachers with each subject having its general district supervisor that is in charge of several schools within his/her district managing teachers with the help of the senior school based teacher in a clear centralized and cascaded process. In this context, it is important to have a clear organizational flow chart that demonstrates the job responsibilities for each of the heads of the school-based Training and Quality unit, the district supervisor and the school principal with respect to conducting and fostering school-based professional development for teachers, which could act as the first building block in establishing professional learning communities. More importantly, there should be a well-structured system and process for monitoring and evaluating the performance of all stakeholders that are accountable for teacher professional learning.

Institutions' failing to fulfill their designated role represent an obstacle in the implementation of school-based professional development for teachers. The Professional Academy for Teachers (PAT), according to some assessment reports, has many gaps to fill in terms of professional development for teachers. El Kharashy's (2010) assessment report summarizes the gaps that PAT needs to fill. He states that PAT has accomplished many achievements, however, it still faces some challenges. Some of the gaps that PAT needs to fill are insufficiency of qualified human resources and lack of assessment tools to evaluate them, absence of internal quality system that ensures ongoing performance self-evaluation, and absence of data base for local and regional professional development needs.

Finally, teachers must be considered as "allies" and not merely "tools" in the process of school-based reform where school-based professional development for teachers occupies the central place. The concept of teacher leadership needs to be emphasized in the policy discourse and this concept must be transferred and communicated at school level. Policy makers need to understand that maximizing the learning outcomes for the students comes in parallel with enhancing and maximizing teacher learning, for if we want to have a generation of life-long learners as students, we need to cater for a generation of "reflective practitioners" and life-long learners of teachers as well.

ACKNOWLEDGEMENTS

I would like to thank the teachers who participated in this study. I would also like to address my sincere thanks to Dr. Nagwa Megahed, Associate Professor, Ain Shams University and The American University in Cairo, for her mentorship and valuable review, feedback and comments throughout the development of this study.

REFERENCES

Butler, D., & Leahy, M. (2003). *The teachnet Ireland project as a model for professional development for teachers*. Dublin: St, Patrick's College of Education, Dublin City University. Retrieved from http://teachersnetwork.org/effectiveteachers/images/CTQ_FULLResearchReport_021810.pdf

Central Agency for Public Mobilization and Statistics. (2012). *Population Demographics*. Egypt. Retrieved from http://www.capmas.gov.eg/Pages/SemanticIssuesPage.aspx?page_id=6155

Egypt's national strategic plan. (2007/2012). Retrieved from http://planipolis.iiep.unesco.org/.../Egypt/

Ministry of Education. (2014). *Egypt's national strategic plan for pre-university education 2014–2030*. Egypt: Misistry of Education. Retrieved from http://www.unesco.org/education/edurights/media/docs/c33b72f4c03c58424c5ff258cc6aeaee0eb58de4.pdf

Egypt. National Authority for Quality Assurance and Accreditation of Education. Retrieved from http://naqaae.eg/

El Kharashy, S. (2010, December). *Arab centers for excellence: Professional academy for teachers, Egypt: Perspectives on the mission and the priorities of building capacities*. (Working Paper) [in Arabic].

Feiman-Nemser, S. (2001). From preparation to practice: Designing a continuum to strengthen and sustain teaching. *Teachers College Record, 103*(6), 1013–1055.

Fishman, B. J., Marx, R. W., Best, S., & Tal, R. T. (2003). Linking teacher and student learning to improve professional development in systemic reform. *Teaching and Teacher Education, 19*(6), 643–658.

Garet, M., Porter, A., Desimone, L., Birman, B., & Koon, C. (2001). What makes professional development effective? *American Education Researcher, 38*(4), 915–945.

Glickman, C., Gordon, S., & Ross-Gordon, J. (2010). *Supervision and instructional leadership*. Boston, MA: Pearson education, Inc.

Lambert, L. (2000). *Building leadership capacity in schools* [Monograph]. Australian Council for Educational Research. Retrieved from http://research.acer.edu.au/cgi/viewcontent.cgi?article=1000&context=apc_monographs

League of Arab states & United Nations children's fund. (2010). *Guiding framework of performance standards for Arab teachers: Policies and programs*. Cairo: League of Arab States & United Nations children's fund.

Leithwood, K. A., & Riehl, C. (2003). *What we know about successful school leadership*. Philadelphia, PA: Laboratory for Student Success, Temple University.

Middle East and North Africa & Organization for Economic Cooperation and Development. (2010). *Business climate development strategy: Phase 1 policy assessment, Egypt, human capital*. Paris: OCED. Retrieved from http://www.scribd.com/doc/46727327/Competitiveness-and-Private-Sector-Development-Egypt-2010-2510041e

OECD. (2008). *Improving school leadership volume 1: Policy and Practice*. Paris: OECD. Retrieved December 13, 2013, from ERIC.

Opfer, V., & Peddar, D. (2011). Conceptualizing teacher professional learning. *Review of Educational Research, 81*(3), 376–407.

Organization for Economic Cooperation and Development. (2005). *Teachers matter: Attracting, developing and retaining effective teachers*. Paris: OECD. Retrieved from www.nefmi.gov.hu/.../oecd_publication_teachers_matter_english_06

Schwille, J., Dembélé, M., & Schubert, J. (2007). *Global perspectives on teacher learning: Improving policy and practice*. Paris: UNESCO.

Stronge, J. H., Gareis, C. R., & Little, C. A. (2012). *Teacher pay & teacher quality: Attracting, developing, and retaining the best teachers.* Moorabbin: Hawker Brownlow Education.

UNESCO. (n.d.). *The global monitoring report 2013/2014: Implications for a renewed agenda for teachers and quality education.* Paris: UNESCO. Retrieved from https://en.unesco.org/events/global-monitoring-report-20132014-implications-renewed-agenda-teachers-and-quality-education.

Wallace, F. (2013). *The school principal as leader: Guiding schools to better teaching and learning, perspective* (Expanded ed.). New York, NY: Wallace Foundation.

Wei, R., Darling-Hammond, L., Andree, A., Richardson, N., & Orphanos, S. (2009). *Professional learning in the learning profession: A status report on teacher development in the United States and abroad.* Dallas, TX: National Staff Development Council. Retrieved from www.learningforward.org/news/NSDCstudytechnicalreport2009.pdf

Amira Abdou
Graduate School of Education
The American University in Cairo (AUC)

SARA TARAMAN

8. STUDENTS' PERCEPTIONS OF THE QUALITY OF HIGHER EDUCATION

A Case Study of a Remote Public University in Egypt

INTRODUCTION

Higher Education (HE) institutions foster intellectual growth, cultural awareness, social interaction, and personal change. Besides graduating productive students, the universities' role has developed to include the development of the surrounding community; what the UNESCO called the "*Third Mission*" (UNESCO, The Role of Higher Education in Promoting Lifelong Learning, 2015). Consequently, there has been a high concern about quality and quality assurance measures in educational institutions, especially in higher education. Speaking of Egypt, since Mohamed Ali's era, establishing a higher education system that offers quality education and professional training has been a priority. Yet, finding the appropriate institutions, recruiting qualified professors, and preparing competent students have always been key concerns (Maḥmūd & Nās, 2003, p. 31). Currently, there are more than 90 different higher-education institutions(Central Agency for Public Mobilization and Statistics, 2013). Yet, none of them were included in the 2012–2013 university top ranking (Thomson Reuters).

Despite the increase in the number of HE institutions, the quality has been always questioned. Egypt's rank, in terms of the quality of higher education, has declined from 80 out of 114 countries in 2005/2006 to 128 out of 139 in 2010/2011 (Reda, 2012). A product of a dictatorship era, which gave birth to the January 25th uprising, the current education system has been too centralized and overly dominated by rigid governmental control. Universities have limited autonomy needed for introducing new curricula that match the continuously changing market demands. Many of the Egyptian universities have inadequate incentives to renovate or internationalize their programs. From 1982 to 2006, the Gross Enrollment Rate (GER) in HE has almost doubled. It moved from 16% to 28.57% (Strategic Planning Unit, Minsitry of Higher Education, 2010). Yet, the unemployment rate among university graduates remains at a high rate of 14% (Strategic Planning Unit, Minsitry of Higher Education, 2010).

In 2012 and as an after-effect of the January 25th Revolution, it was announced that there is a project for building forty public universities in the upcoming period, most of them are in remote areas in Egypt where there is a lack of university graduates who can contribute to the development of their communities (Fathy,

2012). The current routine for establishing a university in Egypt starts with creating a branch from an existing one. Once the branch has seven different colleges, the branch can be turned into a university. One example for that is the Matrouh Branch affiliated with Alexandria University. While HE institutions were widely spread by the 1960s in Egypt, the first college introduced to Matrouh[1] governorate was in 1993. In 2005, only 2% of the total high school students in Matrouh pursued their higher education degrees; this led the government to introduce five more colleges. Currently, there are six colleges as well as three different open-education[2] ones affiliated to the Alexandria University and located in Matrouh. As part of the reform development plan, Matrouh branch is expected to be one of the forty promised universities.

Expected to be a completely separate university with the continuous expansion of colleges, the current quality of higher education in Matrouh-Branch of Alexandria University, represents an interesting case. It exemplifies the status of higher education in remote areas within the Republic. The available colleges at these branches, are designed and established based on the need of the community. Consequently, an assessment for the quality of HE in these areas is necessary to better cater for their needs. The assessment is vital, given the crucial role of higher education in producing agents of change who can contribute to the development of their community and can compete globally.

Particularly, this study examines how students as the first beneficiary of the educational services, in the different colleges available in Matrouh, perceive the quality of education in terms of:

i. The educational environment, with a focus on the availability of efficient educational facilities and the soundness of the organization's culture.
ii. The quality of teaching and learning experience.
iii. The quality of education outcomes, not only for the job pursuit but also for community service.

Before exploring the perceptions of Egyptian students in regard to higher education quality, a discussion of educational quality and the importance of students' voices, especially in higher education is presented and followed by a description of Matrouh governorate as the local context of this study.

QUALITY IN HIGHER EDUCATION INSTITUTIONS

Quality is a multidimensional process that cannot be measured by and in itself. Since quality is a relative term (Harvey & Green, 1993), benchmarks have to be set to measure it. Based on the UNESCO "Policy Paper for Change and Development in Higher Education"(UNESCO, 1995) and the World Conference on Higher Education (UNESCO, 1998), quality of education includes excellent teaching and non-teaching staff, students, and accreditors; it consists of outstanding academic programs, funding agencies, research, infrastructure, and community service plans.

Yet, different groups of stakeholders have a different view of what quality means given their interest/work in HE. As a result, when talking about quality, defining whose quality is being investigated is important. Notably, the variables that define quality change in time and circumstances. In this research, quality is defined by the transformative definition of quality given by Harvey and Green (1993) as well as the definition of quality of graduates given by Crombag (1978). The transformative concept of quality is rooted in the notion of "qualitative change" (Harvey & Green, 1993, p. 24). In that sense, "transformation is not restricted to apparent or physical transformation but also includes cognitive transcendence" (Harvey & Green, 1993); "value added" is used to measure quality of education in terms of knowledge, abilities, and skills of students. Furthermore, Crombag (1978), specifically, distinguished between quality of education and quality of graduates. He defined quality of education as a synonym for "efficiency of education" (Crombag, 1978). He defines it as "the ratio of the average quality of the graduates and the average costs per graduate – costs incurred by the educational institution as well as by the student" (Crombag, 1978). On the other hand, he defined quality of graduates as "the amount of subject matter learned and the depth to which it is mastered by the students" (Crombag, 1978). Thus, the definition of quality in this research refers to the quality of education, which equips students with knowledge, abilities, and skills to be an agent of change in their communities.

Being the main recipients of educational services, students' perceptions of their experience and of the quality of education received have been increasingly a concern for scholars, educators and reformers. In his article entitled "Sound, Presence, and Power: Student Voice in Educational Research and Reform", Cook-Sather states that "young people have unique perspectives on learning, teaching, and schooling; that their insights warrant not only the attention but also the responses of adults; and that they should be afforded opportunities to actively shape their education" (Cook-Sather, 2006). Since they are the direct recipients of education, listening attentively to student's opinions and suggestions about their learning empowers the educational process. Considering students' voice acknowledges their right as active citizens within the school. For their voices to be heard, school culture needs to be positively responsive, friendly, and interactive while addressing student's problems. Teachers and administration should tolerate student's opinion if it was not in their favor and should not use their power against them. This leads to the importance of examining the pillars that constitutes a good quality of higher education institutions.

Resources (human, financial or technical) and infrastructure are essential factors that make up a competitive institution. However, resources alone cannot provide a performing educational institution. Other essential factors are vital, such as governance and leadership policies, quality assurance measures, research produced, community service, the institution's culture, students' engagement, professional development for staff, and student's employability after graduation. These aspects all together shape and contribute to students' experience and their preparation as change agents and lifelong learners, as follows:

Governance and Strategic Management

A strategic plan has a crucial role in articulating the institutional mission and vision, prioritizing resources, and promoting organizational focus. Yet, it usually lacks information about the effective process through which an institution achieves them. According to Wu (2012), Douglas Toma, in "Building Organizational Capacity: Strategic Management in Higher Education", addressed the framework of building capacity of an organization. The framework is based on eight main pillars. The "Institutional Purpose" pillar defines the missions and aspirations embedded in an institution. The second pillar sets the organizational chart of an institution. Continually, "Governance" pillar deals with the leadership and decision-making process, while the "Policies" aspect of the strategic management defines the regulations for the operations of the organization. Furthermore, there should be a way for generating information and communicating data. Finally, institutional "Infrastructure" as well as "Culture" should be defined to constitute the last two pillars of this strategic planning model (Wu, 2012).

Research

Faculty members, who are researchers, are considered reflective practitioners (Rowland, Byron, Furedi, Padfield, & Smyth, 1998; Katz & Coleman, 2001). Research helps identify and solve problems related to teaching and learning. Although Rowland et al. (1998) believe that there should not be a correlation between research and teaching. Anderson (2007), in his response to their article, suggests that collaborative research between students and professors, in higher education, gives better understanding of the subject, strengthens the relationship between students and their professors, and fosters the learning for both. Universities that have a high rate of research have high student enrollment rate and diversified student body (Katz & Coleman, 2001).

Teaching and Learning

Despite the emphasis on academic teaching staff's role, professors' qualifications usually are not equally emphasized (Coates, 2005); the thing which jeopardizes the quality assurance of the students' learning process. The empirical work for Lammers and Murphy (2002) argues that although lecturers in HE have an essential role in delivering information, they do not necessarily stimulate student's thoughts, or change attitudes. Additionally, an assessment of student's perceptions in quality of HE done by Hill, Lomas and MacGregor (2005), students concur that professors who were encouraging and showed enthusiasm, positively affected the learning process. Unfortunately, usually, student's learning is measured by passing an exam. However, what is being neglected is the authentic knowledge that a student has acquired throughout the years (Lammers & Murphy, 2002). Notably, learning is relative to many factors, some of which are: the student's interest, the difficulty of the subject matter being studied, teaching staff qualifications, and whether the student is making an effort to understand the subject (Coates, 2005).

Community Engagement

Currently, performing institutions of HE expand their role beyond teaching and research. The new role of higher education institutions involves real social transformation through community involvement (Bernardo, Butcher, & Howard, 2012). This is what UNESCO (UNESCO, 2015, p. 20) refers to as the "Third Mission" of higher education. The activities of community engagement change by the institution/country. For example, in the Australian context, community involvement is considered as a hands-on experience for what is being studied in class (Bernardo, Butcher, & Howard, 2012). On the other hand, in the United Kingdom, there are two models; the first of which is responding to a specific need of the community regardless of the curriculum and only aims at developing students' sense of belongingness. The second model addresses the academic requirements based on benefiting the community. Hence, community engagement emphasizes the interrelationship between the university and the community (Bernardo, Butcher, & Howard, 2012).

Employability

Employability gives an indication of the qualifications, skills and experiences that a university has equipped its students with (Coates, 2005). Although job opportunities might be considered as an indicator for quality of education, "employment outcomes can be influenced by a range of non-educational factors, such as institutional reputation, personal networks, and labor market conditions" (Coates, 2005). The literature on education and employment is explained through many models, most of which are based on the human capital theory. Concerning Egyptian employment, El-Hamidi (2008) proposed two models of employability in relation to education. The first model advocates the job competition model, which assesses the candidate's educational level in respect to the cost of investing on job training. The second model is the assignment model, where the emphasis is on the ability to accomplish the task efficiently regardless of the candidate's academic level or background (El-Hamidi, 2008). In both cases, there is a mismatch between the graduates' jobs and their education.

Student Engagement

Since learning is influenced by participating in educationally purposeful activities, constructivist theory can best explain the importance of student engagement. Educational institutions (represented in the teaching staff and the administration) have to set up the conditions, opportunities, and expectations that help students participate. The set-up might include better teacher-student relationships, sufficient places promoting group work and collaboration, the use of active learning, and/or depending on hands-on experience (Coates, 2005). On the student's side, learners have to put quality effort and challenge themselves to learn and interact with new ideas. Johnstone believes that "we need to focus more on the student and his or her training, and to be a little less preoccupied with, and critical of, the faculty (and all the rest of the administrative, professional, and clerical support staff of our colleges and universities) in our question for more productivity" (Johnstone, 1993, p. 4). In that sense, learning can be viewed as "a joint proposition" between students and teachers (Coates, 2005, p. 26). Although the process of quality assurance at universities is done through collecting data, there is high emphasis on information about institutions and teaching while less attention is given to what students are actually doing or what they really think about their institution (Coates, 2005). Besides measuring the real impact and performance of educational institutions, examining students' perspectives on the quality of education acknowledges their right as active citizens within the school. It empowers them and gives them a sense of belongingness and ownership. Some of the elements that determine the quality of higher education are: students being proactive in learning, student-teacher relationship, pedagogy techniques, the authentic knowledge acquired, social responsibility and community involvement, as well as internships and job market preparation.

With the ramifications of the January 25th upraising, examining educational quality as perceived by students at the Matrouh-Branch of Alexandria University offers a demonstrated example of youth perceptions of educational quality during the time of political transition and social unrest in Egypt. In addition, given the expected returns of higher education for societal development, in remote areas catering higher education for the needs of the marginalized areas and disadvantaged groups could be a means for empowering youth, developing communities, and providing equal opportunities to different segments of the society.

HIGHER EDUCATION IN MATROUH

As per the latest available data by the CAPMAS (Central Agency for Public Mobilization and Statistics, 2013), in 2006, higher education degree holders counted for only 8.9% of the total population of Matrouh at that time.[3] Until 2005, Matrouh had only one college serving its population, which is the College of Education. In an urge for more university degree holders who can contribute to the development of the city, in 2005, the governor of Matrouh demanded establishing a university. Consequently, more colleges, which are financed through the Governorate Central Office "*dewana'am el mohafaza*" and supported by teaching staff from Alexandria University, started to be established in Matrouh. Currently, there are six regular colleges (Agriculture, Education, Hotel Management, Kindergarten, Nursing, and Veterinary Medicine) as well as three affiliated "Open University" colleges (Education, Commerce, and Law. Due to financial constraints, there is no devoted buildings or one main campus accommodating the different colleges. Currently, colleges are occupying other institutions' buildings. For example, Veterinary Medicine and Agriculture colleges have been renting and sharing a school in Foka city (about 1.5 hours away from the capital). Before establishing the branch, only 2% of the *ThanawyaAmma*[4] (Egyptian secondary school diploma) holders in Matrouh pursued their higher education degrees due to the high cost of living in another town, as well as the conservative nature of the community, which does not encourage traveling for educational purposes. Currently, with the availability of different colleges in Matrouh, the number of students who pursue higher education increased from 2% to 13%.

The affiliated branch in Matrouh follows the organizational and educational structure of Alexandria University—i.e., it follows the same rules and regulations of the main university. Moreover, the curriculum of a given major taught in both locations is expected to be the same. Matrouh was no exception in calling for better living conditions after the January 25th revolution, though it usually went unnoticed due to being distant from the center of events.[5] For example, there were some demands for better infrastructure, enhancement of the facilities in different sectors, and better quality of education in all levels.

RESEARCH METHODOLOGY

This research is a case study that focuses on examining students' opinions on the educational quality of the Matrouh branch of Alexandria University. It intends to analyze the effectiveness of the educational environment, the pattern of teaching and learning, and the role of college in empowering students rather than simply preparing them for a specific job after graduation. A pilot study was the start of this research, through which the sample of colleges and students were designed.

The research was carried out using mixed method (quantitative/qualitative). In this research framework, quantitative data is *complementary* for qualitative data. The sample in this research included four colleges in the Matrouh branch with regular student enrollment that have been operating for more than 4 years. The design of the research strategy included: College of Agriculture, College of Education, College of Nursing, and College of Veterinary Medicine. The targeted student sample included the second and third year students who happened to be the cohorts who joined the different colleges right after the January 25th, 2011 uprising. To make sure that students' perceptions of the educational quality were not affected by the political instability, one focus group discussion per academic year was conducted with students whose course of study preceded 2011 revolution (fourth and fifth year students). A total number of 24 focus group discussions were conducted and lasted on average about 30–35 minutes. Table 1 shows the number of students who participated in the focus group discussions per academic year and gender.

Semi-structured interviews with some administrators and faculty members were conducted to get better understanding of the issues addressed by the students. Finally, a convenient sample was chosen from each of the four colleges to take a survey. The survey was designed, with adaptation, using the Student's Handbook for

Accreditation and Quality designed by the National Authority for Quality Assurance and Accreditation in Egypt (NAQAAE). While the first part of the survey dealt with the respondent's profile, the second part consisted of 17 questions using a 5-degree Likert scale. A total number of 237 valid surveys was collected with Cronbach's Alpha coefficient = 0.838. This sample constitutes about 41% of the total population.

Tables 1 and 2 show the number of students who participated in the focus group discussions and the survey by gender and academic year. It is important to note that the total number of female students is higher than male students. This is more likely because female students, by records, are the dominant gender in these four colleges.

Table 1. Number of students in the focus group discussions by gender

	Females	Males	Total
Second Year	48	25	73
Third Year	55	28	83
Fourth Year	10	8	18
Fifth Year	5	5	10
Total	116	66	184

Table 2. Total collected surveys by gender and acadmic year

		Year Second	Year Third	Total
GENDER	FEMALE	81 (34%)	68 (29%)	149 (63%)
	MALES	38 (16%)	50 (21%)	88 (37%)
TOTAL		119 (50%)	118 (50%)	237 (100%)

FINDINGS

The findings of the research show a general dissatisfaction of the quality provided to students. To understand students' perceptions, I begin by identifying their reasons for choosing specific major/college. Then, I discuss their perceptions of educational quality in terms of institutional facilities/infrastructure, organizational culture, especially in relation to students' freedom of speech, teaching and learning experience, and education for career pursuit and community service.

Students' Reason for Choosing the College

The reasons behind joining the specific college were addressed in the demographics question in the survey. Results show that almost 50% of the sample joined their respective college because of their score in the High School Certificate (*ThanawyaAmma*).[6] The second reason was attributed to the "*Family*" and counted for 32%. Family reasons included: not allowing females to study in another city, students having to look after their parents, or families were worried about sending their offspring to study in another city after the January 25th Revolution with the presence of ongoing protests and demonstrations. Only 14% of the sample had "Passion for the Future Career." Furthermore, 18% of the sample had different reasons including: financial constraints or participants' health problems, as shown in Table 3.

Table 3. Reasons for choosing the college

Why did you join the college?	Gender		Total
	Female	Males	
Score	64 (27%)	45 (19%)	109 (46%)
Family	64 (27%)	11 (5%)	75 (32%)
Passion to the Future Career	11 (5%)	23 (10%)	34 (14%)
Others	10 (4%)	8 (3%)	18 (8%)
Total	149 (63%)	88 (37%)	237 (100%)

Educational Facilities

The findings reveal a general dissatisfaction with educational facilities. About 70% of the surveyed sample disagreed that the college was providing them with quality educational resources/facilities (library, laboratories, lecturing halls... etc.). Reasons for inadequate facilities can be attributed to the fact that the majority of colleges did not have fixed places for lecturing due to financial constraints that hindered providing a decent educational venue. As expressed by participant students, this negatively affected their feeling of belongingness to their respective college. For example, one of the colleges does not have an independent building. The college operates by sharing the building of Ras El Hekma Emergency Hospital (70 kilometers away from the main city). Students confirmed that sharing the place led to many problems for both the college and the hospital.

In the few colleges that have their devoted buildings, auditorium halls were described as underequipped. Some lecturing halls are not supported by appropriate technology (computers and projectors). As one of the students commented "Although lecturing halls are big enough to accommodate the number of students, the technology provided does not support the educational process. The projectors and computers are almost malfunctioned and do not facilitate the professor's mission in class." Further, findings of the fieldwork showed that the laboratories, in all of the surveyed colleges, were also underequipped, an issue that was perceived as negatively affecting students' hands-on, practical experience.

Based on the focus group discussions, the idea of using different available buildings for offering classes seems to be a solution for the lack of resources. However, an efficient HE system is not only limited to providing a meeting space as it includes the extent to which this space is designed and equipped to serve educational purposes and enable achieving the intended learning outcomes. This deteriorated status of facilities was further supported by the survey's results.

Organization Culture and Freedom of Speech

The focus group discussions revealed that the organization's culture was mainly centered on the administration. While 18% of the surveyed sample agreed that the college provided a democratic atmosphere, about 67% opposed that it did. The centralization of the decision-making process was reported in the four colleges, but in varying degrees. Any approval had to be processed by the dean himself. Moreover, students were not encouraged to voice their opinions. Although the administration was supposed to discuss decisions with the student union, students were surprised by decisions made regardless of their opinion on the issue. Moreover, with the current political situation in Egypt, no political engagement, of any sort, was accepted by the administration. One of the students sarcastically commented," In our college, freedom of speech is granted as long as you are not criticizing the administration or talking about politics."

Although students were to fill out an evaluation form every semester about the quality of education, no real change happened in response to such evaluation. "It is just a routine," as noted by all the interviewed students. About 70% of the surveyed sample disagreed about having an effective complaining mechanism, while only 14% agreed. During the focus groups, students agreed that one could approach the administration easily and voice their demands. However, all groups confirmed that they were not courage enough to clearly voice their complaints. As stated by a student, "Clearly, you can complain as much as you want. Yet, the administration has the right to pretend as if they did not hear anything." Students feared that if they complained, the administration would be biased against them and they might fail the academic year. One of the students commented, "I know some students who have been here for 6 years because they voiced their opinion about the quality of education."

There was no precise reason for why the administration was not including students in the decision-making process. Was it about the level of the maturity and proactivity of students? Was it about the governing body who wanted to exclude them in the first place? Or was it a combination of both? To varying degrees, students in the four colleges confirmed that their voices were not taken into consideration. Some of the focus group discussions indicated that few students had protests against the administration. Although this gives an indication about students being proactive, it is important to consider that such protests took place at a time where everyone was calling for their rights in Egypt. In other words, students' enthusiasm might not have been driven by the culture of their educational institution; they were rather timely, following common public actions during the revolution and its aftermath.

It was interesting to see how the examined colleges restricted students' freedom of speech. How can these colleges empower students if they are oppressing them in the first place? It might be true that students were not appropriately expressing themselves and their demands. However, the colleges were not providing venues for students to express their opinions in a democratic atmosphere. This was supported by the survey results where about 67% of respondents disagreed that the college provided a collegial and democratic educational atmosphere.

Teaching and Learning

The majority of students were neutral when it came to the "Formal Teaching and Learning" experience. The survey results displayed almost a symmetry in student's opinions as to the qualifications of the teaching staff (35% of the surveyed sample agreed on their qualification, while 39% disagreed). However, the focus group discussion revealed that there was a lack of educational efficacy on both the students' and the teachers' sides. All students agreed that the majority of professors mastered the subject matter. However, they confirmed that a few were not up to the expected academic level. Sometimes, lecturers assigned materials that they could not easily deliver. Furthermore, although undergraduates were to be taught the same content as the main campus of Alexandria University, students concurred that they ended up having less material than their counterparts. This can give an indication about the fulfillment of the expected learning outcomes. Students confirmed that professors were not interested in investing more time to teach because of two reasons. First, professors believed that students were not competent enough to expand on clarifying the academic content.[7] They believed students were looking for the information to pass the exam. Second, professors came to college, after a three-hour-trip, too exhausted to stimulate the class.[8] On the learners' side, students showed no interest in the subject matter. As a student noted "the lecturers give us what is important for the exam and we do not want more than what is provided."

Moreover, there were different opinions in regards to the use of assessment strategies as well as involving students in the process of teaching and learning. Although 31% agreed that professors use different assessment tools, about 47% disagreed. Based on the discussions, professors used different assessment tools such as quizzes, midterms, research papers, presentations, and end of term exams. However, students did not think such assessment reflected their genuine understanding. A student commented, "Although they might seem different assessment tools, the largest percentage of the grade is divided among the final and midterm exam. The weight of the other activities is very minor relative to the written exams." Moreover, although part of the grade was assigned to reports and research papers, students confirmed that they were not taught how to do proper scientific research.

On another note, according to the NAQAAE standards, students are supposed to be informed about the evaluation of their exam and reflect upon their mistakes. However, in the focus groups, students confirmed that professors did not discuss wrong answers, or grades. As per the survey results, 54% disagreed that professors discuss with students the evaluation of the student exams while only 27% agreed that they do. This actually can give an indication about the teacher-student relationship, and the institution's understanding of the importance of exam in measuring students' comprehension.

It might have been justifiable for lecturers to lessen the academic content given the deteriorated academic level and unwillingness of students; nevertheless, the authentic knowledge students have accumulated, which will empower them to achieve the expected learning outcomes and repay this back to the community (the original goal for which the colleges were built) is very questionable. The problem involves professors, students, and the educational environment. That is, professors did not deliver the required material based on the belief that students were not interested or competitive enough to receive more in-depth information. Yet, as it was presented in the literature review, an effective professor has the responsibility for engaging students and fostering their learning. On the students' side, they did not exert great effort in understanding the subject. They simply studied in order to pass exams regardless of their authentic knowledge. This might be attributed to the lack of efficient educational facilities and the supportive learning environment.

Education for Career Pursuit and Community Service

Since the Matrouh colleges were established mainly to cater for the need of the community, one would expect that the established colleges are engaging students in community service activities. However, according to the majority of respondent students (90%), the colleges did not provide them with academic programs that develop their skills as relevant to the community needs . This actually can be reflected in students' opinions about being equipped with 21st century skills as well as their readiness to the job market. There was a general disagreement that the examined colleges enable the development of the 21st century skills including critical thinking and creativity, communication skills, and collaboration (75%, 54.9%, and 51% respectively).

In addition, the majority of students, 56% of the surveyed sample disagreed that their respective college prepares them for the job market. While higher education should be catering for potential change makers who can contribute to the economic development of their communities, the survey results and the focus group discussions reveal that the majority of respondents (54%) believed that they are not ready or prepared for the job market. Most of the students in the different focus groups did not feel confident in their level of knowledge or skills. About 55% disagreed that the education received leads to a job afterwards that is aligned with students' skills, passion, and academic knowledge, while only 20% agreed.

As one of the interviewed officials clarified, colleges, by law, should provide students with different hands-on experience. For example, in the colleges under review, students in the College of Education have a practicum experience starting from the third year as well as a microteaching course[9] in the second year. The College of Veterinary Medicine has a preclinical training in the first three years and an internship in the fourth year. Additionally, students in the College of Nursing should serve in a hospital in the summer and have a 12-month-training (internship) in a hospital after graduation (*takleef*). Finally, the College of Agriculture should have different fieldwork visits throughout the academic year. However, from students' perspective, most of the practical experience was not corresponding to their needs of pre-service training. Unfortunately, focus group discussions confirmed that, students think they are academically incompetent in comparison to their counterparts from any other university. This feeling, as they explained, stemmed from three reasons. First, due to the students' low scores in *ThanawyaAmma* upon their admission, some professors considered and treated them as low academic achievers, and as a result, this image was reflected upon how they perceived themselves. Second, since professors assumed that students did not have profound knowledge, they gave them the minimum required material. Third, students ended up memorizing the material for the end of term exam without a genuine understanding of subjects taught due to their concern more about obtaining high grades than comprehending the materials or because of the lack of equipped laboratories and efficient teaching strategies.

Since learning experience is a joint effort between the teaching staff, the administration, and students, it was important to consider learner's opinions about the education for community service and engagement and how they are engaged to achieve such a concept. On the students' side, there is almost a symmetry between students who perceived themselves as proactive and those who did not (39% agreed, 26% neutral while 35% disagreed). Although more than one-third of the surveyed sample described themselves as proactive, responses in regards to students' engagement did not support such claim. The majority of students were not engaged in any extracurricular activities (64%) or decision-making (about 70%). Similarly, there was lack of activities for student empowerment in the examined colleges. About 58% disagreed that the college encouraged students' engagement and community service and provided the necessary setting for that, while only 20% agreed.

Even though there were few social and cultural students' clubs in the different colleges, undergraduates confirmed that these activities were not effective nor profound in transforming their characters or unleashing their talents. Based on the different group interviews, this was mainly due to the lack of a clear vision in the different clubs, the absence of an experienced student body, the tedious paperwork, and the limited available budget offered by the administration. Notably, clubs recruited only experienced students and were not willing to invest in new members. When asked about the reason behind recruiting experienced members only, one of the Heads of student activities noted, "We need students who can efficiently execute and produce the required job; we do have neither the resources nor the time to train the members. "In fact, undergraduates pointed out that the limited budget led them to self-finance their activities most of the time.

This poses a question on the value added of these colleges. Is opening a higher education institution, regardless of the quality offered, sufficient for empowering youth and impacting local communities? The main aim of these colleges was to better cater for the need of the community. Yet, given the perceptions of their students of the educational quality offered, achieving this primary goal seems far from reaching.

DISCUSSION AND CONCLUSION

In this study, I examined the quality of higher education as perceived by students during the time of the post-revolution in Egypt, allowing them to reflect on their experience at their respective institution. A special attention was given to students' perceptions of educational quality in terms of institutional facilities/infrastructure; organizational culture, especially in relation to students' freedom of speech; teaching and learning experience; and education for career pursuit and community service. The examined colleges were established to increase higher education opportunities and address community needs in Matrouh. Justly, the colleges offer areas of specializations that are aligned with the needs of local communities. The Marouh-Branch of Alexandria University witnessed a gradual increase in the number of colleges over the past years. Nevertheless, the findings of this study indicated that this quantitative expansion disregarded improving the quality of education provided in the examined colleges. Among the identified problems are the lack of resources and inadequate facilities along with organizational culture that restricts students' freedom of speech and active participation in community services.

Furthermore, employability gives an indication of the qualifications, skills and experiences that a university has equipped its students with (Coates, 2005). Based on the findings of this study, higher education in these communities seems to create a liability on the governorate's budget, more diploma diseases, and unskilled graduates. Although the percentage of students who pursued university degree in Matrouh increased from 2% to 13% during the period of 2006 to 2013, the corresponding unemployment rate increased as per an interview with an official working at the cabinet of Matrouh governorate. Scholars and international organizations, identified several reasons and factors for (un)employment. According to Coates, "employment outcomes can be influenced by a range of non-educational factors, such as institutional reputation, personal networks and labor market conditions" (Coates, 2005, p. 30). On the other hand, unemployment can be attributed to the fact that higher education degree increases the bar of graduates' expectations about their future jobs, refusing to settle for less than what they deserve (World Bank & OECD, 2010). Given that the economic activity in remote areas is very limited and depending heavily on governmental jobs, higher education in these areas need to develop partnerships with local communities and with different public and private organizations and institutions in order to provide opportunities for students to engage in internships and trainings that can enhance students readiness for the job market but also for community service.

For students to become involved in their learning experience, institutions and staff have to set up the conditions, opportunities and expectations that help students participate (Coates, 2005). However, in the case under review, these factors were perceived as ineffective. Although professors are expected to empower students, in reality, some professors were referred to as being a reason for students' discouragement. In the meantime, on the students' side, it is important to highlight that some students expressed their lack of interest in the subject matters or in being proactive and getting engaged in academic or extracurricular activities. Johnstone claims, learners have to put quality effort to be engaged and challenge themselves to learn and interact with new ideas. Learning should be viewed as "a joint proposition" between students and teachers (Coates, 2005, p. 26). Obviously, in the examined colleges, the teaching and learning experience as a "joint proposition" was limited.

It was suggested that the new role of higher education institutions involves real social transformation through community involvement (Bernardo, Butcher, & Howard, 2012). This is what UNESCO refers to as the "Third Mission" of higher education. Yet, 80% of the respondent students in this study were not involved in any community service activity. In addition, they were not instructed to undertake group projects related to the needs of their local communities. Considering that colleges/higher education institutions in remote areas, similar to the examined case, are mainly established to serve marginalized groups and contribute to community development, integrating strategies and designing activities for service learning and community engagement deserve more attention by educators and officials in order to enable the contribution of higher education institutions in the development of marginalized and remote communities.

NOTES

[1] Matrouh is one of the twenty-seven governorates in Egypt. It is located far North West in the boarders between Egypt and Libya. It has a total population of 380,155 as per the Central Agency for Public Mobilization and Statistics report in 2011.

[2] Open education system is a system that grants bachelor degrees for interested students who left education for more than five years; yet, they want to continue their higher education (in case of high school students) or obtain another bachelor degree (in case of higher education graduates).

[3] The total population in 2006 was 280,299.

[4] ThanawyaAmma is the final year of the secondary school stage after which a student is expected to join the higher education system if gained the required score.

[5] As mentioned before, Matrouh is located in far north west of Egypt. About 6 hours away from the capital of Cairo.

[6] Matrouh branch accepts students with the lowest scores for HE enrollment comparing to other Egyptian HE institutions.

[7] This stems from the fact that Matrouh's college accept the lowest enrollment score over the republic.

[8] Professors commute daily from Alexandria to Matrouh to deliver their lectures (three-hour-commute).

[9] In the micro teaching course (*tadressmosaghar*), students are expected to be trained and mock what happens inside a classroom. Each class, there is a role play where a student become a teacher and his colleagues are his students. S/he is put in different situations to test and be trained on how to lead a classroom.

REFERENCES

Bernardo, M. A., Butcher, J., & Howard, P. (2012). An international comparison of community engagement in higher education. *International Journal of Educational Development, 32*(1), 187–192.

Central Agency for Public Mobilization and Statistics. (2011). *The yearly report in 2010/2011*. Cairo: Central Agency for Public Mobilization and Statistics.

Central Agency for Public Mobilization and Statistics. (2013). *The annual statistics book, Arab Republic of Egypt*. Cairo: Central Agency for Public Mobilization and Statistics.

Coates, H. (2005). The value of student engagement for higher education quality assurance. *Quality in Higher Education, 11*(1), 25–36

Cook-Sather, A. (2006). Sound, presence, and power: "Student voice" in educational research and reform. *Curriculum Inquiry, 36*(4), 359–90.

Crombag, H. (1978). On defining quality of education. *Higher Education, 7*(4), 389–403.

El-Hamidi, F. (2008). *Education-occupation mismatch and the effect on wages of Egyptian workers*. 15th Annual Conference of the Economic Research Forum, Economic Research Forum, Cairo.

Fathy, M. (2012, November 27). *100 universities by 2020*. Retrieved from http://digital.ahram.org.eg/articles.aspx?Serial=1109549&eid=1187

Harvey, L., & Green, D. (1993). Defining quality. *Assessment & Evaluation in Higher Education, 18*(1), 9–34.

Johnson, R., Onwuegbuzie, A., & Turner, L. (n.d.). Toward a definition of mixed methods research. *Journal of Mixed Methods Research, 1*(2), 112–133.

Johnstone, D. (1993). Enhancing the productivity of learning. *AAHE Bulletin, 46*(4), 4–8.

Katz, E., & Coleman, M. (2001). The growing importance of research at academic colleges of education in Israel. *Education + Training, 43*(2), 82–93.

Lammers, W., & Murphy, J. (2002). A profile of teaching techniques used in the university classroom. *Active Learning in Higher Education, 3*(1), 54–67.

Maḥmūd, S. T., & Nās, A.-S. M. (2003). *Qaḍāyā fī al-taʻlīm al-ʻālī wa-al-jāmiʻī*. Cairo: El Nahda EL Masria.

National Authority for Qualtiy Assurance and Accreditation in Egypt. (2013). *Overview*. Retrieved from http://en.naqaae.eg/

OECD. (2010). *Reviews of national policies for education: Higher education in Egypt*. Paris: World Bank & OECD.

Reda, M. (2012, January). *Enhancing Egypt's competitivness: Education, innovation and labor*. Retrieved from http://www.eces.org.eg/Uploaded_Files/%7B9D22B058-6BF8-431B-8953-7A4265246B21%7D_WP%20167.pdf

Rowland, S., Byron, C., Furedi, F., Padfield, N., & Smyth, T. (1998). Turning acadmics into teachers. *Teaching in Higher Education, 3*(2), 133–141.

Strategic Planning Unit, Minsitry of Higher Education. (2010). *Higher education in Egypt: Country background report*. Cairo: Ministry of Higher Education.

The World Bank. (2013). *Higher education enhancement project*. Retrieved September 15, 2013, from http://web.worldbank.org/external/projects/main?pagePK=104231&Projectid=P056236

Thomson Reuters. (n.d.). *The world university ranking*. Retrieved from http://www.timeshighereducation.co.uk/world-university-rankings/2012-13/world-ranking/region/africa

UNESCO. (1995). *Policy paper for change and development in higher education*. Paris: UNESCO.

UNESCO. (2015). *The role of higher education in promoting lifelong learning*. Hamburg: UNESCO.

World Bank & OECD. (2010). *Reviews of national policies for education: Higher education in Egypt*. Paris: OECD & The International Bank Reconstruction and Development.

Wu, C.-L. (2012). J. Douglas Toma: Building organizational capacity: Strategic management in higher education. *Higher Education, 63*(1), 153–155.

Sara Taraman
Graduate School of Education
The American University in Cairo (AUC)

AUTHOR BIOGRAPHIES

Amira Abdou has been a passionate high school teacher for 11 years before she decided to pursue postgraduate degrees to strengthen her professional experience by gaining further inquiry-based and academic qualifications. Abdou was among the first graduates to obtain her MA in Comparative and International Education in 2012 from the AUC's Graduate School of Education. During her MA studies, she worked as a research fellow in several research and development projects. She also served as an instructor at the AUC's Professional Educator Diploma Program where she taught aspiring and experienced teachers in the strands of Early Childhood, Teachers of Adolescent Learners, and Educational leadership. Abdou has recently relocated with her family in the United Arab Emirates; she is an adjunct faculty at the University of Wollongong in Dubai. In addition, she is a doctoral student at the School of Education, University of Leicester.

Shereen Aly has obtained her MA degree in International and Comparative Education from The American University in Cairo, and has a Bachelor's degree in Electrical Engineering. She has participated in several research projects in the field of education, namely peace education, non-formal learning settings and science education. She is currently working as an independent consultant, researcher and trainer for educational institutions. Shereen Aly has over 9 years' experience in multi-national corporations before she decided to shift career to education, in these years she realized the wide gap between the skills needed in real life and what the educational institutions are offering their students. Therefore, she shifted towards education with a strong belief that the road to real world transformation is a powerful and holistic learning experience.

Soha Aly has joined The American University in Cairo (AUC) in 2008 as a Program Associate and currently is a Senior Specialist in the area of Student Services. Her professional experiences at AUC also included revamp, pilot, and administer academic and non-academic programs. Soha Aly received her MA in International and Comparative Education, with concentration in Educational Policy and Development from the AUC's Graduate School of Education. She co-taught classes in the Professional Educator Diploma Program at AUC. Soha Aly participated in different international conferences. Recently, she obtained the CCTAFL certificate for teaching Arabic as a foreign language.

Shaimaa Mostafa Awad is a Research Associate at the Department of International and Comparative Education and an Instructor at the Professional Educator Diploma Program in the Graduate School of Education at The American University in Cairo. She holds MA degree in International and Comparative Education, with a

AUTHOR BIOGRAPHIES

concentration in Educational Leadership from the same university. As a holder of BA in English language and literature, she has gained fifteen years of experience in teaching English as a second language for young learners. She participated in several international conferences. Her research interests focus on civil society support to educational development, global citizenship education, character education and reflective teaching and practice in teacher education.

Jason Nunzio Dorio, Ph.D., is a Postdoctoral Scholar at the Graduate School of Education and Information Studies at the University of California, Los Angeles (UCLA). His research interests focus on the relationships between multiple forms of citizenship education, universities, and the state in North Africa and Southwest Asia. Broader interests include comparative and international education, political sociology of education, critical pedagogy, social movements and educational change, in addition to exploring theories and practices of global citizenship education. Jason was formerly a Scholar Without Stipend with the Graduate School of Education at the American University in Cairo (2014–2015). Currently he serves as the Director of Academic Programs for the UNESCO-UCLA Chair in Global Learning and Global Citizenship Education.

Ola Hosny earned her MA degree in International and Comparative Education from The American University in Cairo in 2014. She carries over 14 years of experience working in international organizations on research and development projects (i.e. UNESCO Cairo Office and the Population Council). In addition to 4+ years of experience acting as an independent research and development consultant. She has solid experience in conceptualizing and managing projects working mainly in the areas of poverty, gender and youth. Hosny's work and research interests focus on examining policies and practices pertaining to education development in local and global contexts, acknowledging the influence and power of cultural, political, economic, and social issues. Hosny is also an instructor at the AUC Professional Educator Diploma Program.

Nagwa Megahed is Associate Professor of Comparative and International Education at Ain Shams University and The American University in Cairo. She teaches and conducts research on educational reform (policy and practice) in Egypt, the MENA region and other developing countries. Megahed obtained her Ph.D. in Social and Comparative Analysis in Education from the University of Pittsburgh. She is involved in numerous technical advisory and consultancy capacities in many educational reform projects with international organizations and national authorities. Megahed is a recipient of the 2009 and 2010 Fulbright Scholarship Awards for Teaching and Research. She has published extensively; her record of publications focuses on international organizations and education development; educational policy, administration, and reform; teachers and teacher education; educational quality; gender, religion and education equality.

Sara Taraman has a Master's Degree in International and Comparative Education from The American University in Cairo as well as a BA in Economics from the same university. She has five years of experience working on different capacity building projects funded by international donors. She has been extensively involved in project management starting from the inception phase to the closure of the project. Further, she has intensive experience designing and implementing M&E tools to assess the effectiveness of different initiatives and interventions. Taraman is interested in different topics related to the economics of education as well as economic development.

Printed in the United States
By Bookmasters